OUR GLORIOUS INHERITANCE

Volume Two . . . Entering the Land of Promise

by
MIKE SHREVE

An exhaustive study of the revelation of the titles of the children of God

• **REVISED EDITION** •

DEEPER REVELATION BOOKS

"Holding forth the word of life . . ." Phil. 2:16

Cover art: by Gerry Hattaway

The following are some of the Bible translations used:

King James Authorized Version (AV or KJV)
Phillips Modern English (PME)
Revised Standard Version (RSV)
New International Version (NIV)
New English Bible (NEB)
The Living Bible (LB)
New American Standard (NAS)
Today's EnglishVersion (TEV)
Amplified Bible (AMP)

Other Reference Books:
Unger, Merrill F. *Unger's Bible Dictionary* (UBD). 1957, 1966. The Moody Bible Institute. Chicago, Illinois.

Vine, W.E. *Vine's Expositiory Dictionary* (VED). 1984. Bethany House. Minneapolis, Minnesota.

Young, G. Douglas. *Young's Concordance* (YC). 1984.Tyndale House Publishers. Wheaton, Illinois.

Strong, James. *Strong's Concordance* (SC). 1984. Thomas Nelson Publishers. Nashville, Tennessee.

Dake, Finis. *Dake's Annotated Reference Bible* (DARB). 1979. Dake Bible Sales. Lawrenceville, Georgia.

ISBN: 0-942507-01-0
ISBN: 0-942507-04-5 (8-Volume Set)
Our Glorious Inheritance Volume Two
Copyright © 1986 by Mike Shreve
Our Glorious Inheritance Volume Two (Revised)
Copyright © 1987 by Mike Shreve
Our Glorious Inheritance Volume Two (Second Revision)
Copyright © 1989 by Mike Shreve

All ministry correspondence
should be directed to:
Mike Shreve
P.O. Box 700
Cleveland, TN 37364

All correspondence dealing
with book orders, etc:
Deeper Revelation Books
2427 Fifeshire Dr.
Winter Park, FL 32792

DEDICATION

In deep appreciation of Kent Sullivan, this second volume of OUR GLORIOUS INHERITANCE is sent forth. I thank God for the day when Kent compassionately shared the reality of Jesus with me, opening up my understanding and leading me to the throne of grace.

COVER ART

*This beautiful scene depicts the Promised Land in its Kingdom Age splendor. It also symbolically represents the "chapter one theme" of this volume: that the **title-positions** of the children of God comprise a spiritual "Land of Promise" that we may dwell in all the days of our lives. This is a land of new beginnings (represented by the double-rainbow), a land of transformation (represented by the butterfly), and a land of spiritual fruitfulness (represented by the grapes of Eshcol).*

TABLE OF CONTENTS

The second volume in
an eight-volume series
on

The Revelation
of the
Titles of the Children
of God

ENTERING THE
LAND OF PROMISE

THE LAND OF
SPIRITUAL TITLE-RIGHTS

"...that thou mayest go in unto the land which the Lord thy God giveth thee, a land that floweth with milk and honey; as the Lord God of thy fathers hath promised thee."

(Deuteronomy 27:3)

INTRODUCTORY CHAPTER

ENTERING THE LAND OF PROMISE
THE LAND OF SPIRITUAL TITLE-RIGHTS

"...that thou mayest go in unto the land which the Lord thy God giveth thee, a land that floweth with milk and honey; as the Lord God of thy fathers hath promised thee."

(Deuteronomy 27:3)

• Canaan was a natural land promised by Jehovah God to Abraham and His seed...thus it was called THE LAND OF PROMISE.

This territory, situated between the Mediterranean Sea on the west and the Jordan River on the east, was a land of such great natural abundance that it was described to be *flowing with milk and honey.*

It was also called *"the land of oil olive"* - *"a land which the Lord thy God careth for: for the eyes of the Lord thy God are always upon it."* (Deuteronomy 8:8, 11:12)

This natural Land of Canaan represents, in Biblical symbolism, a spiritual Land of Promise, a realm of "abundant life" that is available right now, in this era, to those who have been born again.

It is a "faithful saying and worthy of all acceptation" that God's main concern was not just leading Israel out from Egypt's bondage. He was even more interested in leading them into the Land of Promise.

In like manner, in the New Covenant, believers are given grace unto salvation, not just to lead them out of sin's bondage, but even more so, this unmerited love is sent from heaven to eventually lead them into their inheritance "in Christ".

This is a spiritual territory that literally flows with the *milk* of the Word and the *honey* of the Spirit...a land where the *"olive oil"* of the anointing is poured forth abundantly...a land that God watches over with even greater care and devotion.

• It is quite interesting also to note that the Hebrew form of the word **Canaan** apparently came from the Hurrian language and it means *belonging to the land of red-purple.* (UBD)

This was an allusion to the use of the murex mollusks in the dye industry of Phoenicia. It also speaks a subtle and beautiful message to those who have ears to hear.

For the spiritual land of Canaan, presently promised to the sons and daughters of God, is a *land of red-purple* as well.

In a sense, the dye was cast, inwardly and spiritually, the very moment we surrendered to the Lordship of Jesus Christ.

For the Saviour brought forth a miraculous *red-purple* change in all of us...washing us in His precious *red* blood and birthing in us a royal *purple* nature.

1

Now, as joint-heirs with Christ, we abide in this spiritual *land of red-purple* - where promises of redemptive grace and regal glory abound - and where blessed inhabitants feast continually on the nourishing and sweet, *milk and honey* inheritance available there.

It is in this land of "exceeding great and precious promises" that we find strong security, perpetual victory, and a glorious destiny.

• **It is in this land of Word-promises that we first ascertain, then boldly claim and possess our full heirship and sonship rights.**

We discover and then appropriate all of these rights, privileges, callings and potential abilities by discovering and comprehending our *titles*...for there is no sonship inheritance available to the children of God that exists apart from our God-given *titles*.

Therefore, the most comprehensive and effective way of "mapping out" the whole "Land of Promise", and the most sure way of guiding the sons and daughters of God into their God-given heritage, is to teach them their many entitlements.

OBTAINING AND MAINTAINING
THE REVELATION OF OUR INHERITANCE

In **Volume One** of **OUR GLORIOUS INHERITANCE** the *title-positions* of the children of God were collectively represented, first, as *hidden manna* that must be eaten - the heavenly bread of revelation available only to overcomers; second, as a *hidden treasure* that must be "discovered and brought forth"; and third, as *the holy place* - that secret place of divine illumination and regal heirship hidden *beyond the veil* of flesh-consciousness in every child of God.

• Now, in **Volume Two**, the *title-positions* of the children of God are represented as a "**Land of Promise**" that must first be clearly seen, then conquered, possessed, and defended.

We see these *title-callings* as we study the intricacies of God's Word under the inspiration of His Spirit.

This is our only source of reference and our only way of seeing.

But the process of conquering, possessing and defending is different for each *title*.

For instance, we attain the *title-position* of being *disciples* when we sincerely attempt to conquer the selfishness and the egocentricity of the carnal nature. We defend this position by consistently striving to possess a yielded, selfless, holy, zealous, and loving, God-like spirit.

On the other hand, we achieve the position of being *more than conquerors* by first conquering unbelief, self-condemnation, depression and fear. We then possess and defend this status primarily by maintaining and exercising a spirit of faith.

• Again it must be emphasized: first we see, embracing with our eyes

2

and then our hearts, the various rights, callings, privileges and potential abilities promised to sons of God.

Then we strive to conquer that which is in opposition to what we see.

By doing so we succeed in securing our "Promised Land Inheritance" for we "enter into and possess" our God-given *title-positions*.

But because we are in a constant warfare, we must always be on guard, aware that whatever spiritual territory we seize, Satan will certainly attempt to reclaim. Therefore, we must constantly defend ourselves against such attacks by diligently and daily renewing our commitment to God and our commitment to both faith and faithfulness.

By doing so we succeed in making our calling and election sure.

• The four steps previously mentioned - *seeing, conquering, possessing and defending* - were all quite evident from the very start of the natural, progressive and highly symbolic acquisition of Canaan Land under the Old Will.

For instance, when Abraham first gazed into the Land of Canaan, God spoke to him audibly and pledged - *"all the land which thou seest, to thee will I give it..."* (Genesis 13:15)

Then almost five hundred years later, when Joshua went in to finally take full possession of this God-given territory, God declared to him - *"every place that the sole of your foot shall tread upon, that have I given unto you...be strong and of a good courage."* (Joshua 1:3,6)

Furthermore, it is also important to grasp that even though the land was already given to the Jews by the Almighty God, still they had to fight in order to obtain what was already rightfully theirs.

Also, once possessed, their claim to that territory had to be constantly defended, and often territory was lost and had to be regained.

• **Now all of these statements are solemn guarantees that spiritually it will work the same way for us.**

First, in an Abraham-like way we must dare to fix our gaze on the portion of the Word that pertains to us, knowing that if we believe, what we see is also what we can receive.

Then, in a Joshua-like manner, we must walk through the pages of "Genesis through Revelation" to boldly stake out our claim in Jesus' name.

We must determine in advance to rise up violently against any power of hell or weakness of the flesh that could hinder us from obtaining what rightfully belongs to us.

Moreover, we must expect the walls of opposition to fall flat before us, even as the walls of Jericho fell before the triumphant shout of the Israelite camp.

Also, after the manner of Gideon, Samson, Samuel, David and a host of others, we must purpose in our hearts to constantly defend our "boundaries" from every enemy attack.

As we fight to defend our inheritance, God will fight our battles for us for - "He is a shield unto them that put their trust in Him." (Pro. 30:5)

He will keep us and preserve us in all of our trials.

"For this God is our God forever and ever: He will be our guide even unto death." (Psalm 48:14)

THE FIRST ATTEMPT
THWARTED BY UNBELIEF

• The first time that the Jews came to the edge of the river Jordan, Moses sent twelve men to spy out Canaan.

They brought back samples of the fruit of the land, including a cluster of grapes, from the valley of the brook of Eshcol, that was so large it had to be carried on a staff between two men. (O, what a land of bounty and blessing God was providing!)

But ten of the spies were not men of vision and faith.

Numbers 13:32 declares that they brought back "an evil report". It was called an "evil report" because it was a report of unbelief. Without question, unbelief is evil; it is sin. "Whatsoever is not of faith is SIN." (Romans 14:23)

These doubters cried out to Israel, *We be not able to go up against the people; for they are stronger than we...we saw the giants...and we were in our own sight as grasshoppers and so we were in their sight."* (Numbers 13:31-33)

The ten unbelieving spies saw the awesome strength of the enemy and the bigness of the land. They should have looked beyond the opposition to the bigness and greatness of their God.

They first saw themselves as small, weak, incapable, easily crushed and easily defeated...*"we were in our own eyes as grasshoppers."* (Numbers 13:33)

But then the enemy saw them the very same way that they saw themselves...*" and so we were in their sight."*

In like manner, it is certain that the devil will view us in the same attitude with which we view ourselves.

If we see ourselves cowering before him, helpless and defeated, then he will behold us there, cringing in fear, and gain the mastery over us.

But if we see ourselves "in Christ"...unconquerable, unshakable, and victorious...then the enemy will shrink away from us in horror, knowing that he cannot penetrate the wall of faith built around our lives.

• We must cultivate the attitude of Caleb, one of the two believing spies, who cried aloud - *"Let us go up at once and possess the land, for we are well able to overcome."* (Numbers 13:30)

• And let us emulate Joshua, the other righteous spy, who declared of the opposition - *"they are bread for us; for their defense is departed from them...the Lord is with us!"* (Numbers 14:9)

For Satan's *defense really has departed.*

He was stripped of his authority and spoiled openly almost two thousand years ago.

All the evil hordes of fallen angels are truly *"bread for us,"* for everything they do against us ultimately works together for our good, our benefit. *The Lord is with us*...and this is all we really need to know, for knowing it we can boldly *"go up...and possess the land"* of our God-given *title-rights.*

This is our golden opportunity...something we cannot afford to miss as did that first generation of Israelites who came out of Egypt.

THE SECOND CHANCE

• The second time that Israel came to cross over the Jordan River, they were ready.

Forty years of wandering in the wilderness had prepared their hearts.

They had learned some extremely necessary lessons. They understood the consequence of sin, the ultimate outcome of rebellion, and the great worth of obedience. God had humbled them.

They had grown accustomed to being led of His Spirit (the cloud by day and the fire by night).

They had learned by experience to trust in God to meet their needs.

They had subsisted almost totally, for four decades, on the heavenly food that came from above and the supernatural water that came out of the rock.

They were healthy in their bodies as a result; there was not a feeble person among them. They were considerably more healthy in their attitudes as well. They were ready to win. They were ready to claim their inheritance. They were ready to cross over.

Feeding on the Word (the bread of life) and drinking in the Spirit (the water of life) will certainly do the same thing for us in a spiritual sense. Spending a season in what appears to be a wilderness of trials and tribulations can ultimately prove to be beneficial in preparing our hearts for the visitation of God.

• **It is noteworthy also that Moses died just before the children of Israel entered the Land of Promise**...because Moses symbolized the law, and the law never could carry the Jews, or anyone else for that matter, into the fullness of the inheritance God intends for His chosen and ordained people.

Instead, God buried Moses and raised up a new leader, *Joshua*, whose very name is actually synonymous with the name *Jesus* and means *"Jehovah is salvation."*

In a similar way, on the day of Jesus' baptism in the river Jordan, when the Holy Spirit came upon the Word made flesh, in a sense, the law was buried and grace was exalted in its place.

We were then given a "new leader", a Saviour *(Jehovah manifested as salvation)* who proved Himself quite capable of bringing us into "abundant life" that we might ever live in the *"land of oil olive."*

• **Moreover, God has given us a definite plan of success similar to the one he gave Joshua of old.**

Three times the Lord commanded this new leader of Israel to be strong and of a good courage, saying - "I will not fail thee, nor forsake thee." Then Jehovah gave Joshua the key to acquiring this strength and fearlessness when He said:

> *"This book of the law shall not depart out of thy mouth; but thou shalt meditate therein day and night, that thou mayest observe to do according to all that is written therein: for then thou shalt make thy way prosperous, and then thou shalt have good success."*

(Joshua 1:8)

This truth is somewhat astounding and the resulting revelation is no less than wonderful.

The book of the law was to a certain degree a book of death. For the law ministered condemnation to those who heard it and served primarily to make sin appear more exceedingly sinful. (Romans 7:13)

So, in essence, the law proved to the Jews not so much "what they were", but rather "what they were not." Yet meditating on the law, speaking the law and observing to do the law, brought them great success.

It is undeniable, though, that now we have an even better opportunity to triumph in all things.

We are not under the law; we are under grace.

We have received a better covenant built upon better promises.

The New Covenant ministers righteousness and strength to us, not condemnation. We have been made partakers of "the perfect law of liberty" - "the law of the spirit of life in Christ Jesus." (Ja. 1:25, Rom. 8:2)

Therefore, how much more should we expect to prosper and succeed, as we confess the life-giving promises of the New Covenant.

• **How much more should we expect to prosper and have good success when we discover our *title-rights* and meditate on them day and night!!**

THE VICTORIOUS ENTRANCE
THE PURPOSE OF GOD REVEALED

• On the day that Israel finally crossed over into Canaan Land, a very significant event transpired. Joshua sent the ark of the covenant before the children of Israel and the waters of Jordan rolled back all the way to a community called - "the city Adam." (Joshua 3:16)

In like manner, Jesus, the eternal "Ark of the covenant", has gone before us, preparing the way.

He passed through the deep, dark, Jordan-waters of death, rolling the curse back all the way to Adam's original sin.

He was the Forerunner, the eternal example, and the Firstborn from the dead...the Firstborn among many brethren.

In dieing to self, He vanquished death.

In tasting death for every man, He secured the victory we never could have attained on our own.

In an Elijah-like manner he smote "Jordan" and parted the impassable barrier. Now He challenges us to take up the "mantle" of His authority that fell from heaven on Pentecost, and in a Elisha-like manner to do the same.

• We find that the very name **Jordan** means *the descender* (most likely because of its rapid descent into the Dead Sea). The Dead Sea is a stagnant body of water approximately thirteen hundred feet below sea level; the very bottom of the Dead Sea is one thousand, three hundred feet deeper still. Its waters are quite nauseating and undrinkable because of the nearly twenty-six percent salt content. Six thousand tons of water are emptied into the Dead Sea every day, yet there is no way for the oily, salty and chemically rich water to flow out. It can rid itself of excess only by evaporation, which often causes the formation of heavy clouds over the area.

All of these facts speak to our hearts in a spiritual sense...for the "old man", the lustful, prideful, covetous, hostile, selfish, self-exalting, self-sufficient and egocentric, fallen Adam-nature in each one of us must die **if we are to enter into the fullness of our inheritance and eat the luscious, supernatural grapes of Eshcol that await us there.**

Jesus was baptized in Jordan, and He exhorted that we must be baptized with His baptism if we are to share His glory.

Therefore, we must be submerged under the chilly waters of Jordan-like death to self that the carnality of the past must be swept downstream, to be buried, in a symbolic sense, in the depths of the Dead Sea.

It is undeniably true that to follow Jesus we must first "deny self" this way. But if we are "buried with Him by baptism into death" - "as Christ was raised up...by the glory of the Father, even so we also should walk in newness of life." (Romans 6:4)

7

This is the sometimes difficult, yet extremely valuable process by which we enter the fullness of **OUR GLORIOUS INHERITANCE.**

As we come forth out of "Jordan" surely the heavenly dove will descend on us with heaven's most enriching blessings and benefits, as the heavenly Father confesses - *"These are My beloved offspring in whom I am well pleased."*

• In all of our trials we can look beyond the present struggle into a glorious future hope. For the prophet Ezekiel, caught up in a spectacular vision of the Kingdom Age to come, described a river of living water that will yet flow out of the temple in Jerusalem, swiftly increasing in size, and finally emptying into the Dead Sea - *"which being brought forth into the sea, THE WATERS SHALL BE HEALED."* (Ezekiel 47:1-12)

This wonderful, visionary insight into the future communicates that the bitter and murky waters of "death to self" will one day be replaced with the sweet, crystal-clear waters of an indescribably beautiful and eternal heritage ...for *"the waters shall be healed."*

This ultimate exchange will prove that the temporary conflict with carnality was truly worth it all.

In fact, if we are enlightened, we can easily echo Paul, the apostle, who asserted - "the sufferings of this present time are not worthy to be compared with the glory which shall be revealed in us" and "all things work together for good to them that love God, to them who are the called according to His purpose." (Romans 8:18,28)

• **God's good pleasure and foundational purpose is to bring us forth in His image. All things revolve around this central theme of creation.**

This is the longing of God's heart, the mystery of His will, and the glory of His promise.

And in the highest sense, for all of God's people, this is the perfection of what it means to successfully enter into and possess *the Land of Promise.*

Therefore, let us arise and cross over Jordan to "possess our possessions" - joyously drinking in the *milk* of the Word and the *honey* of the Spirit, as we thoroughly study one hundred and fifteen of our God-given *titles.*

Let us purpose in our hearts to leave Jordan behind and make the *"land of red-purple"* - the royal *"land of oil olive"* - our continual, spiritual dwelling place.

And as we discover this grand and challenging portion of **OUR GLORIOUS INHERITANCE** may we be ever faithful to - "walk worthy of the Lord unto all pleasing, being fruitful in every good work, and increasing in the knowledge of God; strengthened with all might, according to **HIS GLORIOUS POWER.**" (Colossians 1:10-11)

AMBASSADORS FOR CHRIST

"...God was in Christ, reconciling the world unto Himself, not imputing their trespasses unto them; and hath committed unto us the word of reconciliation.

*Now then we are **AMBASSADORS FOR CHRIST**, as though God did beseech you by us; we pray you in Christ's stead, be ye reconciled to God."*

(II Corinthians 5:19-20)

AMBASSADORS FOR CHRIST

"...God was in Christ, reconciling the world unto Himself, not imputing their trespasses unto them; and hath committed unto us the word of reconciliation.
Now then we are AMBASSADORS FOR CHRIST, as though God did beseech you by us: we pray you in Christ's stead, be ye reconciled to God."

(II Corinthians 5:19-20)

• An *ambassador* is *a representative or a messenger, one who is sent on a specific errand.*

An *ambassador* always seeks to speak, not his own mind, but the perfect will and the very words that the king, the ruling government, or the authority he represents would speak himself.

Therefore, we can define an *ambassador* as a person who has, to great degree, lost his own identity and become a voice of a message - a message that usually has a supreme or royal source of authority.

The very authority of the message is imparted to the ambassador. His words, in a sense, carry just as much weight as if the king, president or potentate represented was speaking himself.

It is as if an invisible host stands behind the *ambassador* to support each statement and lend authority to what he says.

For instance, when an ambassador of the United States speaks, in a very real way, he is sanctioned and supported by all the combined authority of the U.S. Army, the Navy, the Marines, the Air Force, the Pentagon, the Congress, the Senate, the FBI, the CIA, all city and state government officials, even the President, his cabinet and finally - all of the American people.

It is no wonder then that an *ambassador* can sway a whole nation, for he could well say - *"There are more for me than there are against me."*

In like manner, as *ambassadors of Christ,* we are encompassed about with a great cloud of witnesses, for we speak in the name of the kingdom of God. Therefore, we are also, in a very real way, sanctioned by all of the inhabitants of that kingdom and supported by all of their combined authority - from the patriarchs, to the prophets, to the apostles, to the Lord of glory Himself with all His holy angels.

When we speak under the direction of God and under His anointing what we say can potentially bear just as much authority as when the Lord Himself spoke.

Admittedly, we who are so prone to error can in no way compare ourselves to the flawless Saviour who was God incarnate.

But still, we are constrained to declare that there are definitely certain times when it is not we who speak but the Spirit of our Father who dwells

11

in us and speaks out of us.

This is our God-given privilege and the potential of our calling!

Yes, we can now legally and joyously proclaim, as the seventy disciples - "Lord, even the devils are subject unto us through Thy name." (Luke 10:17)

Jesus spoke with all authority, and all of heaven supported what He said. All power, all authority, in heaven and in earth was given unto Him. Anybody who heard His message knew that He was different. His word was with power, for He spoke with authority and not as the scribes.

But now, as Elijah passed the mantle to Elisha, so the mantle that rested upon the firstborn Son has been passed to the church, to perpetuate the work of Christ on earth. And because we are presently seated with Him in heavenly places, we can boldly take authority over sin, sickness, and satanic powers in His name.

This is our *ambassadorship birthright* and this is our inheritance blessing as sons of God.

The works that Jesus did, we are chosen to do also...we are called to carry on the ministry that He initiated.

The words that He spoke, we are chosen to speak also...we are called to perpetuate the message that Jesus initiated.

It is a God-inspired message.

We are His representatives.

We seek to speak as He would speak if He were here.

As *ambassadors for Christ*, through our words, we have the power to bring darkness under our dominion and to bring men into the light.

THE REVELATION OF RECONCILIATION

• One of the greatest responsibilities given to heaven's representatives is the privilege of entreating humanity to be *reconciled* to God.

To effect this end, the Bible declares that we have inherited *"the word of reconciliation"*, for this was Jesus' message to start with. And He has given us *"the ministry of reconciliation"* as well.

*To be **reconciled** means to be restored to a former right and harmonious relationship...in our case, being restored back to intimate fellowship with God.*

If we have been truly reinstated this way...not only can we tell people about it - *the word of reconciliation* - we can bring them into this blessed experience - *the ministry of reconciliation.*

We can reveal, by the Word and the Spirit, the wonderful transforming power of restoration grace, but what is even more wonderful...we can administer it to broken lives.

12

We are caught up in the process of being restored to the oneness with God that Adam lost, and God has given us the privilege and the power to pass this blessing on to others.

The Greek words translated in II Corinthians 5:19-20 into the verb - *reconciled,* and into the noun - *reconciliation*, are *katallasso* and *katallage*, respectively.

These two related words both convey the meaning of *being thoroughly changed...*in our case, being *changed* from a position of enmity with God to a position of fellowship with God.

• **God is unchangeable. God is never reconciled to man; it is always man who must be reconciled to God.**

The whole human race was reconciled to God potentially by Jesus' death on the cross. The price has already been paid, so the opportunity for reconciliation is always present.

This could easily be compared to some benefactor putting a large sum of money in an account in someone's name and then giving that person a blank check book.

Jesus, in a sense, has similarly filled up a heavenly bank account, in each one of our names, with unlimited mercy, measureless grace, and abundant righteousness.

All we are required to do is sign the check with faith, humility and sincerity, and then the door to this heavenly treasury is opened wide.

This is exactly why no man can earn God's forgiveness either before or after salvation...for there is nothing that we can do to merit this abundant life. A human being is merely required to open himself up to the river of mercy that is already flowing from the throne of God.

We cannot earn the unearned favor of God.

We cannot achieve that which has already freely been given.

MAINTAINING OUR RECONCILED STATUS

God gets great joy out of giving generously and **reconciliation** is one of His most precious, free and generous gifts.

Colossians 1:21-23 makes it so plain:

> *"And you, that were sometime alienated and enemies in your mind by wicked works, yet now hath He reconciled*
> *In the body of His flesh through death, to present you holy, unblameable and unreproveable in His sight:*
> *If ye continue in the faith grounded and settled, and be not moved away from the hope of the gospel..."*

Here we see the key to obtaining sweet communion with the Creator, and once we have obtained it, to maintain this full acceptance in His presence.

We must "continue in the faith, grounded and settled."

This passage can be interpreted two ways.

First - it speaks of the vital importance of building our lives on certain religious principles set down in God's Word that promise to keep us in close contact with the Almighty.

We must persist in holding on to these standards in order to *maintain our reconciled status.*

In other words, "continuing in the faith" consists of abiding in the truth and staying sincere before God through prayer, through repentance, through self-denial, through a lifestyle of holiness, through zealous works, and through the study of God's Word.

By doing these things we do not earn the fulfillment of God's promises; we merely keep ourselves in a *position of receptivity* where we can claim our rights as God's New Testament offspring.

Secondly, the command to "continue in the faith" may well mean that no matter what we face in life we are called to "cling to the old rugged cross"..."and be not moved away from the hope" of mercy and restoration being available there.

"MADE NIGH" BY THE BLOOD

• Ephesians 2:12-18 further explains how we, as Gentiles, were "aliens from the commonwealth of Israel, and strangers from the covenants of promise, having no hope, and without God in this world: but now in Christ Jesus ye who sometimes were far off are *made nigh* by the blood of Christ."

Now, if we are "in Christ", and if we have been *made nigh,* the next question is...."How close really are we to the Father?"

The following four-line poem says it well:

> *Near to God,*
> *Nearer I cannot be;*
> *For abiding in Christ the Son of God,*
> *I am as near as He.*

Yes, this is the miracle of it all...that we are just as accepted in the presence of the Father as the firstborn Son, for we are identified with Christ.

This is wonderful news!

And this is the gracious message that we, as *ambassadors for Christ,* must share with the church and with the world.

14

• We have not only received the peace *of* God; Romans 5:1 and Ephesians 2:14 declare that..."by faith, we have peace *with* God, through our Lord Jesus Christ" - "for He is our peace."

He has *reconciled* both Jew and Gentile unto God "in one body by the cross, having slain the enmity thereby."

And because this is true we can boldly confess ...Now we are *reconciled!* Now we are *made nigh!* And now we have peace *with* God!

Right now we have "*access* by one Spirit unto the Father" and we have "*access* by faith into this grace wherein we stand, and rejoice in hope of the glory of God." (Ephesians 2:18, Romans 5:2)

Before, we were nothing but outcasts and rejects, but now we have *access* (entrance rights). We are more than welcome in the very throne room of the King of kings and the Lord of lords.

By faith we abide continually in His sent-forth presence, for we are members of His family.

We dwell under the canopy of His everlasting love.

We are filled to overflowing with His everlasting life.

• For this cause, restoration grace is far more available to us now than it was the day we were saved.

> *"For if, when we were enemies, we were **reconciled** to God by the death of His Son, much more, being **reconciled** we shall be saved by His life."*
>
> (Romans 5:10)

In other words, if we are true sons and daughters of God, we have an even greater right to obtain God's mercy than the erring, yet repentant sinner seeking for salvation, for *divine life* has taken up residence in our hearts.

This is the *"**Much More Reconciliation Covenant**"* of which we are a part, and this is the constancy and faithfulness of the God who has promised His beloved offspring - "I will never leave thee, nor forsake thee." (Hebrews 13:5)

THE TEST OF TRUE SPIRITUALITY

If we are to procure this part of our blessed heritage we must also be willing to generously give like mercy away to others.

This is not an option.

This is a command.

• Jesus told us Himself that - "if thou bring thy gift to the altar, and there rememberest that thy brother hath ought against thee; leave there thy gift before the altar, and go thy way; first be *reconciled* to thy brother, and then come and offer thy gift." (Matthew 5:23-24)

Maintaining this *spirit of reconciliation*, this spirit to restore, is the sign of Christlikeness, the indication of spirituality, and a major fulfilling of the call to *ambassadorship.*

Galatians 6:1 says - "Brethren, if a man be overtaken in a fault, ye which are spiritual, restore such an one in the spirit of meekness."

This scripture proves that our God is a God of restoration for, through it, He clearly reveals that when we become God-like, when we become spiritual, we will rejoice in restoration also!

JESUS - SLAIN FROM THE FOUNDATION

It is an awe-inspiring truth that long before the fall of Adam the **spirit of reconciliation** was already very much a part of God's character...for it had already taken up its abode in His heart.

• Long before the first sin was committed, and before any man needed to be reinstated, the Bible declares that the Lamb of God was slain..."from the foundation of the world". (Revelation 13:8)

God predetermined that the crucifixion would be a definite future event, and in so doing, **God made a way before the way even needed to be made!!**

Knowing this fact alone should establish us in unshakeable confidence and faith for grace, but there is even more evidence to prove this vital point.

The very first thing that the Lord God did when He visited Eden after the fall, was not to vent His fury against the trembling, guilt-ridden parents of the human race, but rather to prophesy the eventual destruction of Satan and restoration of the redeemed.

He turned to the serpent and spoke those piercing, prophetic words - "Because thou hast done this, thou art cursed above all cattle, and above every beast of the field; upon thy belly shalt thou go, and dust shalt thou eat all the days of thy life: And I will put enmity between thee and the woman, and between thy seed and her seed; it shall bruise thy head, and thou shalt bruise His heel." (Genesis 3:14-15)

The prophecy of *the seed of the woman* having His heel bruised speaks of the torturous treatment Jesus went through on Calvary where he was "bruised for our iniquities." (Isaiah 53:5)

But the prophecy that the head of the serpent would be bruised speaks of Satan's power being crushed, and the venom of sin being rendered powerless...and, of course, this was also fulfilled at Calvary.

• **So we see that from the very start God's chief concern and deep desire was** *reconciliation.*

And surely...His character has not changed.

If this was His passion in the beginning, then it is still His passion and the joyous expression of His heart now.

THIS IS THE MESSAGE THAT A HURTING HUMAN RACE NEEDS TO HEAR!!

Someone quite sincere in her love for God once asked me how long it takes to be forgiven. She had made a serious mistake in her life several years before and was still haunted by it.

I immediately answered - *"As long as it takes for you to believe."* Her face lit up with hope at the sound of this *word of reconciliation* (and how many thousands of others are groping through the darkness of guilt and self-condemnation desperately reaching out for the same kind of blessed hope).

For their sake, we must shout it aloud - *"Amazing grace, how sweet the sound"!*

Grace is our answer.

Grace is the everlasting door to life and faith is the master key that opens the door. Grace comes as an immediate response to the repentant heart and the believing spirit, and grace delights in restoration!

Grace is God's goodness overflowing out of heaven into our lives and overflowing out of our hearts into the lives of others.

• This glorious gift called *grace* is the central core and the main thrust of our message if we are *true ambassadors*...a message of God's bountiful provision for those who believe.

THE IMPUTING OF RIGHTEOUSNESS

We know that Jesus did not come to condemn; He came to save.

Jesus came to bring men back into intimacy with God. Jesus, the last Adam, came for the purpose of being a **quickening spirit** (an ambitious and determined life-giver). (I Corinthians 15:45, 47)

Jesus came to bear the judgment for sin, not to release it against His own. Jesus came, not to impute sin, but to impute righteousness.

• Again, II Corinthians 5:19 declares that - *"God was in Christ, reconciling the world unto Himself, not imputing their trespasses unto them."*

To impute means to lay to a person's charge or reckon to his account.

Jesus did not come to lay sin to our charge and prove us guilty before the throne. The law did that.

Jesus came rather to minister a righteous nature, a new nature, a divine nature, to those who accept and believe in the power of the cross.

Jesus came to attribute a standing of holiness in the presence of God to those who dare to trust in His life-giving promises.

He was the most excellent good-will *Ambassador* ever sent from heaven. Now, every son of God has received His commission and His message. We are *a family of ambassadors*, sent by God, to publish the "good news" of the gospel in all the world.

Jesus said - *"as My Father hath sent Me, even so send I you."* (John 20:21)

We speak in His stead.

We do not entreat the Father to condemn the world, we rather entreat the world and erring members of the church to be *reconciled* to the Father.

It is God beseeching the world through us...compassionately pleading with humanity to receive His gift of mercy.

CORRECTLY PORTRAYING GOD'S ATTITUDES

How different this Jesus is from the picture that we have often painted for people with our words! Too many times, we have portrayed him as a harsh, vindictive God, looming over humanity with a heart intent to destroy, instead of portraying Him as the bleeding, suffering Saviour, hanging over humanity with a heart intent to save.

Like unto the beautiful parable that Jesus gave (Luke 15:11-32) when a prodigal son comes home, He runs to that son, when he is yet afar off, swiftly embracing him in His compassion and restoring him to fellowship again.

This *everlasting Father* is quick to put a ring on His son's finger (renewing His covenant of promise) and quick to clothe him in the finest apparel (robes of imparted righteousness and garments of praise).

This *Lord of reconciliation* is quick in issuing orders to his servants to "kill the fatted calf".

In other words, He is quick in commanding his angels to provide the repentant backslider with a spiritual feast of the good things of God.

This is the revelation of the true nature of God. And this is the spirit and the attitude toward others that we should also have if we are to correctly represent this Christ of Calvary. We must champion the rights of the weak, the weary and the downtrodden, and plead their cause.

• We must present the Word to this generation in the spirit and the revelation that heaven wills.

No *ambassador* would be doing his job right if he exhibited anger when his country wished to extend kindness or mercy. Neither would he be right in extending pity when reproof was needful.

He must die to his own feelings and prejudices, and seek only to reflect the attitude of the nation, kingdom or political ruler for whom he speaks! And so it should be with us, the children of the Most High God.

It should be our continual desire to be so crucified with Christ and so dead to our own will, that in every situation we act and react as Jesus would if He were here.

Let us determine to so fully surrender to our Saviour that His thoughts become our thoughts, His ways become our ways, and His will becomes our will.

May our hearts pulsate with the same emotional rhythm as His.

May we love as He loved, forgive as He forgave...and make a stand for righteousness just as firm as the stand that He took. Then this generation will witness the spirit of the Messiah again - in His people.

The world is hungering to see, not just those who profess faith in Jesus, but those who manifest His Spirit and the nature behind His message. When this fully takes place (when heaven has *true ambassadors* in every nation and in every city) the world will never be the same.

THE ULTIMATE EXPRESSION OF
OUR AMBASSADORSHIP CALLING

Even if we were to reach the perfection of this earthly *ambassadorship* calling, we would still only be stepping up on the very first rung of an inheritance-ladder that reaches all the way into eternity.

• For surely the ultimate expression and manifestation of our *ambassadorship* is yet to be unveiled...in the Millenial Kingdom and the New Creation to come.

We will most assuredly be those Spirit-empowered, oracular emissaries sent forth into all the earth to represent His majesty, the King of glory, when He reigns in Jerusalem in great splendor and matchless beauty during the Kingdom Age.

Moreover, in the infinite age beyond, it seems quite certain that all of creation will be our charge, for the elect will ultimately inherit all things and fill the lofty, stewardship position of *celestial envoys,* officially and gloriously representing Jehovah-God throughout His vast universe.

The main thrust of our message and ministry then, as **AMBASSADORS FOR CHRIST**, will necessarily change, for full and complete reconciliation will at that time be an established universal accomplishment and fact.

This is the foundational purpose of God and the ultimate climax of His plan.

• The swirling alpha and omega whirlpool of this fixed, living and eternal purpose is like a "wheel in the middle of a wheel"...incessantly, powerfully and irresistibly drawing all reconcilable things toward that blessed and final goal - THE DAY OF ABSOLUTE RESTORATION AND PERFECTION.*1

Ephesians 1:9-10 explains the mystery of God's will -"which He hath purposed in Himself: that in the dispensation of the fullness of times He might gather together [or *reconcile]* in one all things in Christ, both which are in heaven, and which are on earth; even in Him."

This will apparently happen progressively, beginning with the coming of the Lord - "whom the heaven must receive until the times of restitution of all things" and culminating at the end of the day of the Lord (the thousand-year kingdom) when - "the heavens shall pass away with a great noise, and the elements shall melt with fervent heat, the earth also and the works that are therein shall be burned up." (Acts 3:21, II Peter 3:10)

"Nevertheless we, according to His promise, look for New Heavens and a New Earth, wherein dwelleth righteousness." (II Peter 3:13)

When this comes to pass, and it surely will, every *ambassador* of Jesus Christ will become an eternal fixture - an everlasting pillar in the temple of God. (Rev. 3:12)

We will be fully restored.

We will be unshakeable in our inherited position.

We will be channels of the living Word throughout the healed cosmos...voices of deity throughout the reconciled creation .

And most of all we will find supreme comfort in the everlasting embrace of a loving heavenly Father.

*We will be **ambassadors for Christ** forever...in the highest sense of the Word.*

AN IMPORTANT AFTERTHOUGHT

• Our study of this title would not be complete unless we include this final thought.

An ambassador normally resides at an embassy.

An American embassy is like a tiny little America in the midst of another country. It flies the American flag.

The resident U.S. diplomats and their staffs enjoy all the rights and privileges of being U.S. citizens within that compound, even if they are in the midst of a somewhat hostile country that rejects our philosophy of liberty for all.

They are in a foreign and unfriendly nation, but they are not of that nation.

In like manner, every truly anointed church or fellowship gathering is like one of heaven's embassies.

We fly the blood-stained banner of Jesus...the symbol of our national identity. We enjoy the rights and privileges of being in the heavenly family though we live in a world at enmity with Him.

We have liberty in the Spirit in the midst of a world of bondage.

We have fellowship with God in a world that is separate from Him.

We experience a little bit of heaven right here on earth.

We are in the world, but not of the world!

WE ARE AMBASSADORS!!

---

*1 Ultimate reconciliation WILL NOT include Satan or any of his fallen angels; neither will it include those who are damned....cut off from God forever at the great white throne judgment.

BRANCHES

"I am the vine, ye are the BRANCHES."

(John 15:5)

BRANCHES

"I am the vine, ye are the BRANCHES."

(John 15:5)

These words were spoken by Jesus.

He likened Himself to a *vine*.

He spoke of His believers as *branches*.

The central theme of this analogy is the concept and the revelation of our oneness with the Lord.

This inheritance of oneness with God is undoubtedly one of the most beautiful mysteries of the New Covenant.

No person can discover this truth without being radically transformed as a result.

We will explore this revelation on four separate levels:

Oneness of origin.

Oneness of nature.

Oneness of purpose.

And...oneness of destiny.

ONENESS OF ORIGIN

• A vine and its branches are one with respect to origin, for both come forth from the same seed.

This *seed* could well represent the eternal plan of God, formed in the heart of God in the very beginning.

This eternal Word-plan definitely included the death, burial and resurrection of Jesus, for the Bible clearly stated that He was delivered up unto death - "by the determinate counsel and foreknowledge of God." (Acts 2:23)

This original *seed-plan* also included every born again, blood-washed child of God that ever has been or ever will be, for we were chosen "in Him" before the foundation of the world. (Ephesians 1:4)

• In light of this revelation, it is somewhat easier to comprehend how Jesus could make astounding statements to His disciples such as - *"ye also shall bear witness, because ye have been with Me from the beginning."* (John 15:27)

Certainly Jesus was referring to something far deeper than just the start of His three-and-a-half year ministry when He used the phrase- *"from the beginning."*

The Bible declared that - "He that sanctifieth and they who are sanctified are all of *one*: for which cause He is not ashamed to call them brethren." (Hebrews 2:11)

The Revised Standard Version translated this passage to say that the Sanctifier, and those He sanctifies, are all of -"one origin."

The New English Bible says that we are - "all of one stock."

The entire human family was originally hidden in the loins of Adam, but our spiritual roots go back farther than that. We come from heavenly stock. The entire family of God was originally hid with Christ in God, in the bosom of the Father. This is a great mystery!

The Vine and His branches, the Sanctifier and those He sanctifies, have both come from the same source.

We have been with Him and in Him...from the beginning.

God spoke the following words to Jeremiah:

"Before I formed thee in the belly, I knew thee; and before thou camest forth out of the womb I sanctified thee, and I ordained thee a prophet unto the nations." (Jeremiah 1:5)

- **The meaning of the word -** *sanctify* **- is twofold.**
  First - it means *to set apart for sacred or religious use.*
  Second - it *means to cleanse, purify or free from sin.*
  In this instance, it means the former - *to be reserved and set apart by God for a certain predetermined purpose.*

God sanctified Jeremiah, setting him apart for sacred use, before he ever came forth from the womb.

The Vine ordained in advance that the life-sap of prophecy would flow through this particular branch, producing the fruit of repentance in Israel.

Now, if this be true with respect to an Old Testament prophet, then how much more is it true concerning every New Testament son or daughter of God!

God has certainly elected us and sanctified us to fulfill a certain portion of His great eternal design and He did it before we ever came into this world.

The spiritual roots of this spiritual Vine reach all the way back to the beginning - to the very commencement of all creative expression.

The Bible declared that we live - "in hope of eternal life, which God, that cannot lie, promised before the world began." (Titus 1:2)

What a marvellous unveiling of truth!

The God of ordination actually knew us in the beginning.

He promised us eternal life in the beginning.

He sanctified us at the very inception of creation.

He anticipated our eventual existence in this world and He qualified us to fulfill His original "blueprint plan" before we ever came forth from the womb.

24

Knowing these things should produce and develop in us a spirit of absolute confidence.

We can be confident that our God will watch over us, for we are linked to Him now and forever.

We know that He is mighty to save.

We know that He will keep us.

We can have this blessed assurance for we know that the Vine and His branches are both integral parts of the same foundational Word-plan.

We are extremely important to Him.

We have nothing to fear.

We came from the same seed.

ONENESS OF NATURE

• The same life-sap that flows through the vine, flows through the branches also.

It is normally the same sap, the same watery solution, that flows throughout a plant's entire vascular system, not separate fluids in different parts of the plant.

In like manner, it is definitely the same spiritual fluid, the same "sap", that flowed initially through Jesus and now flows through the heart and life of every believer.

We have all been made partakers of the same divine nature.

In fact, I Corinthians 6:17 declares -*"He that is joined unto the Lord is one spirit."*

Therefore, the supernatural joy that we experience as sons of God is not just joy that comes *from* God, it is the joy *OF* God! In the Vine-Revelation chapter, Jesus proclaimed..."These things have I spoken unto you that *My joy* might remain in you, and that your joy might be full." (John 15:11)

In like manner, the blessed peace that we partake of as children of the Most High is not just a peace that comes *from* God, it is a peace *OF* God. Jesus said - "Peace I leave with you, *My peace* I give unto you..." (John 14:27)

Moreover, the love that is shed abroad in our hearts by the Holy Ghost is not just a love that comes *from* God, it is the love *OF* God. Jesus prayed - "Father...that *the love* wherewith Thou hast loved Me may be in them..." (John 17:26)

So we see that it is undoubtedly His joy, His peace, His love, His holiness, His strength, His authority and His very nature that rises in us daily, springing up from within.

This spiritual sap is the very life of God.

• **To understand this fully it is imperative to know that there are two kinds of life...natural life** *(psuche)* **and divine life** *(zoe).*

25

Whenever natural life is referred to in the Scripture, the Greek word almost always used is *psuche* (such as Matthew 6:25 -"Take no thought for your *life,* what ye shall eat, or what ye shall drink").

Whenever eternal life, or divine life, is referred to in the New Testament, the Greek word is always *zoe* (such as John 6:47 - "He that believeth on Me hath everlasting *life*").

All sons of Adam inherit the same natural life *(psuche)* that produces the potential for certain natural abilities in their human bodies.

All sons of God inherit the same divine life *(zoe)* that produces certain potential supernatural abilities in their spirits.

This is eternal life and these are divine attributes, divine abilities, that were revealed initially in the firstborn Son.

These attributes and abilities can also be manifested in us, for - "if the root be holy, so are the branches." (Romans 11:16)

If the root be strong and if the Vine be strong, then so are the branches.

If the Vine is a channel of wisdom, love, healing, and deliverance, then so are the branches.

We must reemphasize an important fact.

The same life-sap that flows through the Vine, flows through the branches also.

If the Vine can say, "I am one with the sap", then the branches can also say, "I am one with the sap". If the Vine, Jesus, could boldly declare - *"I and My Father are one"* - then we, the branches, can surely, in a certain qualified sense, echo the same claim.

The Vine is the total plant.

The *life-sap* is the Spirit of the living God.

This spiritual sap contains the sum total of the personality of deity.

The branches are just small individual parts of the total, but heirs of the same life and channels of the same divine personality.

From out of our inner being is issuing forth a deep, strong, and constant current of the life of God *(zoe)* that can make us conquerors in any situation.

As long as we keep believing, this river of life-sap just keeps flowing. (John 7:38)

Having this kind of revelation knowledge produces in us a spirit of stick-to-itiveness, perseverance and power...for we recognize who we are and what we have.

• **It has been said that there are two kinds of vines that grow in this world...climbers and crawlers.**

Crawlers edge their way along on the ground, clinging to the dirt, and are unable to rise above their terrible plight.

Climbers have a different spirit.

They are a different breed.

They love to attach themselves to the obstacles that stand in their way and climb above them.

In fact, they actually use those obstacles as a means of rising higher.

We see a message in this.

There was a time when we were connected to the vine of this world.

We crawled through life, inching our way from one defeat to another.

We were bound to the flesh and saw no way out of our grievous condition.

But now we have been grafted into the Vine of God.

We have been born again.

We are climbers now.

We are linked to the Son of God, who, like Joseph of old, was chosen to be - *"a fruitful bough by a well; whose branches run over the wall."* (Genesis 49:22)

Jesus is the *"fruitful bough"*.

We are His *branches*.

We have been planted by a *well* of living water.

We drink of the supernatural, therefore we have the spirit to win.

No *wall* can permanently hinder us!

No obstacle can stop us.

We turn stumblingblocks into steppingstones.

Our inheritance is sure victory.

We do not have to run from pressure now...instead we can attach ourselves to our problems and rise above them, bringing them under subjection.

We have learned this expertise from our Elder Brother.

He attached Himself to the greatest foes of the human race and victoriously rose above them.

And, without question, this is our character now as well...*for we are one with the nature of the Vine.*

ONENESS OF PURPOSE

There is a definite reason that God has included us in this wonderful Vine-Branch relationship.

• Jesus made His purpose very clear when He said - "Herein is My Father glorified, that ye bear *much fruit;* so shall ye be My disciples." (John 15:8)

The Vine expresses itself by producing fruit...in fact, bearing fruit is the highest expression of the life of the Vine.

God is not interested in merely making men religious; but God is quite interested in producing fruit in their lives...spiritual fruit...lasting, remaining fruit.

This spiritual fruit is the manifestation of the divine personality in us, for *"the fruit of the Spirit is love, joy, peace, longsuffering, gentleness, goodness, faith, meekness [and] temperance."* (Galatians 5:22-23)

This spiritual fruit is also the manifestation of divine abilities and the manifestation of the power and authority of God in us as revealed in the gifts of the Spirit - *the word of wisdom, the word of knowledge, faith, healing, the working of miracles, prophecy, discerning of spirits, divers kinds of tongues and interpretation of tongues.* (I Corinthians 12:8-10)

No person should ever be satisfied with just the initial experience of repentance and salvation, for the Bible demands that we - "bring forth therefore *fruits* meet for repentance." (Matthew 3:8)

We may be involved in many church related works, but mere religious works do not necessarily contain the life of God nor the seed of His eternal purpose.

Fruitless religiosity is an abomination to God.

This was the spiritual condition of much of Israel when Jesus first came and unfortunately this is the condition of many professing Christians in this hour.

• Jesus symbolically revealed how He felt concerning Israel's lack of true spiritual fruit by His reaction to a fruitless fig tree. (Matthew 21:18-21, Mark 11:12-18)

Of all the miracles Jesus performed, this is the only dark miracle, the only negative miracle.

The fig tree represented Israel.

The Bible said Jesus hungered and looked for fruit on the tree, but He found nothing but leaves. (And how the Lord for centuries had hungered to see spiritual fruit in Israel only to find, all too often, the rattling leaves of lifeless, religious rituals instead).

He cursed the fig tree, which immediately withered away, as He cried *"No man eat fruit of thee hereafter for ever."*

The very same day He took a strong stand against religious hypocrisy in His preaching.

He furiously cleansed the temple. Shortly thereafter He announced the beginning of a New Covenant and His "setting aside" of the Jewish religious system, which in a certain sense soon "withered away" also, losing its effectiveness in contacting God.

We had better learn from the history of God's dealings with men lest we also offer Him "rattling leaves" (and professing Christendom has been guilty of this quite often).

We know that Jesus is inspecting the church in this hour, for -"judgment must begin at the house of God". (I Peter 4:17)

As a result, the false church system will again be utterly rejected and dry up from the roots, but - "they that know their God shall be strong and do exploits." (Daniel 11:32)

The true church will bear *much fruit* as the end approaches...quite possibly, more than ever before.

• The key to the fulfillment of this is a word found nine times in the first ten verses of John 15...the word **abide** (a word which has multiple, related meanings).

As an intransitive verb (a verb that needs no complement to complete its meaning) to **abide** means *to continue or to remain stable or fixed in some condition or state.* It can also mean *to remain constant, faithful, and unchanging in some relationship.*

At times, it means *to continue in a place, to have a permanent abode...to stay, to dwell, or to reside.*

As a transitive verb (a verb that expresses an action carried over from a subject to an object) **abide** can mean *to look for, or to watch for...to await expectantly.*

It can also mean *to endure without yielding when faced with some hard trial or task.*

How these definitions enhance the meaning of Jesus' words - "If a man *abide* not in Me, he is cast forth as a branch, and is withered; and men gather them, and cast them into the fire, and they are burned."

If we continue in His commandments, and if we remain firm in our commitment, we *abide* in His love.

If we continue humbling ourselves before Him and if we remain persistent in believing God, we *abide* in His grace.

Jesus said - *"abide* in Me, and I in you. As the branch cannot bear fruit of itself, except it abide in the vine; no more can ye, except ye *abide* in Me."

To *abide in the Vine* is to constantly, fervently walk after the fulfillment of the Word of God and to zealously and continually seek after the leadership of the will of God...as we joyously await His return.

Those who passionately and persistently pursue this goal will surely become one with the ordination of the firstborn Son...for we find our abode in God and the Father finds His abode in us.

When this takes place we can patiently and confidently endure any trial for we know that **the purpose of God** that resided initially in the firstborn Son has taken up residence in us as well.

We can expect opposition for we have been sent even as He was sent, but we can also expect to win in His name.

The Bible declares -"for this **purpose** the Son of God was manifested, that He might destroy the works of the devil." (I John 3:8)

This is God's ordination and purpose in the Vine.

This is also God's ordination and purpose in the branches.

The life-sap is God's ability flowing through us to perform this important task.

We are fruit bearers.

We are purpose producers.

We are well able to destroy the hold of sin, guilt and depression in the lives of those who have been captivated by the same.

We can do all things through Christ, for it is really His Spirit moving through us.

We have spiritual weapons to fight with that are mighty through God.

In the name of Jesus, we will continue to destroy the works of the devil.

We are bold in declaring this, for we are one with the Vine.

Therefore, we are one with the purpose of God.

ONENESS OF DESTINY

The Vine and His branches are destined to share a similar inheritance eternally.

This is His great joy as well as ours.

This is His supreme goal for us.

We recognize that our oneness with Him is presently only partially manifested...but we are soon to enter a relationship of great depth, a spiritual *land of red-purple* that will far exceed anything we have ever known.

We thank God for what we are now, but we long for what we will be.

• In the resurrection chapter of the New Testament (I Corinthians 15) we find that the Vine, Jesus, is going to keep growing and taking over more territory in this world until, when He comes again - *"all things shall be subdued unto Him."*

Jesus must reign, and this Vine must grow, until all enemies are put under His feet.

"The last enemy that shall be destroyed is death." (I Cor. 15:26)

"Then cometh the end, when He shall have delivered up the kingdom to God, even the Father...*that God may be all in all.*" (I Corinthians 15:24,28)

• In other words, in the resurrection, when the plan of God is brought to perfect fulfillment, the fullness of the Godhead will be beautifully and gloriously expressed in every son of God.

The fruit of the Vine will reach full maturity.

God will be all in all.

The life-sap of the Holy Spirit will finally find fullness of expression in us.

Of course, in no way does this or any other statement made in this chapter imply that we will ever reach the absolute of oneness with the Father that Jesus possessed, for He was, and is, and ever will be, God Almighty. We are only the sons of God.

But we do know that this fullness will manifest in us to the highest degree of expression possible in the offspring of the Most High and that this will perfectly transpire, first at the resurrection, and then, quite possibly, to an even greater degree when the New Creation is birthed into being.

And yet, even then, we will still continue to grow...infinitely (for - "of the *increase* of His...peace there shall be no end.") (Isaiah 9:7)

Through the revelation of this scripture we assume that throughout eternity God will be creating within Himself, and within His sons, greater heights and depths of supernatural expression.

Of the increase of His peace there will be no end.

Of the increase of His joy there will be no end.

Of the increase and development of His personality and character there will be no end...within the Vine and within the branches. Of His acts of creativity there will be no end, for God is unlimited in power.

It is therefore impossible for Him to be bound to a certain level of creative expression.

In a sense therefore, we may never be able to fully reach the ultimate, for as we discover and experience greater depths and heights in God, He is able to simultaneously create, within Himself, depths and heights of divine character infinitely deeper and higher than anything we have known Him to be.

In like manner, when it seems that the indwelling presence of God has expressed itself fully in us, suddenly another wave of glory will roll our direction - swelling, cresting, then crashing over our souls. The creative life-sap of the Spirit of God within us will suddenly surge forward, thrusting us into an even deeper revelation of the heart of God and lifting us into an even higher unveiling of that same divine character in us.

• Again, this will be God's great joy as well as ours.

It was also Jesus' fervent plea, for He prayed - *"Father...that they may be one, even as We are one."* (John 17:21-22)

It is certain that His petition was answered.

It is certain that His prayer will come to pass.

And it is certain that Jesus meant what He said when He used the astounding phrase - *even as.*

• THE BRIDE •

THE LAMB'S WIFE

THE CHILDREN OF THE BRIDECHAMBER

THE ATTENDANTS OF THE BRIDEGROOM

HIS SISTER, HIS SPOUSE

THE PRINCE'S DAUGHTER

A WALL

A PALACE OF SILVER

"...Come hither, I will shew thee
THE BRIDE, THE LAMB'S WIFE."
(Revelation 21:9)

"And Jesus said unto them, Can **THE CHILDREN OF THE BRIDE-CHAMBER** *mourn, as long as the bridegroom is with them? but the days will come, when the bridegroom shall be taken from them, and then shall they fast."*

(Matthew 9:15)

*"Thou hast ravished My heart , **MY SISTER, MY SPOUSE...**"*

(Song of Solomon 4:9)

*"How beautiful are thy feet with shoes, **O PRINCE'S DAUGHTER!**"*

(Song of Solomon 7:1)

*"If she be **A WALL**, we will build upon her **A PALACE OF SILVER...**"*

(Song of Solomon 8:9)

THE BRIDE, THE LAMB'S WIFE

"...come hither, I will shew thee THE BRIDE, THE
LAMB'S WIFE."

(Revelation 21:9)

In the beginning, during the first six days of creation, God regularly confirmed the progress of His plan by making a certain positive and conclusive observation.

Five times the Bible recorded that God looked upon the completion of certain stages in the drama of creation and - "God saw that it was good."

On the sixth day - "God saw everything that He had made, and behold, it was very good." (Genesis 1:31)

It seems that God was quite content with the heavens and the earth as they were. God was satisfied. God was pleased.

• But then God made His first negative observation; He noticed something that was not good. Genesis 2:18 states that the Lord voiced his concern saying - *"It is not good that man should be alone."*

This was a flaw in creation that had to be corrected, so God decided to immediately remedy the situation.

He said, concerning Adam - *"I will make him an help meet for him."*

This word - *meet* - means *suitable, fit, worthy or sufficient.*

God knew that the animals, even in their perfect state, could not supply suitable, fulfilling fellowship for Adam.

Adam needed a companion, a helper, capable of communicating with him on his level...someone who could sufficiently meet his needs.

Adam needed an earthly partner...someone he could give of himself to...someone with whom he could share the beauty of life.

• God easily recognized this need in Adam, for apparently God beheld the same need within Himself. So God created the woman for Adam and, at the same time, began symbolically unveiling the plan that would eventually bring forth an eternal bride for the Creator Himself. Here is the account in Genesis of how this miraculous event took place:

> *"And the Lord God caused a deep sleep to fall upon*
> *Adam, and He slept: and He took one of his ribs, and*
> *closed up the flesh instead thereof;*
> *And the rib, which the Lord God had taken from*
> *man, made he a woman, and brought her unto the man.*
> *And Adam said, This is now bone of my bones, and*
> *flesh of my flesh: she shall be called Woman, because*
> *she was taken out of Man.*
> *Therefore shall a man leave his father and his*
> *mother, and shall cleave unto his wife: and they shall be*
> *one flesh.*

And they were both naked, the man and his wife,
and were not ashamed."

(Genesis 2:21-25)

It is quite obvious that certain details in this passage, concerning the creation of the woman, prefigure and symbolize the bringing forth of the bride of Christ. Compare the following similarities:

• Even as Adam was placed in a deep sleep, so also Jesus was over-whelmed by the deep sleep of death on the cross of Calvary.

• The substance that God used to make the woman, one of Adam's ribs, was brought out of Adam's side.

In like manner, the "substance" that God would use to "make" the *bride of Christ* flowed out of Jesus' side on the cross. The soldiers pierced Him with a spear and *blood* and *water* poured out.

The blood was given to cleanse us and prepare us for the indwelling of the Spirit and the Word.

The Spirit and the Word are both represented by the water, for Jesus promised that His Spirit would be in us "a well of water springing up into everlasting life" and that He would cleanse the church "with the washing of water by the Word." (John 4:14, Ephesians 5:26)

These two substances, the blood and the water, came forth from Jesus, both literally and in a spiritual sense also, to heal, transform, recreate and fill all those who make up the everlasting "wife of the Lamb."

• How significant it is that blood is manufactured in the marrow of the bones. Therefore, Eve's blood came from the same source as Adam's. In like manner, the spiritual blood that constantly flows through every member of the bride came from Jesus, the Bridegroom. We share the same life, the same blood.

• It is undeniable that originally the woman was hidden deep within Adam, near to his heart. She was then separated from him for a season, to be molded and shaped unto perfection. Finally, she was presented to Adam to be joined to him forever in a complete, beautiful and sacred union, sealed with the unction of the Spirit.

In like manner, every member of *the bride of Christ* was originally "hid with Christ in God" - near to His heart. "According as He hath chosen us in Him before the foundation of the world..." (Ephesians 1:4)

We were then born into this world of sin and separated from the full glory and manifest presence of our Creator for a season.

We walked for an appointed time in spiritual darkness and ignorance until He came into our lives.

Now, as sons of God, we still walk through various trials, tribulations and persecutions, but we know that, through it all, we are being molded and shaped unto full maturity. We shall come forth perfected in His sight, presented in the bonds of holy matrimony to our Saviour/Groom forever...a complete, beautiful and sacred union, sealed with the unction of the Holy Spirit.

• When the Lord presented the woman to Adam, immediately the man ✗ lifted his voice and said - "This is now bone of my bones and flesh of my flesh; she shall be called Woman, because she was taken out of Man."

In like manner, speaking of *the bride of Christ*, Paul said - "...we are members of His body, of His flesh, and of His bones." (Ephesians 5:30) The Bridegroom has poured His very being into us; we therefore contain His fullness; we are one with Him. He dwells in us, and we dwell in Him. We are vessels of the life of God; we are destined to be full expressions of that divine life. He reveals Himself in us, and through us, and will do so forever. O, what marvellous truth this is!

• Next Adam prophesied of the institution of marriage saying -"There- ✗ fore shall a man leave his father and his mother, and shall cleave unto his wife: and they shall be *one flesh*."

It is interesting to note that four thousand years later Paul finally unveiled the hidden symbolism behind the marital union by quoting this prophecy of Adam and then explaining - "this is a great mystery: but I speak concerning Christ and the church." (Ephesians 5:32)

For - *"he that is joined unto the Lord is one spirit."* (I Cor. 6:17)

How thrilling it is to know that our spirits have merged with His Spirit and we have become one. Because of this present relationship, this spiritual union, we can truthfully say that in one sense we are definitely united to Him in marriage now. In fact, in Romans 7:4, Paul explained "ye also are become dead to the law by the body of Christ; that ye should be MARRIED to another, even to Him that is raised from the dead, that we should bring forth fruit unto God."

THE SPIRITUAL KIDDUSHUN

• Though spiritually speaking we can declare that we are already married to the Bridegroom, technically and scripturally we are described as only being *"espoused...to one husband...a chaste virgin to Christ."* (II Corinthians 11:2)

It must be stated though that an espousal was treated quite seriously by the Jews of Jesus' day, as serious as marriage itself.

This matrimonial agreement was called a *kiddushun* or *erusin* in the Hebrew language and was considered a permanent commitment. When God saved us, we were then formally betrothed to the Son of God, and it is certain - God does not intend to break off this engagement and neither should we.

We have entered into a spiritual *kiddushun,* and this is recognizably a covenant-commitment on the part of both the Bridegroom and the bride.

•   In order for us to comprehend more fully all the many facets of this *kiddushun* relationship that we presently have with Jesus, it is quite important for us to reflect upon the beautiful symbolism contained in certain details of the early Jewish espousal customs.*1

It is accepted that normally the prospective groom would first visit the home of that girl or woman to whom he desired to be engaged and discuss with her father the terms of marriage. The value of the bride would be ascertained and a dowry price would be agreed upon and paid (called a *mohar* in the Hebrew). Then, the espousal having been sealed, the bride-to-be was consecrated or set apart unto her groom.

To confirm this status, the engaged couple would share a cup of wine, drinking from the same vessel. This represented the fact that in anticipation of becoming one flesh, the couple would vow to each other a willingness to "drink in together" both the burdens and blessings that their future lives would bring. The sorrows and joys, the defeats and victories, would be either patiently endured or happily enjoyed in a joint, mutual way.

Yet this *shared cup* meant more: it represented as well a oneness in spirit even prior to marriage...one in their love for each other, one in the joy of expectation, and one in their commitment of faithfulness. After this ritual, the bridegroom would then depart to his father's house for a waiting and preparation period that was usually to last no longer than a year.

Such betrothal vows and ceremonies were extremely binding, so much so, that in order for the couple to annul their agreement to marry, literal divorce proceedings had to take place.

It is also an interesting and sobering fact, that if the espoused woman violated the betrothal vows, such infidelity was punishable by death and was considered adultery. (Deuteronomy 22:23-24, Matthew 1:19)

All of these intriguing, historical facts speak deeply to our hearts right now in a present-truth way.

The Saviour/Bridegroom visited our home, this world, almost two thousand years ago to establish the terms of marriage.

A *mohar* had to be paid and it was the decision of deity that all the riches of earth and heaven combined would still be an insufficient dowry.

Mountains of gold and silver, studded with diamonds, rubies, opals and emeralds would have still fallen far short of the necessary purchase price. The precious blood of the Lamb, His life outpoured, was decided upon as the only just, suitable and effective *mohar.*

Such a thought should melt our hearts and bring us to our knees in devotion, gratitude and praise...that our Bridegroom would pay such an awesome price to win our hand in marriage and to cleanse us that we might be worthy of such a union.

SHARING THE CUP SPIRITUALLY

• To confirm our response of commitment to this marriage proposal we have been called upon to echo Psalm 116:12-14 from the heart:

> *"What shall I render unto the Lord for all His benefits toward me?*
> *I will take the cup of salvation, and call upon the name of the Lord. I will pay my vows unto the Lord now in the presence of all His people."*

We are called to share with the Lord of hosts, even now, a golden cup of new wine, a symbol of our commitment to each other. We must be willing to drink in, and partake of, both the blessings and burdens of this holy union, for this wine is simultaneously both bitter and sweet.

• Jesus, the Bridegroom, presented this marital demand to James and John, who apparently desired the honor of sitting on the Lord's right and left side in the kingdom of God to come.

Upon receiving their request, Jesus said:

> *"Ye know not what ye ask. Are ye able to drink of* ***the cup*** *that I shall drink of, and be baptized with the baptism that I am baptized with?"*
>
> (Matthew 20:22, Mark 10:38)

This was not only a demand placed upon two of the original disciples. This is a common requirement placed upon any and every person who becomes a member of *the bride.*

To share Jesus' cup this way is to drink in both the blessedness of His divine nature and the burdensome demands that were placed upon His life as the firstborn Son.

It involves every necessary facet of true sonship.

It is to know Him in both the power of His resurrection and the fellowship of His suffering.

Although it involves sharing in His relationship with the Father, it also involves times of being hated, despised and rejected...yes, even targetted by hell itself for destruction.

Although it often results in joy unspeakable and full of glory, it also at times results in sorrow that seemingly knows no bounds.

But this is the commitment of love, the result of the covenant-bond to which we have dutifully agreed, and it is only right that we do so.

In one aspect, this shared cup speaks of being filled with the Holy Spirit, a blessing that we can only experience in a comparatively subdued way now...for the mortal frame that we inhabit could never contain the absolute ecstasy that will be our infinite inheritance as glorified saints.

Such unutterable bliss will only be known when this cup is filled to the brim with a new and more glorious "wine" obtainable only in the celestial state. But first, this earthly cup must be finished.

Jesus began sipping this earthly cup Himself when He was born into this woeful world, then in an even more profound way when the Holy Spirit came to Him at His baptism in the river Jordan. In a spiritual and emotional sense, He reached the dregs at the bottom of the cup during the last supper when He announced:

> *"This cup is the new testament in My blood...which*
> *is shed for many for the remission of sins."*
> (Luke 22:20, Matthew 26:28)

But then He presented the heart-gripping demand, passing the cup to all His disciples and urging them:

> *"Drink ye all of it."*

They may not have understood the fullness of what was happening, for as individual members of *the bride of Christ* they were being called upon to share Jesus' suffering, His burden for lost humanity, His cross of self-denial and His submission to the will of the Father.

But the early disciples were not alone in partaking of this marital cup of mystical union, for Jesus commanded all believers who would yet trust in Him to also - *"Do this in remembrance of Me."*

The communion cup has definitely been passed into our hands as well. Now we must be willing and eager to put it to our lips, for love constrains us to make such a choice.

We know that in doing so, we will inherit both His blessings and His burden. But we are not afraid of the latter, for we have the promise of a glorious new day. Right before Jesus ascended into heaven He pledged:

> *"But I say unto you, I will not drink henceforth of*
> *the fruit of the vine, until that day when I drink it*
> *new with you in My Father's kingdom."*
> (Matthew 26:29)

This speaks of the coming age in which the Holy Spirit will abound to such degree that "the mountains shall drop down *new wine* and the hills shall flow with milk." (Joel 3:18)

Our cup will then overflow..with an ecstatic heavenly elixir, the likes of which we have never known.

Our hearts will be overcome with emotion...flooded with His love...revelling in that great and glorious victory that will be a signet ring stamping triumph over all the adversity of our earthly exile.

THE PROMISE OF BECOMING
A PALACE OF SILVER

Until that wonderful era arrives, it behooves every one of us to recognize that our engagement is still actually in the testing stage.

We are courting the Creator and He is courting us.

Our love is being tested. Our sincerity and devotion are being tested.

One patriarch, in realization of this, said: "What is man, that Thou shouldest magnify him? and that Thou shouldest set Thine heart upon him? And that Thou shouldest visit him every morning, and try him every moment?" (Job 7:17-18)

• This constant and necessary trying or testing process is further unveiled in the Song of Solomon in a mysterious passage set aside for the "choir of friends" to sing concerning the Shulamite bride:

> *"We have a little sister, and...what shall we do for our sister in the day she shall be spoken for?*
> *If she be A WALL, we will build upon her A PALACE OF SILVER; and if she be a door, we will enclose her with boards of cedar."*
>
> (Song of Solomon 8:8-9)

It is a possibility that the members of this choir - entitled *the daughters of Jerusalem* - sang these highly symbolic lines as if they were discussing the future of the prospective *wife of the Lamb* (or at least a portion of the bride yet to come into maturity).

"If she be a *wall*, we will build upon her *a palace of silver*" - this means that if she keeps her virtue and resists the sensual entrapments of the world, *the bride* will be greatly rewarded, enriched beyond description. For God will augment her efforts toward perfection by making her to emerge in even greater beauty still...as *a palace of silver*...a perfectly elegant and supernaturally luxurious dwelling place for deity.

"If she be *a door*, we will enclose her with *boards of cedar*" - this could be speaking of spiritual wantonness and its resulting judgment...*a cedar coffin* enclosing the one who opened up the door of her heart to the lust conceived that brings forth sin, and the sin finished that brings forth death. But praise be to God this will not be the case!

The bride of Christ will emerge pure and mature by the grace of God. The next line in this peculiar, poetical and prophetical book is itself a prophecy of *the bride*'s commitment to holiness and her ultimate victory.

> *"I am A WALL...then was I in His eyes as one that found favour."*
>
> (Song of Solomon 8:10)

41

We will find favor in the presence of His majesty, the King of kings at His coming if we have made the choice to be *a wall*...impenetrable and unyielding when it comes to the spirit of the world.

We will reach full maturity at the resurrection.

Having passed through the testing period, we will finally arrive at that indescribably blessed moment when infinite vows will be exchanged irreversibly.

The marriage will then be consummated and fully recognized in heaven. On that glorious day, we will be made utterly one with Him - body, mind, soul and spirit - forever and ever!

SHARING THE NAME OF THE BRIDEGROOM

Concerning the highly symbolic details of Adam and Eve's union, there is another key revelation that needs to be unveiled. It involves the peculiar fact that the woman did not even receive her own individual name until after the fall.

•   In the beginning, the man and the woman were so identified with each other that God - *"called their name Adam."* (Genesis 5:2)

They actually bore the same name.

Then when sin entered in, the guilty pair plunged into an abyss of flesh-consciousness. A veil was cast over their minds, and apparently, simultaneously, they were locked inside the prison of the five senses.

They lost their oneness with God, and they lost the full awareness of that initial, pure, and absolute oneness that they had with each other.

They were still one flesh, but it is very believable that the full depth and the full beauty of that first relationship were gone.

A spiritual gulf came between them, so a separate name was given by Adam to the woman God gave him. (Genesis 3:20)

This chosen name is rendered **Eve** in English and is translated from the Hebrew word *Chavvah* which means *life-giver*. (SC)

Adam chose this name for the woman because - *"she was the mother of all living."* In a similar though spiritual sense, *the bride of Christ* is also *"the mother of all living"*, for all who come into the life of God receive this life-changing and life-imparting experience through the witness and work of *the bride of Christ* on earth.

•   Now, concerning the acquisition of a name paralleling and indicating a spiritual condition, the opposite is also very true.

For a season we have all borne exclusively earthly names that indicate and emphasize both our earthly ties and our separateness from God...for we have inherited these names from our Adamic forefathers.

But thank God we have been born again!

We are the blessed recipients of a *New* Covenant. We are *new* creatures - *new* creations - in Christ Jesus, a part of a *new* family.

As individual members of *the bride of Christ*, it is an irrefutable truth that we have each received a *new name* which no man knows except the recipient of the name and the Lord who gave it. (Revelation 2:17)

It is possible that this particular name will only be used by the Master toward us when we are alone together, roaming through His boundless creation, sharing unspeakable joy in each other's presence.

It is also quite possible that this mysterious *new name* will be a kind of compound name, linked somehow with the very name of our Bridegroom/Saviour.

Ephesians 3:14-15 declares that the whole family of God in heaven and in earth is named with His name...the name of Jesus.

His name shall be upon our foreheads.

The name of God, the name of the city of God, and the new name of the Son of God, will all be somehow written on each child of God. (Revelation 3:12, 22:4)

Even as a woman in this world normally renounces her maiden name on the day of marriage to take the name of her husband, so it is with *the bride of Christ!*

He is our husband - now and forevermore.

We have taken on His name and His nature.

We are not ashamed of His name. We love His name.

We tremble inwardly with gratitude at the very mention of His name.

Eternally, we will be called by His name.

WHAT GOD HAS JOINED TOGETHER...

Now, concerning the earthly institution of marriage and its heavenly counterpart, there is another vital point that should be brought out.

God hates divorce. God hates putting away. (Malachi 2:16)

Strong words about the sanctity of marriage came from Jesus' lips.

He said - *"What therefore God hath joined together, let not man put asunder."* (Matthew 19:6)

This very statement marries us to a firm conclusion.

• If God is so adamant in His stand against divorce in the natural, then surely He is even more adamantly against any divorce taking place in the spiritual.

If God is so firmly against that which is one flesh being separated, then surely He is even more vehemently opposed to the separation of that which has been made one spirit.

This is a fact to which we can cling! This is revelation knowledge that imparts strong security and blessed assurance!

We are certain that God will go to extreme measures to preserve those who are presently a part of *His espoused bride*.

43

We are certain that God will marshall all the host of heaven if necessary to rescue, defend or keep those who trust in His love!

In an attempt to reveal this concept of security and marital oneness, naturally and spiritually, Paul said - *"He that loveth his wife loveth himself."* (Ephesians 5:28)

On a natural level, this is simply an exhortation to husbands about the attitude they should have toward their wives.

But on a higher and greater level this is a sure revelation of Jesus' attitude toward His everlasting bride.

He loves us as He would love Himself.

We are inseparably linked together.

We hurt together. We rejoice together.

If a stone is thrown into our spirits, the water ripples in His Spirit. We belong to him; we are very much a part of Him, and He is very much a part of us.

• Paul went on to say - *"For no man ever yet hated his own flesh; but nourisheth it and cherisheth it, even as the Lord, the church!"*

Hallelujah! We can shout His praise!

In times of spiritual hardships, He will not forsake us.

If we maintain faith and humility before Him, He will *nourish* us and restore us to strength and health spiritually. We can be sure of this, for we know that He *cherishes* us! We are very dear to Him.

Thank God! We have made a grand discovery!

This is not a fear relationship; this is a love relationship!

WHO IS IN THE BRIDE?

• The angel spoke to John, the Revelator, and said, "Come hither, I will shew thee *the bride, the Lamb's wife.*" (Revelation 21:9)

Then he was carried away in the Spirit to a great and high mountain, and he saw that great city, the holy Jerusalem, descending out of heaven from God...*"prepared as a bride adorned for her husband."* (Rev. 21:2)

Undoubtedly, it is not merely the city, but rather the inhabitants of the city, that make up **the bride!**

This would include, not only New Covenant saints, but also those who were redeemed under the Old Covenant as well.

There are several reasons why it is necessary to include both groups.

First of all - even as Joshua brought twelve stones out of Jordan, when the ark of the covenant passed over into Canaan land, so also Jesus, when He came through the violent, churning waters of death, brought out of the lower parts of the earth the righteous, the faithful, and the worthy dead of the Old Covenant (for the twelve stones represented those members of the twelve tribes of Israel who were firm and solid in their commitment to Jehovah-God under the Old Will).

There is no question that after the crucifixion, Jesus went down into Sheol...into Abraham's bosom...where the departed saints of that era had their temporary abode.

There, in the heart of the earth, Jesus preached the Gospel to the dead who apparently could not enter the kingdom of heaven until they were born again.

Surely at that point these righteous ones, who had so patiently waited for the Messiah, promptly accepted Him and were regenerated...for it is not the flesh but the spirit that receives this rebirth.

Then, as bloodwashed and redeemed believers, they ascended up to paradise, to their heavenly "Promised Land Inheritance", and captivity was led captive. It is only logical to conclude that, immediately coincidental to this wonderful salvation and translation experience, the Old Testament saints spiritually became a part of *the bride of Christ* (which is also called - "the church...His body, the fullness of Him that filleth all in all"). (Ephesians 4:8-10, I Peter 3:18-20; 4:6, Luke 16:22)

Second - it is quite clear that both covenants are linked to the holy city *(the bride)* for the twelve *foundations* of the heavenly Jerusalem are named after the twelve apostles of the Lamb, but the twelve *gates* to the city are named by the twelve tribes of Israel. (Revelation 21:12-14)

For through the *gateway* of the Law, Old Testament saints entered into a bridal relationship with Jehovah-God that would eventually be built on a New Testament *foundation.*

Besides, we know that Abraham "looked for a city which hath foundations, whose builder and maker is God" (Hebrews 11:10), and that all the Old Covenant saints were rewarded with this same heritage and destiny.

Furthermore, Hebrews 11:16 declares -"God is not ashamed to be called their God: for He hath prepared for them a city."

This is also a promise to New Covenant saints as well, for Paul said to us - "here have we no continuing city, but we seek one to come." (Hebrews 13:14)

Again, the heavenly city is *the bride* and all the blessed inhabitants of that city make up *the bride*.

Third - We know that in Jeremiah 3:14, God pleaded with Israel saying - "Turn, O backsliding children saith the Lord; for **I am married unto you!**"

We recognize that, in a sense, God did divorce the nation of Israel as a whole when He changed from the Old to the New Covenant because He stopped dealing with man on the basis of Old Testament precepts and laws.

But it can be stated loudly and clearly that He never divorced those individuals who were faithful to Him during that former age. By their faithfulness under that covenant, those who were consecrated to the Lord secured a relationship and inheritance destined to be just as infinitely deep, rich and full as that procured by any New Covenant son or daughter of God. (Jeremiah 3:8, Romans 7:1-4)

• It is important also to note that according to Isaiah 54:1-9, Hosea 1-3 and Zechariah 12-14, a vast majority of present-day Israel, the temporarily estranged and divorced wife of Jehovah-God, will be reinstated in a profound way in the last days by an apparent widespread acceptance of the Messiah among the Jews. For God has prophesied of old:

> *"...thou shall forget the shame of thy youth, and shalt not remember the reproach of thy widowhood any more.*
> *For thy Maker is thine husband; the Lord of hosts is His name; and thy Redeemer the Holy One of Israel; The God of the whole earth shall He be called.*
> *For the Lord hath called thee as a woman forsaken and grieved in spirit, and a wife of youth, when thou wast refused, saith thy God.*
> *For a small moment have I forsaken thee; but with great mercies will I gather thee."*
>
> (Isaiah 54:4-7)

In light of all these scriptural facts, we come to several logical and firm deductions:

It seems quite possible that *the bride of Christ* is not, as some believe, a certain denomination or a small, select group, chosen out from the rest of the body of Christ.

Moreover, it is only sensible to believe that any person considered worthy to partake of the splendor of heaven, will surely be considered equally worthy of being included in *the bride.*

Furthermore, it is irrefutable that all those, from the beginning of time, who have loved and served the Lord, will be married to Him forever!

• THEREFORE, IT APPEARS TO BE A VALID AND SCRIP-TURALLY SOUND ASSUMPTION THAT **THE LAMB'S WIFE** WILL BE COMPOSED OF THE REDEEMED OF ALL AGES!

It is also quite sure that the questions surrounding this controversial issue will be satisfactorily answered in the very near future, when "the Lord Jesus shall be revealed from heaven with His mighty angels in flaming fire." (II Thessalonians 1:7-8)

HIS SISTER, HIS SPOUSE, HIS DAUGHTER

One thing is certain! We are presently caught up in the romance of the ages!! Our souls have been knit together with the soul of the Almighty and He loves us as His own soul.

Our minds reel with wonder that He would ever set His gaze upon us in such a way. We are stricken with awe as we realize that the mighty Creator of the universe is actually in love, and that His heart, so high and lofty, has actually been captured by the beauty of His earth-born bride.

He is from above and we are from beneath, yet such contradiction means little to Him, for in another sense we are of a similar origin.

• In fact, it is quite interesting to see that our peculiar relationship with this Lord of glory was foreshadowed long ago by the marital union of Abraham and Sarah, for they were both man and wife, and brother and sister...having the same father, but different mothers.

In like manner, we are both wife and sister to our heavenly Bridegroom, for we have the same Father - the Everlasting Father - but different "mothers". Jesus came, so to speak, from the "womb" of heaven, for He was heavenly, while we have come from the "womb" of the earth, for we are earthly .

Another important facet of this analogy is the fact that the name **Abraham** means *father of a multitude*, for this great patriarch represented God Himself who would beget a *multitude* of spiritual offspring. But the name **Sarah** means *princess, queen of princes, or mother of princes*, for she represented the very wife and sister of the King of kings (the bride of Christ who would be a mother of princes, "giving birth" to all of the royal seed of God in the earth).

This portion of the revelation must be reemphasized.

• In the Song of Solomon (God's love song) the Bridegroom-King (Jesus) declared to His espoused bride and princess (the church) - "Thou hast ravished My heart, MY SISTER, MY SPOUSE; thou hast ravished My heart with one of thine eyes, with one chain of thy neck. How fair is thy love, **MY SISTER, MY SPOUSE**! How much better is thy love than wine!" (Song of Solomon 4:9-10)

The chosen bride-to-be, thrilled over being the delight of her prospective groom, responded (her heart simply racing with excitement)..."My beloved is mine, and I am His...His desire is toward me." (Song of Solomon 2:16; 7:10)

Can we not see by this revelatory book, which the Holy Spirit entitled *the Song of Songs*, that the heart of Jehovah is literally throbbing with a holy desire to be joined to His bride!

We hear Him exclaim - "How beautiful are thy feet with shoes, O **PRINCE'S DAUGHTER**...How fair and how pleasant art thou, O love, for delights!" - and we are awakened to a wondrous truth, though it seems almost beyond belief. (Song of Solomon 7:1,6)

We have ravished the heart of the Messiah and He has ravished ours.

We can claim not only the *title-positions* of being *sister* and *spouse* to this Prince of peace, this King of glory; we are also referred to as *the daughter of the prince* whose feet have been beautifully shod with the preparation of the gospel.

Yes, we are at once *sister, wife* and *daughter* to the Lord of all creation and His majestic nature is emerging in us in ever-increasing ways.

We are God's porphyrogenitos. We have been "born in the purple"...royal not only by marriage, but royal by birth as well.

WHAT IS GOD DOING RIGHT NOW?

We know that our God is daily overwhelmed with emotion toward us, especially when He sees the beauty of the divine nature reflected in us. He is utterly overtaken with desire toward us...desire as infinitely deep as the heart of God Himself.

Surely His whole being is stirred with a yearning that grips and a love that aches. By His own choosing, though, He must wait until His *bride* is fully conditioned, qualified, and prepared, before He concludes this intermediate step.

• Revelation 19:7 gives the prophetical announcement, soon to be fulfilled - *"Let us be glad and rejoice...for the marriage of the Lamb is come, and His wife hath made herself ready."*

This scriptural passage clearly indicates that *the bride of Christ* is presently in the preparation stage. We are in a divinely ordered training program, a program in which much effort is required on our part.

Every life experience is essential, from the budding of a flower to the blossoming of a nation. Everything has an eternal value and purpose.

The Queen who will share God's throne must be educated to qualify her for certain infinite and royal responsibilities.

All events in heaven and in earth revolve around this central theme.

Our little victories now are simply day-to-day lessons in manifesting the authority God has given His offspring and heirs.

Winning the lost, tackling problems with prayer, laying hands on the sick, casting out devils, conquering temptations - all of these are really quite elementary compared to that which God is training us to inherit!

In fact, many of the events of our lives that we consider to be wasted time, even the most negative, may not necessarily be so.

Impossibilities become God's opportunities; disappointments are sometimes His divine appointments...to teach us, to build character in us, and to eventually bring us forth as mature, resurrected, eternal sons and daughters of God. O blessed be the Lord! The heavenly Bridegroom is totally involved in readying all those in *the bride* who are totally involved in readying themselves.

• A Jewish bride-to-be would sometimes spend weeks bathing in perfumes and ointments, preparing her garments and training her entourage of servants and handmaidens for the "day of her visitation".

The prospective groom would spend the ensuing months after the espousal, preparing a place to which he would take the bride on the day of marriage, usually in his father's house.

Once these preparations were completed the groom would return to take his beloved unto himself.

His coming would be unannounced and would usually take place at night, involving much fanfare and celebration.

Normally, a large procession of rejoicing, singing, torch-carrying friends and family members would walk from the groom's house to the bride's home.

The best man and the male escorts would go before the company, shouting - *"Behold, the bridegroom is coming"*.

All this noise and shouting would alert the bride, forewarning her that the time of "catching away" had finally come. All the many weeks and months of watching and waiting were finally over. No longer would her heart ache; no longer would the tears of loneliness flow.

Surely a minor tempest would suddenly stir in the home of the bride as she and her attendants would rush, in a flurry of activity, checking one last time, to make certain that every detail was right.

The groom would then receive his bride, whose face would be covered by a veil, and both of them would return, accompanied by a great host of celebrants, to the father's house. Upon arriving, the couple would then be escorted into the bridal chamber (called the *huppah* in the Hebrew language) where they would remain seven days, hidden from the eyes of the wedding party. After a week in the *huppah* the couple would emerge and, for the first time, the bride would come forth unveiled for all to behold and admire.

As we meditate on all the various details of these ancient Jewish marriage customs we realize that, in a spiritual sense, something quite similar to this is happening now.

We know that we are referred to as both *the children of the bridechamber* and as individual members of *the bride*.

As *the children of the bridechamber* or *the attendants of the bridegroom* we are seeking to do all we can to *attend* to the will of the everlasting Groom and minister to His needs. (See Matt. 9:15 AV, NAS)

As individual members of *the bride* we are constantly involved in readying ourselves for our soon-to-come union with Him (and it is definitely true that we can fill both positions simultaneously).

We remember the parting words of the Shepherd/King/Bridegroom well, for they echo in our hearts day and night:

"Let not your heart be troubled: ye believe in God, believe also in Me.

In My Father's house are many mansions: if it were not so, I would have told you. I go to prepare a place for you.

And if I go and prepare a place for you, I will come again, and receive you unto Myself; THAT WHERE I AM, THERE YE MAY BE ALSO."

(John 14:1-3)

We do not know the day nor the hour, but we do know that Jesus is returning. As we patiently and watchfully wait, we are called to continually uphold one another and exhort one another that we might prepare one another for such a momentous happening.

The desire of our hearts is - "to see Him as He is."

The cry of our souls is to be ready when it happens.

We know that God is preparing us as we simultaneously prepare ourselves for this grand event.

We are being cleansed daily by the washing of water by the Word.

We are being bathed in the very perfume of praise that we send upward to His throne. Every hour we are being anointed afresh with the poured-forth ointment of His wonderful name.

Every moment we spend longing after him in sincerity, we are purified by his love and empowered by His Spirit. We are undergoing an inward transformation daily on our journey toward perfection.

We know that the Bridegroom is near, at the very threshold, for prophetic pulpit voices are sounding out like trumpets all around the world, saying - *"Behold, the Bridegroom cometh; go ye out to meet Him".* (Matthew 25:6).

The celestial procession of ten thousand times ten thousands saints, marching forth out of the past six milleniums, is soon to appear with the Lord in the eastern sky.

The attending angels, who continually minister to the heirs of salvation, are in a flurry of activity. Every detail has to be right.

Every member of *the bride* must be clothed with the right spiritual attire in order to be acceptable (garments of praise, cloaks of zeal, feet shod with the preparation of the Gospel, and, most of all, robes of righteousness).

Only those who dress in this manner will be swept away to the heavenly *"huppah"* and be included in the marriage supper of the Lamb (that great and joyous feast that will celebrate the glorious day of the restoration of all things).

THE CORRECT BRIDAL GARMENTS
THE RESERVOIR OF OIL

• We are reminded of the parable that Jesus gave in Matthew 22, concerning the marriage feast that the king gave in honor of his son. A certain young man came in to the feast without the proper wedding garments and was cast into outer darkness.

This wedding garment is nothing less and nothing more than the beauty of true holiness!

Revelation 19:8 explains it clearly - *"And to her [the bride] was granted that she should be arrayed in fine linen, clean and white: for the fine linen is the righteousness of saints."*

This righteousness is necessarily twofold. It includes the righteousness that is self-achieved through a sincere desire to please God; but even more so it involves the imparted righteousness that comes through the covering of the precious blood of Jesus. Both kinds of righteousness are woven together in one garment. (And it must be said that only those who sincerely attempt the former are worthy of claiming the latter.)

It can easily be said again and again...*the bride* must make herself ready! We must prepare to meet our God!

• In **the Parable of the Ten Virgins** (Matthew 25:1-13) Jesus unveiled some additional spiritual truths that we need to cover concerning this preparation stage. If we are to be included in *the bride of Christ*, we must first be as virgins spiritually - undefiled by the world - modest, chaste, virtuous and clean. But these character qualities in themselves are still not enough.

Each of the ten virgins had a lamp and a vessel that needed to be filled with oil.

The **lamps** represent the Word (for the Bible declared -"Thy Word is a **lamp** unto my feet, and a light unto my path"). (Psalm 119:105)

The **oil** represents the Spirit (for - "thou anointest my head with **oil**; my cup [my heart] runneth over"). (Psalm 23:5)

Unfortunately, many present day churches build various doctrines, creeds, rituals and ceremonies around the Word, but oftentimes very few, if any, of the people in the congregation are truly born again. In order for us to be included in *the bride,* therefore, we must have more than just a knowledge of the Word (the oil-filled lamp); we must be born of the Spirit and thus, have oil in our vessels.

If we are depending only on theology we may well end up being among those who mournfully declare - "our lamps are gone out" - for the life of the Spirit in the Word is not enough: it must be in us.

It seems clear that this parable compares possessing Christians to those who are merely professing Christians. It is not a comparison between those who only claim salvation and those who have the baptism of the Holy Spirit.

It is a faithful saying and worthy of all acceptation that all born again believers have the influence of the Spirit in their hearts and lives (the oil) though some may not necessarily have the full enduing with power that others go on to receive.

One thing is certain though: all sons and daughters of God must awake out of spiritual slumber, and ready themselves, fully believing that - *"all things are now ready."*

We know that the door leading to the marriage feast will soon be shut.

Sinners, compromisers, and hypocrites will truly be shut out... shut out from the presence of God and shut out from the great inheritance available "in Him". But simultaneously, the sons and daughters of God who make up *the Lamb's wife* will be shut in..."caught up" into the Father's presence...sealed into the anointing and sealed into the very nature of the Lamb of God... forevermore!

Though we have always been hidden behind a veil of flesh, thank God, in that wondrous age to come, the veil will be finally removed.

We will eternally then shine like the sun in the kingdom of our Father.

WHAT IS GOD'S ULTIMATE PURPOSE
CONCERNING THE BRIDE?

• Jesus began His New Covenant ministry at a marriage feast in Cana by turning water into wine.

In a parallel way, He will bring this same covenant to a beautiful conclusion at another marriage feast, transforming those earthly vessels full of the water of His Word into vessels overflowing with the celestial wine of His Spirit, His manifest redemptive love.

And surely on that day we will confess to the Master (but not incredulously) how mysterious it is that the best wine was saved for last. (John 2:1-11)

O, how this Bridegroom has longed through the centuries for the day of supreme ecstasy when He will finally embrace *His bride* in the fullness of His compassion and restoration grace.

How this heavenly Husband has waited in faith-filled anticipation for the dawning of the Kingdom Age when He will finally be free to fully share the most intimate secrets of His heart with His chosen eternal *help meet*...face to face. "For there is nothing covered, that shall not be revealed; and hid, that shall not be known." (Matthew 10:26)

• Surely on that wondrous day, *the bride of Christ* will come out of the wilderness, leaning on the arm of her Beloved, shouting - *"His love was stronger than death. Many waters could not quench love, neither could the floods drown it."* (Refer to Song of Solomon 8:6-7)

• We will have learned two very valuable lessons...the great power of His love and our utter dependence on His strength and grace. Then, having passed the test, *the wife of the Lamb* will become the object of God's total attention and devotion forever...His most intimate companion.

She will be elevated to the most exalted position available in the universe, second only to the position God occupies Himself.

The perfection of all of the emotions of deity will be poured out on this God-ordained heiress.

Even as a magnifying glass gathers many individual light rays, and then condenses them with burning intensity on one spot - so also, the great wealth, the sum total, of all of God's compassion, all of His grace, all of His mercy and all of His power will be condensed together and focused on this Queen of heaven.

This stunningly elegant *wife of the Lamb* will rule in regal glory over all the works of God's hands...a universal *land of red-purple.*

She will reign in splendor over both natural realms and spiritual realms....both earthly kingdoms and boundless celestial expanses. All things, in heaven and in earth, will be presented as a love-gift to this choice one the infinite Groom has surnamed *His beloved, His darling.*

During the Kingdom Age, the *bride* will rule over the world and judge angels. Eventually in the New Creation, she will be given dominion over all of God's vast domain (an immense supernatural realm that will certainly far exceed the present natural cosmos, with its billions of gigantic galaxies and star systems).

All of this will forever be the charge of the bride-elect.

What an astonishing realization!

What an unspeakable gift! What a breathtaking destiny!

We almost stagger at the magnitude of such bold claims, and yet these great and precious promises are dwarfed by the greatest promise and privilege of all.

Just to see Him...to gaze deeply into His compassionate eyes...such all knowing, all seeing eyes...such brilliant mirrors reflecting the glory of eternity itself. Just to be near enough to actually touch Him and feel His life-giving breath...just to lay our head on His bosom or fall at His feet in utter worship...knowing that He really loves and understands and that all is forgiven.

O surely, millions of years spent experiencing all the other delights of heaven will fade away and seem as nothing compared to the rapture of spending one moment in the presence of His majesty, the King of kings.

His voice will no longer be distant and difficult to distinguish, but a continual flow of love-words will echo in our hearts, resounding in our inner being, like gentle waves crashing over and over on the shoreline of our souls.

We will be perfected in His likeness.

We will know even as we are known. In other words, our knowledge of the Father will, in a certain sense, equal His knowledge of us.

• Even as Adam and Eve were originally naked in each other's presence, yet unashamed, so also the Bridegroom and *His bride* will be infinitely transparent in each other's presence.

We will know every detail about God and He will know every detail about us, yet we will be unashamed.

The love of God will prevail; total understanding will be our inheritance, for we will see it all from God's perspective.

Jesus will not be ashamed of us, for He has been a partaker of flesh and blood and He knows all about our struggles.

It is certain that we will not be ashamed of Him for we will be able to boldly declare that He kept all of His promises.

Our union with Him will be complete. His wisdom will be our wisdom. His joy will be our joy. His love will be our love. His throne will be our throne.

We will be caught up in the bliss of paradise forever.

We will be continually absorbed in surveying the perfection of that heavenly **Land of Promise** that will ever be **OUR GLORIOUS INHERITANCE!**

Time will merge into eternity.

We will be fully in love...entranced by His beauty and caught up in the joy of His presence...in that blessed realm where one note on an angel's harp will surely sound like the combined music of ten thousand earthly orchestras.

O, how blessed - how very blessed - are they which are called to **the marriage supper of the Lamb!**

---

*1 Almost all the information on ancient Jewish marriage customs was kindly supplied by Paul Sorko-Ram out of the first chapter of his book, **Only One Beloved.** A few statements were transferred almost verbatim into this title-essay.

• THE CHURCH •

THE CHURCH OF GOD

THE CHURCH OF THE LIVING GOD

THE WHOLE CHURCH

THE CHURCHES

THE CHURCHES OF CHRIST

THE CHURCHES OF GOD

• A GLORIOUS CHURCH •

---

*"And the Lord added to **THE CHURCH** daily such as should be saved."*

(Acts 2:47)

"Take heed therefore unto your-selves, and to all the flock, over the which the Holy Ghost hath made you overseers, to feed **THE CHURCH OF GOD...***"*

(Acts 20:28)

"But if I tarry long, that thou mayest know how thou ought to behave thyself in the house of God, which is **THE CHURCH OF THE LIVING GOD,** *the pillar and ground of the truth."*

(I Timothy 3:15)

"Salute one another with an holy kiss. **THE CHURCHES OF CHRIST** *salute you."*

(Romans 16:16)

"That He might present it to Himself **A GLORIOUS CHURCH,** *not having spot, or wrinkle, or any such thing; but that it should be holy and without blemish."*

(Ephesians 5:27)

THE CHURCH

*"And the Lord added to **THE CHURCH** daily such
as should be saved."*

(Acts 2:47)

• The word *church* comes from a Greek word *ekklesia* which literally
means *a calling out* - hence *"the called out ones"*.

This word *ekklesia* comes from two foundational Greek words - *ek*
which means *from* or *out of,* and either *klesis,* which means *a calling,* or
kaleo which means *to call.*

This word is used 119 times in the New Testament (83 times in the
singular and 36 times in the plural).

It is usually translated to mean *church* or *churches,* but three
times it is rendered *assembly* (and in those cases -Acts 19:32,39 & 41 - it
simply means *a gathering of people*).

The word *church* is, therefore, a very simple though expressive *title*
given by God to those blessed individuals who have been *called out* of the
world into fellowship with Him.

The true New Testament *church* consists of all those who have been
born again - regenerated by being washed in the sanctifying blood of Jesus
- *"called out* of darkness into His marvellous light" - the marvellous light
of eternal life. (I Peter 2:9)

This makes it clear that the *church* is not a certain denomination or
group organized by man, for this is a multitude that no man can number.
(Revelation 7:9) The *church* contains members of many denominations
and some who have no affiliation with any organization at all; this matters
little.

Every true member of the true *church* has been *called out* of a dependence on mere religious doctrines and creeds into a real relationship
with the living Christ. Every true member of the true *church* has been
called out and brought out of a spiritual state of being dead in trespasses
and sins into the life of God...salvation by grace.

• We are singularly called **"the church of God,** which He hath purchased with His own blood", **"the church of the living God,** the pillar
and ground of the truth" and **"the whole church"**. We are collectively
called **"the churches"**, **"the churches of Christ"**, or **"the churches of
God"**, a composite whole made up of individual units. (Ac. 20:28, I Ti.
3:15, Rom. 16:23, I Cor. 7:17, Rom. 16:16, I Thess. 2:14)

Those *titles* which use the phrases - *of God, of the living God,* or *of
Christ* - agree in the idea and concept of divine ownership, for we belong
to Him. We are of Him and in Him. And if we are truly "of Him and in
Him" then we have received of what He is.

Moreover, those individuals, accepted and included in the church, are born - "not of blood, nor of the will of the flesh, nor of the will of man, but of God." (John 1:13)

Therefore this is a work of the Spirit, not a work of the flesh. This is not so much men calling men to salvation, but rather - it is God calling men.

THREE WAYS THAT GOD CALLS

• *A calling is normally defined as an invitation, but at times it can be almost a demand to appear.*

God calls both ways and in various ways.

God called Israel with a national calling.

God has called the world to salvation with a universal call, an invitation - "Whosoever will, let him come" - and any and all can respond. (Revelation 22:17)

But there is also an individual call of ordination sent out to certain individuals God chooses to profoundly reveal Himself to, that they might be included in *the church*. This is more than just a general invitation; this is an unavoidable and compelling revelation and visitation from above.

It is important to keep in mind that this depth of divine election still hinges on the individual's choice to willfully respond and submit.

But it also goes without saying that if a person is chosen to receive such a specific and unique call of God, it is almost irresistible.

Whether human beings respond to God's universal invitation or His personal manifestation, though, they can all be a part of *the church* and thus be numbered among *"the called out ones"*.

THE CHURCH COMPARED TO A BRIDE

The church never has been, and never will be, just a cold institution or a mechanical-like organization. It is vibrant, living and full of love.

• Ephesians 5:25-26 reveals this love-factor by declaring that "Christ....loved *the church,* and gave Himself for it; that He might sanctify and cleanse it with the washing of water by the Word."

Paul also stated that as "the husband is the head of the wife" so "Christ is the head of *the church*: and he is the saviour of the body". (Ephesians 5:23)

Comparing our relationship with Him to the beautiful and mysterious oneness of a marriage relationship, the apostle further related -

> *"For this cause shall a man leave his father and mother, and shall be joined unto his wife, and they two shall be one flesh.*

This is a great mystery: but I speak concerning Christ and the church."

(Ephesians 5:31-32)

GOD'S PURPOSE IN THE CHURCH

• The Saviour/Redeemer constantly pours His very being and essence into *the church*, for we are all ordained to eventually come forth in His image. This is why "all things work together for good to them that love God" for we are - *"the called according to His purpose."* (Rom. 8:28)

> *"For whom He did foreknow, He also did predestinate to be conformed to the image of His Son, that He might be the firstborn among many brethren.*
> *Moreover whom He did predestinate, them He also* **called**: *and whom He* **called**, *them He also justified: and whom He justified, them He also glorified."*

(Romans 8:29-30)

It is a fact to be pondered that even though the day of the glorification of the saints is yet in the future - it is stated in the above scripture in the past tense (which is God's way of revealing the certainty of the event and God's way of declaring that He fully intends to do a complete work in every "called out" member of *the church*).

It behooves us all to remember that "God hath set some in *the church*, first apostles, secondarily prophets, thirdly teachers, after that miracles, gifts of healings, helps, governments, diversities of tongues." (I Cointhians 12:28-30)

Some of those filling these God-ordained ministry positions are called - *"the messengers of the churches, and the glory of Christ."* (II Cor. 8:23)

In the beginning of the book of the Revelation, each pastor of the seven churches in Asia was referred to as *"the angel of the church."*

The word translated **angel** is *aggelos* and is, in other portions of Scripture, translated into the word *messenger* as well.

These key positions in *the church*, and many others, are unquestionably given to individuals who are chosen before the foundation of the world to occupy such places of influence and service to the rest of the body of Christ.

This may seem difficult, confusing and out of reach to some people, but it is a simple thing for the infinite, omniscient God, the great I Am, who dwells simultaneously in the past, present and future.

If God in advance could touch the hearts of a certain band of men and compel them to present themselves in service to King Saul, then it should certainly not be unthinkable that God can also touch the hearts of certain persons well in advance, compelling them to present themselves in service to the King of kings Himself! (I Samuel 10:26)

Of course, all members of *the church*, both leaders and laity, are required to maintain their position through consistency and submission. But as long as we remain sincere in our desire for God, Jesus will powerfully remain both the Author and the Finisher of our faith.

He preserved the garments of the Jews for forty years in the wilderness. We can confidently say that He will preserve us.

We are "kept by the power of God through faith." (I Peter 1:5)

God begins the work. God continues the work. God perpetuates the work. And God brings it to completion. This salvation-transformation, from the beginning to the end, is undeniably an act of God.

• Acts 2:47 declares - *"the Lord added to the church daily such as should be saved."*

From the start it was primarily the Lord who did the work, not so much the disciples.

They were merely channels of His power, Word and will.

• Jesus enhanced this revelation when He said - *"No man can come to Me, except the Father which hath sent Me, draw him."* (John 6:44)

Therefore, if Jesus could not come to us without being *sent,* it makes sense to believe that we cannot go to Him without being *drawn.*

• Even prior to the spiritual birth of the church in the upper room, the apostles did not appoint themselves to their notable position. Luke 6:13 says that Jesus - *"called* unto Him His disciples: and of them He *chose* twelve."

In Luke 10 we find that - "the Lord *appointed* other seventy also, and sent them two and two before His face into every city."

They did not merely volunteer.

They were picked. They were called out and chosen.

They were appointed and anointed at the will of God.

For this is exactly what gives divine stability to the true church. IT IS A WORK OF GOD.

THE SOLID ROCK

THE REVELATION OF JESUS' DIVINITY

In Caesarea Philippi, Jesus asked His disciples -"Whom do men say that I the Son of Man am?"

"And they said, Some say that thou art John the Baptist: some, Elias; and others, Jeremias, or one of the prophets."

But Simon Peter answered - "thou art the Christ, the Son of the living God."

Jesus then said - "Blessed art thou, Simon Barjona: for flesh and blood hath not revealed it unto thee, but My Father which is in heaven...and **upon this rock I will build** *My church;* and the gates of hell shall not prevail against it." (Matthew 16:13-18)

The "rock" that Jesus said *the church* would be built on was definitely not a reference to Peter, neither was Jesus referring to Himself.

- **The solid rock-like foundation of *the church* that Jesus referred to was and is the fact that the true *church* is something built by divine revelation.**

Those who become a part of *the church* do not do so because they are just intellectually convinced by a man, by flesh and blood, that Jesus is the Messiah. Rather, this divine truth is revealed to those privileged and blessed of God to receive.

This is the solid rock.

This is the strength of our election and the harder-than-concrete, substructural base of **OUR GLORIOUS INHERITANCE.**

For if revelation is unveiled from heaven, it cannot be challenged or refuted successfully. Nothing and no one can cause believers of revealed truth to doubt their revelation, if it truly comes as a spiritual experience from God. No wonder Paul said - "The foundation of God standeth sure."

The *true church* has received this life-giving breath of divine inspiration, therefore the *true church* will "stand sure" for all time and eternity.

BINDING AND LOOSING

- The *true church* has God-given authority, for it is comprised of men and women who fully recognize the Lordship of Jesus.

Even as the Son of God gave the keys of the kingdom of heaven to Peter, when this former disciple proclaimed Jesus as Lord and Christ, so has He given them to us. (See also Matthew 18:18)

We recognize that these keys were given to Peter in a more profound and manifest way than most ordinary members of *the church* will ever experience. But Peter certainly did not possess the exclusive rights to these keys. All who sincerely recognize Jesus as "the Christ" receive of His authority, for Jesus said:

> *"...whatsoever thou shalt bind on earth shall be bound in heaven: and whatsoever thou shalt loose on earth shall be loosed in heaven."*
>
> (Matthew 16:19)

As "called out" members of *the church*, God expects us to boldly and continually take authority over sin, over satanic powers, and even over sickness...*binding* the same through the Word and by the Spirit.

We are called to perpetuate Jesus' work by setting the captives free...opening "prison doors" to *loose* them in the name of the Lord.

• The "keys of the kingdom" that effectively accomplish this goal surely include: the blood of Jesus, the name of Jesus, the Word of God, the power of confession, faith, hope, charity, and all the other gifts and fruits of the Spirit. For through these things we open the door to victorious kingdom-living, both for ourselves and others, and we lock the door on defeat.

It is so true, though, that we should never expect these promises to be fulfilled unless we are first willing to incorporate into our lives and our relationship with God, the very essence of what it means to be in *the church*.

We are a "called out" people.

And because we are in the world, but not of the world...God expects us to live separated and sanctified lives.

Only then can we expect to experience that dominion Jesus described as being - "power...over all the power of the enemy." (Luke 10:19)

THE CHANNEL OF DIVINE REVELATION

• **The true *church* is the channel through which the mystery of God's infinite plan is revealed.**

Paul exhorted that we - "make all men see what is the fellowship of the mystery, which from the beginning of the world hath been hid in God...to the intent that now unto the principalities and powers in heavenly places might be known *by the church* the manifold wisdom of God." (Ephesians 3:9-10)

What is this hidden mystery?

Colossians 1:26-27 speaks that - *"the mystery* which hath been hid from ages and generations...is *Christ in you, the hope of glory."*

Paul said - "Behold, I shew you a *mystery*; We shall not all sleep, but we shall all be changed..at the last trump..the dead shall be raised incorruptible, and *we shall be changed*." (I Corinthians 15:51-52)

All the other divine mysteries mentioned in the Scripture revolve around this central mystery - that God intends to miraculously bring forth a nation of sons and daughters, resurrected and glorified in the full image of the Son of God who dwells in their hearts. He also intends to grant these divine offspring the eternal calling and destiny of reigning with Him as kings, ultimately inheriting ALL THINGS.

This is our hope of glory!

This is the core of God's original purpose from the dawn of creation.

This is the absolute *"land of red-purple"* to which we are bound and the *"milk and honey"* witness that we drink in deeply every single day.

But why has this *mystery* of the plan of God been hidden in God from the foundation?

Apparently not even the angels, the "principalities and powers in heavenly places", have known the full plan of God from the beginning. Why?

It is certain that some messenger angels have known the small portions of the prophetic plan that they were commissioned to bear to some prophet or oracle of God, but apparently they have not known the full scope of what God has done, and what He is going to do for His heirs.

• This complete understanding was first to come to *the church* and then *"by the church"* the angelic principalities of heaven would see and understand...as *"the mystery"* is unveiled in us.

• No wonder the Bible said that when we gather together, angels desire to come in our midst to see and hear what the Holy Ghost sends down from heaven. (I Peter 1:12)

They certainly participate in what God does in our gatherings, and they rejoice with us, for they are created to be ministering spirits, ministering to the heirs of salvation.

But more than all of that...they are piecing the mystery of the ages together. They are joyously watching the unfolding of the plan of God as He works in our midst.

They know that the "spirit of revelation" has been committed to *the church*, and thus they recognize our intimacy with the Father and our importance to Him.

It seems quite certain that God has done this, at least partially, for the purpose of honor.

• We know that the Father committed "the spirit of judgment" to the Son for the purpose of honor (esteem and recognition).

> *"For the Father judgeth no man, but hath committed*
> *all judgment unto the Son:*
> *That all men should honour the Son, even as they*
> *honour the Father."*
>
> (John 5:22-23)

In a parallel way, "the spirit of revelation" has been committed unto *the church*, so that all of heaven and all of earth might honor and highly esteem *the church*, and that this recognition might redound to the glory of God.

THE CHURCH - HIS BODY AND HIS BRIDE

It is significant to note that *the church* is also referred to as *His body* (Ephesians 1:22-23, Colossians 1:18) and *His bride* (Ephesians 5:27-33).

The church, the body of Christ, and *the bride of Christ...*in the absolute and everlasting sense, these all speak of the same group of people
(God's people). Therefore, the terms are synonymous ultimately.

• And does this include the Old Covenant saints, some of whom were
called *"the church in the wilderness"*? (Acts 7:38)

In a technical sense, the answer is *No,* for *the church* is totally a New
Covenant institution, but in a certain, qualified sense, the answer is a loud,
resounding *Yes.*

All Jews delivered from Egypt were considered to be a part of *"the
church (the assembly or congregation) in the wilderness,"* but still many of
these rebelled and did not enter into "God's rest". (See Acts 7:38 NIV)

Only the faithful of the Old Covenant ever became bona fide members
of *the church of the living God* as defined in the New Testament and in
this *title-essay.*

So it is possible that a person could have been a member of *"the
church in the wilderness"* without ever becoming a member of God's eternal *church.* This alone proves that these two terms are definitely related,
but not totally synonymous.

To further explain this mystery, we know that Abraham was first
"called out" from his country and his kindred to the Promised Land, His
offspring were later "called out" of Egypt first, then "called out" from a
temporary enslavement in Babylon many years afterward.

Throughout their relationship with Jehovah, the Jews were constantly
being "called out" of the bondage of sin into holiness and "called out" of
lawlessness into submisssion to the commands and precepts of the law.

Also, as stated in the previous chapter, it is certain that after Jesus
died on the cross, He brought full salvation to the "called out" saints of the
Old Covenant who were at that time held in abeyance in Abraham's
bosom (for the law of sin and death had still reigned over them to a certain
degree).

But God made a way for His "called out" and chosen ones. When
Jesus "led captivity captive" and "called out" the righteous who were in
the lower parts of the earth, they all had to be born again in order to enter
paradise ((the third heaven). This definitely had to take place, and
could have, for it is the spirit, not the flesh, that receives this rebirth.

If so, by virtue of this experience, and at the time of this experience,
they surely, in a certain sense, became members of the body of Christ to
await with the rest of us, the wonderful day of resurrection when our
Bridegroom/Saviour will finally return for His bride, presenting unto Himself and establishing forever - *"A GLORIOUS CHURCH, not having spot,
or wrinkle, or any such thing...holy and without blemish."* (Ephesians 5:27)

Called out of vanity into absolute perfection!

Called out of time into eternity!

Even so, come Lord Jesus.

· CITIZENS OF HEAVEN ·

FELLOW-CITIZENS WITH THE SAINTS

THE COMMONWEALTH OF ISRAEL

GOD'S CHOSEN COMMUNITY

THE GENERAL ASSEMBLY AND CHURCH OF THE FIRSTBORN

THE ASSEMBLY OF THE FIRSTBORN

THE ASSEMBLY OF THE FIRSTBORN CITIZENS OF HEAVEN

· FIRSTBORN SONS ·

*"We, by contrast, are **CITIZENS OF HEAVEN,** and from heaven we expect our deliverer to come, the Lord Jesus Christ."*

(Philippians 3:20 NEB)

*"Now therefore ye are no more strangers and foreigners but **FELLOW-CITIZENS WITH THE SAINTS,** and of the household of God."*

(Ephesians 2:19)

*"That at that time ye were without Christ, being aliens from **THE COMMONWEALTH OF ISRAEL..."***

(Ephesians 2:12)

"But ye are come unto mount Sion, and unto the city of the living God, the heavenly Jerusalem, and to an innumerable company of angels,

*To **THE GENERAL ASSEMBLY AND CHURCH OF THE FIRSTBORN,** which are written in heaven..."*

(Hebrews 12:22-23)

CITIZENS OF HEAVEN

THE COMMONWEALTH OF ISRAEL

THE GENERAL ASSEMBLY AND CHURCH OF THE FIRSTBORN

"We, by contrast, are CITIZENS OF HEAVEN, and from heaven we expect our deliverer to come, the Lord Jesus Christ."

(Philippians 3:20 NEB)

"Now therefore ye are no more strangers and foreigners, but FELLOW-CITIZENS WITH THE SAINTS, and of the household of God."

(Ephesians 2:19)

The second scripture quoted above was Paul's reassurance to the converted Gentiles that they were fully accepted in **"the commonwealth of Israel"** though at one time they had been considered aliens from the covenants of promise -"having no hope and without God in this world".

But the apostle protested - "now in Christ Jesus ye who sometimes were far off are made nigh by the blood." (Ephesians 2:12-13)

To fully understand and appreciate this particular facet of **OUR GLORIOUS INHERITANCE** we must realize that a **commonwealth** is defined as being *some kind of political unit, such as a nation or a state.*

Prior to the incarnation, this biblical phrase - **the commonwealth of Israel** - would have only been used in reference to the natural offspring of Abraham. But now it definitely refers to a spiritual nation, comprised of spiritual citizens, who have been spiritually "born into" a heavenly citizenship.

This commonwealth - also referred to as **God's chosen community** - is therefore presently made up of all those who have been saved, the whole family of God in heaven and in earth. (Ephesians 2:12 PME)

• For this cause Philippians 3:20 states in the present tense that we are **"citizens of heaven"** and that right now "our citizenship is in heaven" - "from whence also we look for the Saviour, the Lord Jesus Christ." (NEB, RV, AV)

O, glory to God! We may be presently earthbound, but our names are written in heaven in that celestial roster called - "the Lamb's Book of Life"! We are in the world, but not of the world.

We are citizens of another sphere, temporarily exiled in the realm of time.

- The word - **citizen** - is defined as *a person owing allegiance to, and entitled to the protection of, a sovereign state.*

We can certainly relate to this definition - for we owe everything that we are, and all that we ever will be, to the heavenly theocracy of which we are a part.

We have therefore made the decision to be "faithful unto death" if need be, to promote the furtherance of this kingdom and to enhance its influence presently in this world.

This is the commitment of citizenship!

In return we are promised divine protection and security if we abide by the laws of this kingdom.

We know that He has given His angels charge over us to keep us in all our ways. We are sure that "He preserveth the souls of His saints." (Psalm 91:11; 97:10)

Therefore, we can be bold in echoing the statement Elisha made to his servant when the Syrian soldiers were coming to take them into custody. (II Kings 6)

The undisturbed prophet said - "Fear not: for they that be with us are more than they that be with them."

Then God opened the eyes of Elisha's young assistant - "and he saw; and behold, the mountain was full of horses and chariots of fire round about Elisha."

What utter confidence must have gripped his spirit!

What supernatural strength must have surged through his inner being!

To view the merging of the two worlds, and the subduing of the natural with such ease, must have left a permanent imprint of adamant faith on the spirit of this unnamed servant.

As the Syrian soldiers fell under a curtain of blindness and had to be led away, surely the revelation of God's ordination penetrated his heart, branding him with a prophet-like stance from that day forward...not arrogance or cockiness...just blessed God-given assurance (total confidence in the rights and privileges associated with heavenly citizenship).

Now, as sons of God and *citizens of heaven,* we can go through life with this same intrepid attitude of mind.

We can be courageously resolute - undaunted in the face of any danger or difficulty, for this is part of our *commonwealth* inheritance.

The King of glory is the Head of this blessed nation and He is a sovereign Potentate and supreme Lord over all.

This great and glorious God is for us; therefore, who and what can possibly be against us.

Whatever the ultimate outcome of any situation may be, one way or the other it is an absolute surety that God's populace always emerge as winners.

THE CHARACTER OF THE COMMONWEALTH

• If there are two words that describe the character and the atmosphere of this blessed, heavenly *commonwealth* to which we belong...those words are *freedom* and *liberty*.

In John 8:36 Jesus said - "If the Son therefore shall make you free, ye shall be free indeed."

In other words, whether they are earthbound or in paradise, all *citizens of heaven* have been compassionately set free from the dominion of sin and the bondage of the Adam-nature.

We are as free as men can possibly be, by virtue of our inherited position "in Christ".

• James 2:12 says - "So speak ye, and so do, as they that shall be judged by *the law of liberty.*"

This liberation law that overshadows every son of God is also known as - *"the law of the spirit of life in Christ Jesus."* (Romans 8:2)

It involves the gift and provision of immediate restoration and reconciliation to God, always available in response to faith, humility and sincerity.

The blood of Jesus, and *the life of God* contained in the blood, is our constant source of mercy, forgiveness, righteousness and victory. The *"spirit of life in Christ Jesus"* is stronger than any death-dealing entrapments this world may set for us. Therefore, if we keep our hearts melted before the Lord, and keep our attitudes right, it is absolutely impossible for us to be slaves to sin or circumstance any longer.

We choose, first of all, to live above all contaminating influence, for we are righteous by nature, but if by chance we are stained, we obtain cleansing by appropriating God's promises of grace and forgiveness into our lives.

Under the covering of God's love and by the indwelling of divine life, we are free from condemnation, free from fear, free from depression, free from sickness, free from guilt, and free from the past.

• This is the *perfect law of liberty* and these are some of our fundamental rights of citizenship.

But in order to enjoy these privileges we must stubbornly - "stand fast therefore in the *liberty* wherewith Christ hath made us free" and refuse to be again "entangled with the yoke of bondage." (Galatians 5:1)

This kingdom of absolute, joyous, spiritual freedom, both in its present state and in its future level of manifestation, is that "better country" - that supernatural *"land of oil olive"* - for which Abraham and all the other patriarchs and prophets so diligently searched.

Though these notable Old Testament personages knew Jehovah-God, they were all still bound to one degree or another by the law of sin and death...whether they were in Egypt, in the wilderness, or in Canaan land.

The blood of their animal sacrifices only provided partial and temporary relief from the dreadful entrapment of the fallen flesh-nature.

But then God, incarnate in human flesh, visited this earth to revolutionize man's relationship with God, bringing His chosen people out of spiritual bondage into the glory of the Lord.

A "JUBILEE" COMMONWEALTH

Shortly after receiving the Holy Ghost in the river Jordan, Jesus announced His ministry in the temple at Jerusalem by quoting Isaiah 61:

> *"The Spirit of the Lord God is upon Me; because the Lord hath anointed Me to preach good tidings unto the meek; He hath sent Me to bind up the brokenhearted, to proclaim liberty to the captives, and the opening of the prison to them that are bound; to proclaim the acceptable year of the Lord."*

• It is quite illuminating to understand that the term - *the acceptable year of the Lord* - directly refers to a great festival that took place in Israel every fifty years called *the year of Jubilee.*

During this festive and jubilant year - at the command of God - all debts were forgiven, all Jewish land, with only a few exceptions, was restored to its original owners, many prisoners were released, all Israelite slaves who had sold themselves because of poverty were set free, the land was given a sabbatical year of rest, and the Jews were ordered as well not to oppress one another. (Leviticus 25)

It is noteworthy that God promised to command His blessing on the Jews' crops in the forty-eighth year and they would bring forth such an abundant yield that it would last three years.

This wonderful *year of Jubilee* was definitely chosen of God to symbolize the great salvation and the spiritual liberty, rest, deliverance, restoration and bounty that would eventually be available through the New Covenant to believers of every nation, kindred and tongue.

Jesus entered the world to proclaim and inaugurate the institution of a new *commonwealth*, a spiritual kingdom, in which there would be a perpetual celebration of *Jubilee.*

This is definitely happening now and has been happening since the Day of Pentecost.

Under the Old Covenant, *the year of Jubilee* would be joyously ushered in by the blowing of trumpets all over the land of Israel on the Day of Atonement.

In fact, the word - *Jubilee* - is translated from the Hebrew word -

yobel - which actually means *the blast of a trumpet or a time of shouting.*
(UBD, YC)

• But what happened primarily "in the natural" for the Jews of old has become primarily a spiritual experience for God's people now.

At the dawn of the New Covenant, one hundred and twenty "trumpeteers" in the upper room began proclaiming the "Good News" of a new and greater *Jubilee* as they lifted their voices like trumpets, speaking in tongues and preaching to Jews of every nation "the wonderful works of God."

Since then, by countless millions, *the feast of Jubilee* has been experienced and enjoyed, not as a symbolic feast celebrated every fifty years, but as a supernatural reality available constantly to those who trust in the atoning price that Jesus paid.

• We celebrate *Jubilee* every day.

Indebtedness to God is continually being forgiven whenever and wherever men repent and call on the name of Jesus.

Prisoners of sin are constantly being released from iniquity's bonds through the precious blood of the Lamb.

Those who have been *slaves* to oppression, doubt and fear are continually being set *free,* as believers cease from their own works and enter into *"the rest"* of God's imparted righteousness and grace.

Victims of spiritual *poverty* (backsliders stripped of their fellowship with God and the manifestation of His gifts) find the *restoration* of their inheritance whenever they go to the cross in humility and faith.

Moreover, the Jubilee command *"not to oppress one another"* has found a perfect channel and means of expression and fulfillment in *the citizens of heaven,* because the love of God has been shed abroad in our hearts by the Holy Ghost.

The regenerated spirits of true, mature sons of God overflow with the forgiving character and the merciful nature of the One who rejoiced in the very beginning to institute *Jubilee* as a foreshadowing of the New Covenant Age.

During this wonderful year of rejoicing in Israel, the Jews were exhorted by God to remember the poor, and not to demand usury of one another (interest on money or goods loaned out). This speaks of the fact that we must "bear the infirmities of the weak" (those who are *poor spiritually)* and also that we should never demand more love, forgiveness, service or consideration from others than we are willing to give. We must be fair, selfless and just in our dealings with others, especially the brotherhood.

This should not merely be a self-imposed duty; this should be the rejoicing of our hearts, for we are loyal and devoted citizens of that celestial kingdom birthed out of the womb of heaven that could well be called "a *Jubilee* Commonwealth".

And without a doubt, God has *commanded His blessing* upon us.

We did not work our way into such spiritual abundance; it came as a free gift of grace.

Now our great passion is to obey the laws of this kingdom, and to see the fulfillment of the promises of this kingdom, in our daily lives. And one of the greatest of all its laws and promises is simply - "Give, and it shall be given unto you." (Luke 6:38)

If we live by this standard, laying down our lives for the brethren, surely all men will know that we are definitely *citizens* of another world, where selfishness has been dethroned and love reigns supreme.

ELEVEN OTHER LAWS OF THE COMMONWEALTH

We have already mentioned three vitally important and related laws that govern the kingdom of which we are part - **The Perfect Law of Liberty, The Law of the Spirit of Life in Christ Jesus**, and **The Law of Giving and Receiving.** (James 1:25; 2:12, Romans 8:2, Luke 6:38)

There are eleven others that are quite worthy of being mentioned in this study. By closely inspecting some of these major laws of God's kingdom, we simultaneously gain an even greater insight into the full beauty and personality of this everlasting commonwealth to which we belong.

The Law of God after the Inward Man - *"For I delight in the law of God after the inward man..."* (Romans 7:22)

This law is the undeniable truth that whenever individuals are truly born again, God immediately writes the law on the fleshly tables of their hearts. Automatically, such privileged persons receive an inward craving to fulfill God's purpose - loving what the Creator loves and hating what He hates. This spiritual desire is resident, not in the carnal part of our being, but in the *"inward man"*, the "hidden man of the heart."

The Law of Faith - *"Where is boasting then? It is excluded. By what law? of works? Nay: but by the law of faith. Therefore we conclude that a man is justified by faith without the deeds of the law."* (Rom. 3:27-28)

To be justified is to be reckoned righteous in the sight of God. According to the above scripture this can never be achieved by works. It can only come through *faith* in the blood of Jesus. Therefore, no man can boast over righteous deeds and if we do we are greatly deceived. Whatever we receive from God is freely given, not because of our worthiness, but because of the "price" Jesus paid and the sincere *faith* we have in that "price". This is our only source, and by this rule the kingdom advances in many areas.

The Law of Righteousness - *"But Israel, which followed after the law of righteousness, hath not attained to the law of righteousness. Wherefore? Because they sought not by faith."* (Read Romans 9:30-33)

This law Paul called *the law of righteousness* works in close conjunction with *the law of faith.* "For with the heart man *believeth unto righteousness;* and with the mouth confession is made unto salvation." (Romans 10:10) Also, concerning the Jews mentioned in the foregoing scripture, Paul said - "For they being ignorant of God's righteousness, have not *submitted* themselves to the righteousness of God." Therefore, New Covenant righteousness is something *believed for* and *submitted to.* Jesus Christ is the end of this quest for "every one that believeth." (Romans 10:3-4)

The Law of Christ - *"Bear ye one another's burdens, and so fulfill the law of Christ."* (Galatians 6:2)

The law of Christ is the command that we should walk as He did in this world - full of compassionate caring. Our goal as followers of Christ is to be oriented to the needs of others as He was...seeking above all to relieve the pain of the pained, assuage the grief of the grief-stricken and lift the burdens of the burdened. To accomplish this we must develop a feeling heart...for this law can never be effectively fulfilled just out of a sense of duty or obligation.

The Royal Law - *"If ye fulfill the royal law according to the Scripture, Thou shalt love thy neighbor as thyself..."* (James 2:8)

The *royal law* is the chief of all the laws of the commonwealth of Israel. It should reign supreme in our lives. By it the body of Christ functions effectively and properly in this world - for love is the fulfilling of the law. If we truly love, we will never transgress the law of God bringing harm to others. We will treat them as we desire to be treated ourselves. We will grant each person the respect and dignity that he or she deserves. We will even love our enemies and do good to them that hate us.

Other Pertinent Laws

The Law of Humility and Exaltation - *"For whosoever exalteth himself shall be abased; and he that humbleth himself shall be exalted."* (Luke 14:11)

The Law of Losing and Finding - *"He that findeth his life shall lose it: and he that loseth his life for My sake shall find it."* (Matthew 10:39)

The Law of Dying and Living - *"For if ye live after the flesh, ye shall die: but if ye through the Spirit do mortify the deeds of the body, ye shall live."* (Romans 8:13)

The Law of Suffering and Reigning - *"If we suffer [with Him] we shall also reign with Him."* (II Timothy 2:12)

The Law of Sowing and Reaping - *"Whatsoever a man soweth, that shall he also reap."* (Galatians 6:7)

The Law of True Greatness - *"But whosoever will be great among you, let him be your minister; And whosoever will be chief among you, let him be your servant."* (Matthew 20:26-27)

THE SUPREME WORTH OF
EVERY CITIZEN OF HEAVEN

In the twelfth chapter of Hebrews, Paul contrasted the vast difference between the Old Covenant that ministered death and the Gospel of grace that ministers life and righteousness.

He rejoiced to tell God's New Covenant offspring that we have not come to Mt. Sinai - the mountain of the revelation of the Law that could not be touched - "that burned with fire" and was covered with "blackness, darkness and tempest."

Rather he declared - "Ye are come to mount Sion, and unto the city of the living God, the heavenly Jerusalem, and to an innumerable company of angels, to **THE GENERAL ASSEMBLY AND CHURCH OF THE FIRSTBORN,** which are written in heaven..." (Hebrews 12:22-23)

This scripture is the only place that this particular *title - the church of the firstborn* - appears in the Word of God.

It brings to light a unique and marvellous revelation concerning the supreme worth of every individual member of the church in the sight of God and the splendid future that awaits us.

THE MYSTERY OF THE FIRSTBORN STATUS

The term *firstborn*, on the first level of interpretation, simply refers to the first son born to any man, the *"beginning of his strength"* as Deuteronomy 21:17 puts it.

This *firstborn* son, among the Jews, was the legal heir to certain privileges, rights, advantages and responsibilities that none of the other offspring possessed.

• The *firstborn* son normally received a double portion inheritance of his father's estate.

• The *firstborn* also received the commission of being the priest of the family. The *firstborn* son was expected to exercise authority over his younger brothers and sisters in a measure similar to the father and in the event of the father's death, this elite son was also responsible for the welfare of the others.

In the revelation of the New Covenant this term is first used, and primarily used, in reference to Jesus.

He is called "the *firstborn* of every creature", "the *firstborn* of all creation" and "the *firstborn* from the dead; that in all things He might have the preeminence." (Colossians 1:15,18 RSV, AV)

74

He is titled "the *firstborn* of the poor" who is "higher than the kings of the earth" and "the *firstborn* among many brethren." (Isaiah 14:30, Psalm 89:27, Romans 8:29)

In all these and other references as well, the expression *firstborn* means not only the first to accomplish or to be a certain thing (a forerunner or a beginner) but it also takes on the added, symbolic meaning of *that which is most excellent, preeminent, supreme or choice.*

We know that these words are easily descriptive of Jesus, who is also called -"the Head of the church" in Colossians 1:18.

• But what is most amazing is the fact that these words also aptly describe our rank in God's great universal plan...for we are His *most excellent* achievement in time and eternity, destined to inherit a *preeminent* position of paramount importance in His vast creation. We are His *supreme* pleasure and, of all entities and beings in heaven and earth, we are His *choice* way of expressing Himself.

The New English Bible, in translating Hebrews 12:23, declares that we are - **"THE ASSEMBLY OF THE FIRSTBORN CITIZENS OF HEAVEN."** The Revised Standard Version says - **"THE ASSEMBLY OF THE FIRSTBORN** who are enrolled in heaven."

In other words, as joint-heirs with Christ, we have been lifted to a similarly elite status with Him in the kingdom of God...*a firstborn status.*

Not only is our elder Brother a King, destined to sit on the throne of David, and a High Priest, after the order of Melchizedek, but He has - "made us unto our God kings and priests, and we shall reign on the earth." (Revelations 5:10)

We will forever share His throne and share His priesthood.

It is evident by this irrefutable scripture alone that Jesus has not reserved the glory, privilege, and honor of being the *firstborn* Son unto Himself alone...rather, He has lovingly and joyously divided His inheritance with us.

Our spirits soar as we meditate and speculate on the various ways that such a promise could be fulfilled.

We know that Jesus, the original *firstborn* Son, possessed a **double portion inheritance** - the life of the Father indwelling and eternal life in the future celestial state. So we, His many brethren, have received a double portion heritage blessing as well. We have "the promise of life that now is, and of that which is to come." (I Timothy 4:8)

Also, as Jesus was the Word made flesh and was given the Spirit without measure, so we, His joint-heirs have been begotten of the Word and born of the Spirit. This could also be considered our **double portion inheritance.**

Only eternity itself will reveal the full ramifications of such generous gifts from the Father above.

IDENTIFYING WITH ISRAEL
THE EVERLASTING COMMONWEALTH

- As sons of God we have all spiritually become a part of Israel, therefore it is significant to note that in Exodus 4:22 God said - *"Israel is My son, even My firstborn."*
The interpretation of this passage is simply wonderful, for it is surely a reference that includes us.

Apparently, not only is Jesus the *firstborn* Son of the family of God (what is spiritually called *Israel*)...the family of God as a whole is apparently the *"firstborn group"* of something far more marvellous, and for the most part undisclosed, that God intends to bring forth in the New Creation to come.

We are *"the beginning of His strength"*, the first step in a plan so vast that it spans the eternities.
Even now, in this humiliating earthly state, heaven's attention is on us to such degree that even the hairs of our heads are all numbered.
How much more so will this attentive care intensify when our heavenly Father fully expresses Himself in every one of His redeemed sons and daughters!!
This will all transpire in the twinkling of an eye - at that final and ultimate celebration of *"Yobel"*, when the *"trump of God"* shall sound and the dead in Christ shall rise incorruptible!

O, what a *"time of shouting"* that will be!
O, what singing, what rejoicing will resound in the heavenlies when we are fully restored...set free forever from the bondage of this vile Adam flesh!
It is so true that we daily "groan within ourselves" to experience this glorified state that will finally be our irreversible and infinite inheritance. But as we journey toward such a glorious destiny it is also true that with every faith-filled step we can have *"a time of shouting"*.
Every day can be fully orchestrated with heavenly trumpets blasting out the joy of the Lord as we meditate, deep down in our spirits, on the manifold promises of God and the spectacular future set before us.

- What a blessing it will be when all the laws of the commonwealth are brought to total fulfillment and fruition in all of us:
    - the law of God after the inward man in full control of our hearts.
    - the laws of faith and righteousness splendidly manifested.
    - the perfect law of liberty permeating the heavenly atmosphere.
    - the royal law overflowing out of our hearts toward every other member of **GOD'S CHOSEN AND ETERNAL COMMUNITY.**

What joyous freedom! What a feast of charity !
What a celebration of victory! What an inheritance of spiritual plenty!

• Imagining these things, we are filled to the brim with expectancy. And being filled, we are all the more compelled to quote yet another translation of Hebrews 12:22-23 that brings this *title-revelation* to an ecstatic grand finale.

> *"What you have come to is Mount Zion, and the city of the living God, the heavenly Jerusalem, where millions of angels have gathered for the festival, with the whole church in which everyone is a 'first born son' and a citizen of heaven."* (JB)

The festival is...JUBILEE.

The eternal position for each one of us is that of a **FIRSTBORN SON.** *1

The everlasting *title* is...**A CITIZEN OF HEAVEN, A MEMBER OF THE COMMONWEALTH OF ISRAEL.**

---

*1 This concept of our firstborn status will be explored in even greater depth in the chapter entitled **His Son, His Firstborn** in Volume Five of **Our Glorious Inheritance.**

• A CITY SET ON A HILL •

THE CITY OF THE LIVING GOD, THE HEAVENLY JERUSALEM

THAT GREAT CITY, THE HOLY JERUSALEM

AN ETERNAL EXCELLENCY

JERUSALEM WHICH IS ABOVE

HEPHZIBAH

• THE SONS OF HEPHZIBAH •

"Ye are the light of the world. A CITY that is SET ON A HILL cannot be hid."

(Matthew 5:14)

*"But ye are come unto mount Sion, and unto **THE CITY OF THE LIVING GOD, THE HEAVENLY JERU-SALEM,** and to an innumerable company of angels."*

(Hebrews 12:22)

*"And I John saw **THE HOLY CITY, NEW JERUSALEM,** coming down from God out of heaven, prepared as a bride adorned for her husband."*

(Revelation 21:2)

*" But **JERUSALEM WHICH IS ABOVE** is free, which is the mother of us all."*

(Galatians 4:26)

*"Thou shalt no more be termed Forsaken...but thou shalt be called **HEPHZIBAH**...as a young man marrieth a virgin, so shall thy **SONS** marry thee..."*

(Isaiah 62:4-5)

A CITY SET ON A HILL

THE CITY OF THE LIVING GOD, THE HEAVENLY JERUSALEM

"Ye are the light of the world. A CITY that is SET ON AN HILL cannot be hid."

(Matthew 5:14)

• In the first *title-scripture* above, Jesus likened His people to a city...*a city set on a hill.*

The hill is certainly, symbolically, the hill called *Golgotha.*

This hill is the foundation of the entire city; it is a common foundation for every building and every citizen in this spiritual city.

And, without controversy, the Bible said that - "other foundation can no man lay than that is laid, which is Jesus Christ." (I Corinthians 3:11)

The foundation is nothing more and nothing less than the Son of God Himself and the redemptive work that He accomplished.

This foundation is solid and eternal; II Timothy 2:19 declares that it *"standeth sure".*

Therefore we can loudly proclaim that this luminous city is *set* eternally on a sure and dependable base...the passion and death of the one who is called Shiloh and Immanuel.

• The word - **set** - can be interpreted to mean *permanently fixed or established.*

This quality of stability marks the inhabitants of this spiritual city, for they are trusting in, and building their lives upon, the finished work of Calvary.

Those people who build their present existence and their eternal future on religious rituals, denominational ties, or mere intellectual, theological concepts are on a shaky, unstable foundation.

They are building on temporal, lifeless things that will soon pass away. They are building on sinking sand, not on the solid foundation that supports and upholds every true member of the family of God.

Isaiah said it this way..."Thus saith the Lord God, Behold, I lay in Zion for a *foundation* a stone, a tried stone, a precious corner stone, *a sure foundation...*" (Isaiah 28:16)

• **Because Jesus was the *tried stone* of Calvary, He could become the *sure foundation* of the church on Pentecost.**

Those who refuse to build on this Calvary-foundation will find that their "covenant with death shall be disannulled" and their "agreement with hell shall not stand." (Isaiah 28:18)

When a person receives the revelation of Jesus and the inward experience of His reality, the spiritual emphasis from then on must be

81

placed, not on denominations and doctrines of men, but rather on the precious blood of the Lamb and the power that is present in the blood to remit sin.

Those who receive, and yield to, this life-transforming illumination of the inner man become radiant lights shining forth brightly in a world that has been swallowed up in the gross darkness of religious deception.

They shine like *a city set on a hill.* They cannot be hid.

The light of truth is just too bright.

The glory of His presence is just too brilliant.

The change of lifestyle is just too obvious.

The difference in attitudes is just too radical.

To hide or quench the light of God's anointed sons and daughters is nearly as impossible as hiding or quenching the light of the sun.

We have been chosen to take authority over darkness and conquer it, as our God did in the beginning.

We have been commanded to let our light so shine before men that they might see our good works and glorify our Father which is in heaven.

To even make an attempt at hiding this light would be a terrible sin against humanity.

Even as the gentle light of a hill-set city reaches out as if to warmly embrace the weary wilderness traveler, so also the light of God's love, emanating from His people, reaches forth to embrace every sin-sick soul, journeying through the realm of time.

In every generation, this vibrant and *living spiritual city* becomes a refuge from the darkness of the night...a place of blessed rest and loving protection in the midst of a world filled with chaos and confusion.

The natural light of a hill-set city will frighten and even repel the wild beasts that lurk in dark places, seeking whom they may devour. In like manner, evil powers and principalities, seeking to destroy and devour us spiritually, are repelled and even frightened away when they see God's people dwelling together in unity, as *a city set on a hill.*

Therefore achieving and maintaining a spirit of unity among ourselves is of the utmost importance.

A LIVING CITY
UNITED IN THE LOVE OF GOD

• What great strength and what great love we discover when we truly learn that we are more than an organization; we are an organism - *a living city* - a spiritual community perpetually bound together by a common experience, inheritance and destiny!

What great security becomes ours when we learn that we are actually one with other members of the body of Christ and that we function as a unit! What great exploits result when we learn to pool our faith and share one another's burdens!

What great miracles can transpire when we learn the effectiveness of agreeing together in prayer!

• In Genesis 11, we read of the inhabitants of Babel building a tower, quite possibly a ziggurat, to be used for astrological and idolatrous purposes.

These tower builders said - "Let us build us a city and a tower, whose top may reach unto heaven; and let us make us a name, lest we be scattered abroad upon the face of the whole earth."

Although their motives were evil, self-centered and seditious, still God said - "Behold, the people is *one*, and they have all *one* language...and now nothing will be restrained from them, which they have imagined to do."

The essential point to be made is this: if such unity in an evil endeavor could open the door to nearly impossible tasks being fulfilled, then what could a godly people united in the Holy Ghost - and in a desire to lift up the name of God - achieve if they dare to throw their differences to the wind and reach for *oneness* of purpose.

• In line with this, the Psalmist David wrote -"Behold, how good and how pleasant it is for brethren to dwell together in unity" (in real, spiritual fellowship). (Psalm 133:1)

That is why the Bible commanded that we forsake not - "the assembling of ourselves together." (Hebrews 10:25)

We are commanded to uphold one another...for we are part of the same community, the same city.

The strong are called to bear the infirmities of the weak and not to please themselves.

We are commanded to be watchful over the spiritual condition of those around us, knowing that we are our brother's keeper.

We are commanded to exhort one another daily and, as the writer of Hebrews put it - "so much the more as ye see the day approaching."

Another translation of the same passage says -

> *"Let us do all we can to help one another's faith and this the more earnestly as we see the final day drawing nearer."*

(Hebrews 10:25 PME)

Now, more than ever before, we must strive for unity as members of the same family and fellow-citizens of the same city, for we are living in that perilous era in which Jesus said - "the love of many shall wax cold". (Matthew 24:12)

We must strive to fully arrive at the unity of the Spirit, the unity of the faith, and the unity of the knowledge of the Son of God, for then, and only then, will we reach the perfection of what God has for us in the last days. (Ephesians 4:3-13)

This *city set on a hill* must shine brighter than ever as we near the establishment of the kingdom of God in this world.

This must come to pass and this will come to pass, for the prophecy has already been given - "...the path of the just is as the shining light, that shineth more and more unto *the perfect day*." (Proverbs 4:18)

THE CAPITOL CITY OF THE NEW CREATION

•   When this *perfect day* comes that Solomon prophesied about, *the city set on a hill* will be lifted up to a much more lofty and luminescent inheritance.

God has already determined that on that day - all things will be made new.

There will be a New Heaven and a New Earth.

The first heaven and the first earth will pass away.

The restoration, renovation, and recreation of all things will come to pass...as foretold and revealed in God's infallible Word.

In the book of the Revelation, the antichrist, apostate church of the last days was likened to both a woman (the Great Whore) and a city (Mystery Babylon).

In a positive parallel truth, we see that the true church is also jointly represented as a woman (the bride of Christ) and a city (New Jerusalem).

John the Revelator said - "I...saw **THE HOLY CITY, NEW JERUSALEM**...coming down from God out of heaven, prepared as a bride adorned for her husband." (Revelations 21:2)

This eternal city is called - "the bride, the Lamb's wife...**THAT GREAT CITY, THE HOLY JERUSALEM**...having the glory of God: and her light was like unto a stone most precious." (Revelation 21:10-11)

This is the city that Abraham looked for - "whose builder and maker is God" and the city that God has promised to all His elect. (Hebrews 11:10,16)

Hebrews 12:22 entitles this glorious dwelling place - "**THE CITY OF THE LIVING GOD, THE HEAVENLY JERUSALEM**" where there abides "an innumerable company of angels."

And Paul describes it as - "**JERUSALEM WHICH IS ABOVE**" - not a place of bondage but "free...the mother of us all." (Galatians 4:26) For those who are free in Christ will eventually enjoy absolute freedom there forever.

Surely, this will be a literal city - the capital city of a literal New Heaven and a literal New Earth.

• **But it is also certain that this glorious city symbolically represents the eternal bride of Christ, for the members of the bride are destined to be its inhabitants.**

Therefore, certain details concerning the appearance of the city are revelations into the nature, character and destiny of the bride.

We will explore the depth of these revelatory details now!

SYMBOLIC CELESTIAL ARCHITECTURE
THE REVELATORY DESIGN

• **That great city, the holy Jerusalem, is beheld by John from a great and high mountain.** (Revelation 21:10)

This represents the fact that the little despised hill of suffering called Calvary, and the Rock of Ages cleft there for us, will ultimately become a great and glorious mountain, the kingdom of God, filling the whole earth. (Daniel 2)

• **The city has a "wall great and high" - about 144 cubits high (app. 228 feet) according to the measure of a man.** (Revelation 21:17)

There has never been any earthly city fortified to such degree.

This spectacularly high wall, therefore, speaks of the great grace that has always acted as a hedge of divine protection for God's people throughout their journey from time into eternity.

No wonder the prophet prophesied to Jerusalem saying - *"Thou shalt call thy walls Salvation and thy gates Praise."* (Isaiah 60:18)

The God that began a *salvation* work in us will perform it, and continue it until the end. This is His promise and we enter the gate of this security-promise through faith and praise.

Such preservation power is exceedingly and indescribably *precious* to us and to God as well.

It is quite understandable, therefore, that these walls, representing God's keeping power, appear extravagantly *costly* -"like a stone most *precious,* even like a jasper stone, clear as crystal" - for these walls really were quite expensive.

The purchase price was the very life of Jesus poured out in sacrifice and the blood that He shed on the earth.

Quite notable also is the fact that jasper is an extremely hard stone, nearly indestructible - even more so is God's shield of defense around those who trust in Him.

• **The city is - "pure gold, like unto clear glass."** (Revelation 21:18)

The brilliant appearance of the entire city also speaks of the great value of the bride in the eyes of the Creator, for gold is one of the most expensive metals in the world.

This spectacular, celestial picture also speaks of the infinite purity and divinity of God's people...for all who enter this eternal city must first be refined by fire, purged of impurities, and brought forth as gold.

God must have used this particular symbol in the Scripture because many of the detailed aspects and qualities of this metallic substance produce a perfect similitude of various aspects and qualities of the bride of Christ. (See Job 23:10)

Gold is one of the most *malleable* metals (a metal that is more easily formed and beaten into shape by the hands of a craftsman). Therefore, this city of gold symbolizes the final success of God's eternal purpose in us, molding and sculpturing us into His image.

This golden, eternal, dwelling place also represents the outstanding eternal excellence of the bride, for something golden is always something that transcends and surpasses the normal...being *superior* and exceptional in quality.

The resemblance of gold also speaks of the infinite stability and unchangeableness of our inheritance in the kingdom of God, for gold is one of the most perpetually *lustrous* metals - it will not tarnish or change in its color.

Finally, the golden appearance of the city symbolizes the *two opposite character* qualities that are being developed in us by passing through this valley of the shadow of death.

Gold is one of the most *enduring* metals and yet, at the same time, it is one of the *softest* metals.

The resulting metaphor speaks of the fact that in like manner, God is creating in us the traits of strength, firmness, and immovability, while simultaneously developing in us the qualities of gentleness, tenderness, mercifulness and compassion.

Enduring and strong, yet soft and pliable...able to make a firm stand for truth, yet equally able to feel the infirmities of others.

This is part of what it means to come forth as gold.

This is what God is doing in us right now.

And this is what God will perfect in us forever.

• **The city - "lieth foursquare...the length and the breadth and the height of it are equal."** (Revelation 21:16)

This speaks of the absolute flawlessness and the ultimate perfection of the heavenly state.

No earthly city could ever claim such an amazing architectural design (a perfect cube)...but, of course, the spirit of the world has never produced any perfect and flawless men either.

Heaven can claim such a structure, for heaven will surely generate an innumerable host, that no man can number, of - "*just men made perfect*". (Hebrews 12:22-23)

What a mighty God we serve! How great is His miracle-working power! He is well able to - "change our vile body, that it may be fashioned like unto His glorious body, according to the working whereby He is able even to subdue all things unto Himself." (Philippians 3:21)

He is well able to make us perfect, even as our heavenly Father is perfect.

- **The city is adorned with - "the glory of God."** (Rev.21:2,11)

This speaks of the eternal, ethereal *beauty* of God, being freely and lovingly bestowed on the bride...the matchless *beauty* of His inward nature and the radiant beauty of His outward appearance.

To be **adorned** means - *to be beautified.*

Therefore, to be adorned with the glory of God means to be brought forth in the supernatural image of the One who is described as being "altogether lovely" (Song of Solomon 5:16) - the mighty God who clothes Himself "with light as with a garment." (Psalm 104:1-2)

We will forever - "behold the *beauty* of the Lord...in His [heavenly] pavilion: in the secret of His tabernacle." (Psalm 27:4-5)

But simultaneously, this excellent loveliness will blossom in us, for He has promised to give us..."*beauty* for ashes, the oil of joy for mourning, and the garment of praise for the spirit of heaviness." (Isaiah 61:3)

"For the Lord taketh pleasure in His people: He will *beautify* the meek with salvation." (Psalm 149:4)

We will share His honor. We will partake of His majesty.

We will be clothed with a divine, heavenly light so bright that there will be no need for the light of the sun or the light of the moon. The glory of God will itself lighten the city...powerfully emanating from the Lamb of God and from all His many brethren.

Surely we will dwell with our God surrounded by and endued with indescribable splendor.

"The *beauty* of the Lord our God" will be upon us and He will "establish...the work of our hands." (Psalm 90:17)

No wonder Peter declared that in anticipation of this supernal inheritance, we all rejoice with joy unspeakable.

This joy is unutterable, for to meditate on such a future glory lifts us high above the plane where words are sufficient in communicating ideas. In fact, we would dare say that it is impossible for us now to fully envision, or to fully describe, what awaits us in the kingdom to come, for God "is able to do exceedingly abundantly above all that we ask or think." (Ephesians 3:20)

- **The city will be called - "by a new name, which the mouth of the Lord shall name."** (Isaiah 62:2)

It seems that everything and everyone participating in the New Creation will receive a new name...even the Son of God Himself. (Rev. 3:12)

A new name always speaks of new beginnings.

One new name of the city of God is **Hephzibah** - which means, *My delight is in her*. (Isaiah 62:4)

Surely God's everlasting *delight* will not be focused on just the literal city of God itself. His extreme pleasure will be rather in the beloved sons of God that inhabit that city.

So, we can easily conclude that this name is applicable to both the city and the bride that the city represents.

It is important to note that the word **Eden** means *delight.*

It is certain therefore that those who dwell in this eternal city - *Hephzibah* - will be restored to the delightful *Eden-paradise* relationship that Adam and Eve once possesed with God. God will *delight* Himself in us and we will *delight* ourselves in the Lord.

Because of this the prophet Zephaniah declared to Jerusalem - "Fear thou not...the Lord thy God in the midst of thee is mighty; He will save, He will rejoice over thee with joy; He will rest in His love, He will joy over thee with singing." (Zephaniah 3:16-17)

If **THE HOLY CITY, NEW JERUSALEM** is the bride, and it is - then the bride, the Lamb's Wife, is actually **HEPHZIBAH** (His *delightsome* companion, His eternal delight...His everlasting satisfaction and His ultimate joy).

Yes, we will be God's greatest source of fulfillment and happiness...infinitely.

Our relationship will never become stale.

The Bridegroom will eternally be ecstatic over His bride, and in like manner, we will never cease to be utterly thrilled with Him. He will continually pour out His best on us...for He has promised to make us "**AN ETERNAL EXCELLENCY.**" (Isaiah 60:15)

Concerning the everlasting city of God - **HEPHZIBAH** - Isaiah prophesied - "For as a young man marrieth a virgin, so shall thy **SONS [the sons of Hephzibah]** marry thee: and as the bridegroom rejoiceth over the bride, so shall thy God rejoice over thee." (Isaiah 62:5)

Regarding this future state the Psalmist David also declared - "The meek shall inherit the earth; and shall delight themselves in the abundance of peace." (Psalm 37:11)

We know that the word **Jerusalem** means *possession of peace.*

So to be a part of **THE HEAVENLY JERUSALEM** will surely involve the experience of a deeper peace than we have ever known.

And it will certainly be our possession forever - for we are that **CITY SET ON A HILL**...that *living city* in which the Almighty God will rapturously dwell throughout the ceaseless ages.

Yes, we can say with all confidence...our future is absolutely secure.

DISCIPLES

"And seeing the multitudes, He went up into a mountain: and when He was set, His **DISCIPLES** came unto Him:

And He opened His mouth, and taught them..."

(Matthew 5:1-2)

DISCIPLES

"And seeing the multitudes, He went up into a mountain: and when He was set, His DISCIPLES came unto Him: And He opened His mouth, and taught them."

(Matthew 5:1-2)

• **In the beginning of the New Testament Age, the word *disciple* was the term most often used to signify a follower of Jesus.**

The title *believer*, used quite often in recent years, is still only found twice in the Scripture (Acts 5:14, I Timothy 4:12).

The other present-day traditional title *Christian* is only found three times (Acts 11:26, 26:28, I Peter 4:16).

• But the term *disciple* appears two hundred and fifty-five times in the New Testament.

Therefore we conclude that because God has placed a far greater emphasis on this entitlement, it is of exceeding great importance that we fulfill its demands.

The standard definition of the word *disciple* is - *one who accepts, and assists in spreading, the doctrines of another.*

The New Testament Greek word that is translated *disciple* is *mathetes* - meaning, *one who is trained or taught.*

But a *disciple* is more than merely a student; a true *disciple* aspires to be an imitator, attaining the stature of his teacher and walking in his footsteps.

• **The term - *disciple* - appears only once in the Old Testament, in the eighth chapter of Isaiah.**

It is apparent that in this particular prophecy Isaiah is not even referring to anyone under the Old Covenant.

He is prophesying concerning New Covenant believers.

First, Isaiah predicts that the Messiah will come and that He will be - "for a sanctuary." This can mean either a place of refuge or a place of worship...and Jesus is definitely both.

He then reveals that Jesus will be rejected and become - "a stone of stumbling and...a rock of offense, to both the houses of Israel." Finally, Isaiah foretells that there will be a number of adherents who will follow the Messiah and preserve His message for future generations. Concerning them, he prophesies - *"bind up the testimony, seal the law among My disciples."* (Isaiah 8:16)

Again, this is the only place in the Old Testament where the word *disciples* appears, and it is clearly referring to New Testament believers who would see *the law sealed* and brought to final fulfillment right before their eyes, through the death and resurrection of the Messiah.

91

Then these disciples would go forth into all the world with the testimony of Jesus Christ, proclaiming His power to save, to heal, and to deliver.

Through them, *the testimony* would be *bound up*...protected and preserved within their hearts, promulgated and perpetuated through their preaching.

It is quite clear that God intended well in advance to confirm their word by manifesting the supernatural, for two verses later, the following prophecy was given:

> *"Behold, I and the children whom the Lord hath given Me are for signs and for wonders in Israel from the Lord of hosts."*
>
> (Isaiah 8:18)

God explains here that His express purpose for raising up *disciples* is to manifest *signs* and *wonders* through them.

We know that these words were definitely spoken concerning New Testament believers for Paul confirmed it later in his letter to the Hebrews. (Hebrews 2:4, 13)

• In line with all of this, it is important to note that the word rendered - *disciple* - in Isaiah 8:16 is the Hebrew word - *limmud.*

This same Hebrew word was translated into the English word - *learned* - two times in Isaiah 50:4 when he prophesied:

> *"The Lord God hath given Me the tongue of the* **learned** *[limmud], that I should know how to speak a word in season to him that is weary: He wakeneth morning by morning, He wakeneth Mine ear to hear as the* **learned** *[limmud]."*

When taken in context it is quite clear that this is a prophecy of Jesus. In essence, Isaiah was prophesying that the Son of God Himself would be given the tongue and the ear of a *disciple.*

He would be sensitive enough spiritually to speak as an oracle of God, a mouthpiece of the Almighty, a channel of the living Word. **He would have the tongue of a disciple.**

He would be sensitive enough spiritually to fully hear and respond to, the inspiration of the Almighty. **He would have the ear of a disciple.**

This was definitely fulfilled, for Jesus, during His earthly sojourn, openly declared - "I have not spoken of Myself; but the Father which sent Me, He gave Me a commandment, what I should say, and what I should speak. And I know that His commandment is life everlasting: whatsoever I speak therefore, even as the Father said unto Me, so I speak." (John 12:49-50)

This discipleship inheritance-possession was in a sense fully stirred up in Jesus when He was baptized by John in the river Jordan and simultaneously baptized with the Holy Ghost descending from heaven above.

At that moment He filled up the measure of a *true disciple*, for He was empowered to do the works of the Father that sent Him.

• He was the original New Covenant Disciple who set the pace for all those who would run the race of discipleship after Him.

Now He is challenging us to be true disciples also, and it is certain that this can only be accomplished if we fully surrender our lives to Him. Remember, disciples are highly disciplined believers who have been expertly trained and effectively taught - through the Word and by the Spirit - in the deeper things of God.

Obviously, this only happens for those who show themselves willing to count the cost and pay the price of discipleship. In fact, this very statement leads us to the first of seven major requirements and signs that Jesus said would be evident in the life of a true *disciple*.

FORSAKING ALL - LUKE 14:26-33

• Consider carefully the following statement that Jesus made concerning discipleship:

> *"If any man come to Me, and hate not his father, and mother, and wife, and children, and brethren, and sisters, yea , and his own life also, he cannot be My disciple.*
>
> *...For which of you, intending to build a tower, sitteth not down first, and counteth the cost, whether he have sufficient to finish it?*
>
> *Lest haply, after he hath laid the foundation, and is not able to finish it, all that behold it begin to mock him,*
>
> *Saying, This man began to build, and was not able to finish.*
>
> *Or what king, going to make war against another king, sitteth not down first, and consulteth whether he be able with ten thousand to meet him that cometh against him with twenty thousand?*
>
> *Or else, while the other is yet a great way off, he sendeth an ambassage, and desireth conditions of peace. So likewise, whosoever he be of you that forsaketh not all that he hath, he cannot be My disciple."*

These scriptures unveil the great cost required in order to attain the stature of a *disciple*.

How strange it is that Jesus said that we must actually *hate* our families and even our own lives!

93

Normally, the accepted meaning of the word **hate** is - *an intense feeling of dislike, aversion or hostility.*

Certainly Jesus did not mean that we should cultivate negative feelings such as these for our loved ones, or even for ourselves, for this would be directly contrary to other commands given in His Word.

He rather meant that all human relationships must be secondary to our relationship with God. We must not compromise what we know God expects of us in order to please our families or even our own corrupt Adam-flesh.

• **We have laid the foundation:** our faith in the grace of God and the finished work of Calvary.

Now each one of us is building a tower that reaches into heaven.

This tower, if completed, represents the hundredfold fruitfulness that we can have in God if we fulfill His perfect will. It represents reaching upward and attaining our full potential - through a consecrated life and the works that result. To successfully build this tower we must be totally committed to the purpose of God and the calling of God in our lives.

This tower will potentially cost us everything.

Whether or not it actually does depends on circumstance, but still, we must be willing to pay that extreme of a price if necessary.

• Not long ago, in a certain cemetery in West Virginia, I saw a memorial to those who lost their lives in World War I and World War II.

The memorial itself was very impressive, but the inscription upon it impressed me even more. Written near the top was the heart-gripping phrase:

"All gave some, but some gave all"

In my mind, I immediately related this statement to the varying degrees of commitment found in individuals in the body of Christ, but then I realized that unfortunately the analogy was somewhat imperfect, for the following reason.

Any soldier going out to war has to resign himself over to the possibility of having to give his life, whether he wants to or not...so, in a sense, all go forth prepared to give all. In contrast, only a few professing Christians view their future with this attitude of complete sacrificial service, yet this is the *spirit of discipleship.*

God does not demand that every believer aspiring to discipleship literally forsake his career, his family, all his material possessions and everything he counts dear; but God does demand that, in a spiritual sense, all these things be placed on the altar.

The patriarch, Abraham, ultimately did not have to sacrifice his son Isaac, but He did have to place him on the altar, proving that he was willing. In like manner, we must willingly give up to God, in our spirits, every earthly thing, so that we have no attachments on our lives stronger than our attachment to the purpose of God.

As radical as the preceding statements may seem, they still only constitute the first basic step in imitating the Great Teacher at whose feet we sit in admiration and adoration.

• We must also consider that the moment we determine in our hearts to become *true disciples* we walk right into the front ranks of an intense, spiritual warfare. We become the target of the devil, for *true disciples* are a threat to him.

Attaining our goal will be no easy matter, for the power of the flesh and the powers of Satan will do all they can to keep us from progressing in God.

We will win only if we cultivate an attitude similar to the one possessed by the soldiers of ancient Sparta. These Grecian warriors always went into a battle with the point of view that they would come home *with their shields* or they would come home *on their shields*, but they would never come home *without their shields*.

In other words - they refused to entertain even the thought of retreat as a possibility. They purposed to either win the battle or die trying. They were almost always invincible as a result.

In like manner, we must dare to make up our minds that the truth we have discovered is well worth living for, and certainly worth dying for - and then proceed into the battle, never intending to drop our "shield of faith" regardless of what adversity we face.

This is part of what it means to forsake all...forsaking even the luxury of being able to entertain thoughts of quitting.

This is definitely our duty, for He forsook all for us.

This is definitely for our benefit, for He promised that everything we sacrifice will return to us a hundredfold. (Mark 10:29-31)

This truth was beautifully expressed by Jim Elliot, a notable missionary-martyr who once said:

> *"He is no fool, who gives away that which He cannot keep, in order to obtain that which He cannot lose."*

CONTINUING IN THE WORD - John 8:31-32

• Jesus said - *"If ye continue in My Word, then are ye My disciples indeed. And ye shall know the truth, and the truth shall make you free."*

To *continue in the Word* is to reach for much more than just the initial experience of salvation.

It involves pursuing the more intimate relationship with God that

95

comes through the Baptism of the Holy Spirit. It means pursuing the stirring up and the manifestation of the supernatural gifts and fruits of the Spirit, that we might be more effective in the kingdom.

But *to continue in the Word* also means to remain committed to all the statutes and precepts of holiness and righteousness contained in the Word.

This is not the bondage of legalism; this is the liberty that comes through submission, for God will only lead and disciple a yielded vessel.

He has promised to send the Spirit of truth to all who are yielded to lead and guide them into all truth. (John 16:13) We know that this "spirit of revelation" is God's attempt to help us *continue in the Word,* for Jesus pledged that -"the Comforter, which is the Holy Ghost, whom the Father will send in My name, He shall teach you all things." (John 14:26)

BEARING MUCH FRUIT - JOHN 15:8

• Jesus said - "*Herein is My Father glorified, that ye bear much fruit; so shall ye be My disciples.*"

Spiritual abundance and great fruitfulness are God's perfect will for those He counts His *disciples.*

This speaks of both yielding to and bringing forth the divine personality. It also speaks of abounding in the works of the Lord...having impact on this world for the glory of God.

A king would not be glorified by sending forth common tramps to represent him; neither does God receive glory from representatives that are spiritually fruitless, ignorant and ineffective.

It pleases God for us to be highly successful in spiritual matters. In fact, God's people should excel even in many natural endeavors of life...and thus, even in natural ways, reflect the greatness, perfection and excellency of our Father.

Heretofore, many believers have suffered from some kind of false humility syndrome. They have somehow convinced themselves that God was glorified by the defeated and the inferior, so they made cheap, sloppy and second-rate attempts at doing His work.

This false concept is exactly what Jesus was talking about when He said that "the children of this world are in their generation wiser than the children of light." (Luke 16:8)

The world knows how to make something a success.

They have learned how to reach humanity with their message.

Too often God's people have willingly taken a back seat spiritually.

They have lacked drive and self-confidence, so to defend their own crumbling self-image, they falsely labeled their condition - *meekness.*

It is high time that we be awakened out of this pitiful state of self-deception and realize that God wants us to abound in such fruitfulness that

- "the plowman shall overtake the reaper, and the treader of grapes him that soweth seed." (Amos 9:13)

PERSECUTION - MATTHEW 10:24-25

• Jesus was warning us of the opposition that we will most likely face if we fully walk after Him when He said:

> *"The disciple is not above his master, nor the servant above his lord.*
> *It is enough for the disciple that he be as his master, and the servant as his lord. If they have called the master of the house Beelzebub, how much more shall they call them of His household?"*

Jesus is the Master of the house, a household of disciples.

Beelzebub was the name of a Philistine god who was considered by the Philistines to be the head of all evil spirits. This name is thought to mean either *lord of the flies* or *god of the dung.*

Jesus used this heathen title to refer to the devil.

It is a degrading term referring to the filthiness and inherent uncleanness of the one we know as Satan.

Jesus in essence was saying that if He was accused of being under the influence of the devil, then they may well say the same thing about us. If He was falsely charged and degraded this way, then His true disciples can plan on being degraded and falsely charged also.

If He was persecuted, scorned and rejected, then we can expect the same kind of treatment.

The world hated Jesus because He was not of the world and His Word cut against the grain of what the world considered to be right.

In like manner, Jesus described His disciples as He prayed to the Father, saying - "I have given them Thy Word; and the world hath hated them, because they are not of the world, even as I am not of the world." (John 17:14)

We are walking in Jesus' footsteps. We speak the same Word.

We are commanded to - "have no fellowship with the unfruitful works of darkness, but rather reprove them." (Ephesians 5:11)

No wonder the Bible promised - "yea, and all that will live godly in Christ Jesus shall suffer *persecution*." (II Timothy 3:12)

If we are not being persecuted, chances are, we are not living godly enough - for as reprovers of darkness, we will surely make many enemies. Jesus warned that we would be hated of all nations for His name's sake. And He even foretold that - "a man's foes shall be they of his own household." (Matthew 10:36)

If and when this happens we must therefore not be crushed by it, nor compromise as a result, for Jesus said, -"He that loveth father or mother...son or daughter more than Me is not worthy of Me." (Matt.10:37)

We must always strive for harmony, love, forgiveness, and understanding that we might "follow peace with all men". But if rejection burns against us, we are called to rejoice before God that we have been "counted worthy to suffer shame for His name." (Acts 5:41)

Although this is only a potential price of discipleship, we must be prepared for the same if it happens to come. Jesus summed it up in Matthew 10, the discipleship chapter of the Bible, when He instructed us how we should react to persecution - *"Be wise as serpents, and harmless as doves...fear them not...endure to the end."*

LOVE - JOHN 13:34-35

- Jesus spoke these astounding words right before He died:

> *"A new commandment I give unto you, That ye love one another; as I have loved you, that ye also love one another.*
> *By this shall all men know that ye are My **disciples**, if ye have love one to another."*

Notice that Jesus said this was *a new commandment.*

In the Old Will they were commanded to love God and to love others, but not with the same kind of love.

The main words translated *love* in this passage are the Greek words - *agape* and *agapao.*

This *agape-love* is a spiritual love, birthed in heaven, that goes far beyond the limits of mere human love. This is the kind of totally selfless, divine love that Jesus first possessed and manifested.

The majority of men have no capacity for such depth of love. They can only love within the boundaries of the fallen Adam-nature. They are not born again partakers of the divine nature as we are.

We possess an inward potential of attaining a level of love that they cannot reach, for Jesus lives in our hearts and we can yield to His influence. Jesus even prayed specifically that this great love of God would dwell in us. (John 17:26)

Now He has commanded us to manifest it.

Surely this is why He called it *a new commandment.*

We have been called to love one another even as He loved us...faithful unto death. Even when strife arises, if we are *true disciples,* we remain committed to one another.

We die to our own feelings and seek instead to feel the infirmities of others and see things from their point of view.

We are called to forgive seventy times seven times in a day if necessary, and that's one time every three minutes.

Even when it feels like situations and certain human relationships are killing us mentally or emotionally, we must still make the attempt to keep loving one another with an everlasting love. This is the kind of love that God said He felt toward Israel. (Jeremiah 31:3)

• **This everlasting, undying, unchanging, irreversible, unconquerable kind of love is called** *"charity"*.

Charity is the God-kind of love, the highest form of love...a love that can even be freely bestowed on enemies. Charity is what constrained Jesus to forgive His murderers while on the cross. Charity is what compelled Stephen, in like manner, to pray for those who were stoning him, saying - "Lord, lay not this sin to their charge." (Acts 7:60)

By reacting in such a way, this first martyr of the Church imitated his teacher and proved that he was truly a *disciple*.

It is quite important to note that the word *charity* is another English translation of the Greek word *agape*.

The Greek words *eros* (sensual love) and *phileo* (brotherly love) are never translated into the word *charity* - only *agape*.

This *agape-love (charity)* -"suffereth long and is kind...is not easily provoked, thinketh no evil."

This *agape-love (charity)* - "beareth all things, believeth all things, hopeth all things, endureth all things."

Human love is not really able to bear, believe, hope and endure all things, though at times it may come close.

Human love can fail, but - *"charity never fails."* (I Corinthians 13)

• **Possessing charity is the sign of a true disciple; it is called "the more excellent way".** (I Corinthians 12:31)

Manifesting this *agape-kind of love* is a sign to the world that Jesus still lives - in and through the hearts of those who have been touched by His amazing grace.

Jesus did not say - "By this shall all men know that ye are My *disciples*, if ye have *phileo* (brotherly love) one to another."

He rather said - "By this shall all men know that ye are My *disciples*, if ye have *agape* [the God-kind of love] one to another." (John 13:35)

BEARING THE CROSS - LUKE 14:27

• Jesus gave this as a necessary condition and demand for true discipleship. He said - *"Whosoever doth not bear his cross, and come after Me, cannot be My disciple."*

Notice the possessive pronoun - *his* - before the word, *cross*. Jesus did not say that the disciple must bear *a cross*; He said that each disciple must bear *his cross*.

It is apparent, therefore, that each Christian has received a certain cross that he alone can bear. It has been given to him by God and is uniquely fitted to his spiritual development and the purpose of God in his life.

This cross may be a certain ministry, work, burden, gift or spiritual responsibility that demands death to self if it is to be performed properly.

Therefore, *"bearing the cross"* is usually not just the enduring of personal suffering - it is fellowshipping with Jesus in His suffering, which necessarily involves sharing the burden of humanity.

To become a channel of His resurrection power, in helping others, we must first of all be crucified with Christ.

* **This has never been explained any better than in the following essay, written by Evangelist Pat Hayes:**

"I am crucified with Christ: nevertheless I live; yet not I, but Christ liveth in me: and the life which I now live in the flesh I live by the faith of the Son of God, who loved me and gave Himself for me." (Galatians 2:20)

Jesus was born into this world by the Holy Ghost - the Spirit of God.

From the moment of His birth, His life took only one direction - to Calvary. What an example - what a precedent for us!

We have been born into the kingdom of God's Son by the Holy Spirit, and it behooves us to set our pathway to the same destination as the first Son of God.

The goal in life for every Christian must be no more and no less than the same goal of Jesus' life - *the cross.*

It is easy and quite common to label oneself by the name of "Christian" but it is not so easy to follow Christ or to be Christ-like.

To call yourself a "Christian", all you need is a seat in a church building; but to be Christlike, you must bear a cross, and your life, your desires, your plans, yes, your love and all that you are must eventually be nailed to that cross.

Paul says that the true sons of God are they who are led by the Spirit of God. This must be understood - the Spirit of God will lead us in one direction only - towards Calvary.

As this becomes true to us, we find that every great lesson to be learned in life is taught to us only when we are under the weight of the wood on the cross road, or when our lives become nailed to that wood at Calvary.

Only at Calvary can we learn how to love; not in the arms of some perfumed woman or handsome Romeo - but in the whip-striped arms of Jesus.

Only at Calvary can we learn how to pray; not the selfish, spoiled-child prayers of our self-seeking selves; but the dying-to-self prayers that Jesus prayed through bruised and scab-crusted lips. We learn to pray forgiveness and good to those who hurt us and use us; blessing for them that curse us; love for them that hate us. No man will learn to pray this way without the weight of the wood on his back.

Only at Calvary can we learn how to have peace; not the empty, short-lived peace that humans try to purchase by owning possessions or attaining "status"; but the long, deep, strong, eternal peace that comes from being dead to ourselves - alive in Christ.

Only at Calvary can we learn how to rejoice; not the imitation joy and plastic praise that we sometimes manufacture in our church meetings by the pounding of tambourines and ringing of guitar strings; but the high-flying and eagle-winged joy that is set before everyone who endures the cross.

No true Christian must lose sight of this fact:

You can go to heaven without stained-glass windows or tall steeples.

You can go to heaven without shouting.

You can go to heaven without money and dressed in rags.

But you cannot go to heaven without a cross.

[This is still correct in spite of the lecturing of certain modern day "teachers" who have lessened the standards and watered down the demands of God's Word. Having ears "itching" for the praise of men they have turned their ears away from the truth and turned to fables...producing, alas, a "comfortable Christianity."]

All true sons of God, though, accept the splintered wood of the cross as their teacher. Their seminary course is the bloodied footprints pressed into the dust of the Calvary trail.

And here someone will say, "I speak with tongues, shout, prophesy, and do many wonderful works in the name of Jesus. This is the proof that I am a Christian."

I tell you these are shallow and hollow proofs that will never add up to true evidence of your "Christianity" in God's final court of law. You see, the devil can counterfeit tongues and duplicate prophecy. Our enemy has proven that he can shout with the best of us and will even do so under the cover of Jesus' lovely name, like a wolf in sheep's clothing.

In fact, the devil can falsely imitate almost anything a Christian can do, except for one thing; the devil cannot live a crucified life. And with terror Satan fears those who have crucified their lives with Christ.

This alone is the final proof and the core of truth and the heart of gold in every true child of God.

It is now incumbent upon us as mature Christians to let go of the "sucking pap" of [certain childish, off-balance, self-exalting, religous philosophies of the day] and aim our footsteps with determination towards Golgotha. We must let go of every goal but Calvary for our lives.

There is no room for selfishness at Calvary.

No one can go where his desires would lead him if his feet are nailed to a cross. No man can work to serve himself or "help himself to the good things in life" with his hands stapled by spikes to a cross.

(Many, many there are who will come back from Calvary with unscarred hands and unbloodied feet).

But we must not only go to Calvary, we must give our lives there, be crucified there. It was Jesus who said, "If any man will come after Me, let him deny himself, and take up his cross, and follow Me." (Matthew 16:24)

We must sacrifice every whim, every plan we have schemed out for our own future. We can no longer dream of "many things" to do in life, but now we must declare with Paul, "this one thing I do." (Philippians 3:13-14)

We must then, press on towards the mark of the prize of the high calling that is in Christ Jesus. (End of essay by Pat Hayes)*1

POWER - MATTHEW 10:1, LUKE 9:1-2

• Matthew 10:1 says that - *"when He [Jesus] had called unto Him His twelve disciples, He gave them power against unclean spirits, to cast them out, and to heal all manner of sickness and all manner of disease."*

• Luke 9:1-2 says that He gave His disciples - *"power and authority over all devils...and He sent them to preach the kingdom of God, and to heal the sick."*

Both of these scriptures sound quite similar, but there is a definite, significant difference between the two.

The Greek word translated *power* in Matthew 10:1 is *exousia* and it means either *authority* or *privilege.*

This is the word that was used in the scripture where Jesus said to His seventy disciples - "behold, I give unto you *power (authority)* to tread on serpents and scorpions, and over all the power of the enemy: and nothing shall by any means hurt you." (Luke 10:19)

It was also used in the Gospel of John, where the beloved disciple wrote - "as many as received Him, to them gave He *power (the privilege)* to become the sons of God." (John 1:12)

The Greek word translated power in Luke 9:1 is *dunamis*, from which we get our modern word - *dynamite,* and it means *ability.*

This is the word used in the scripture where Jesus told His disciples to tarry in Jerusalem until they be -"endued with *power* from on high." (Luke 24:49)

It was also used in I Corinthians 2:5 where the Bible declared that our faith should not be in "the wisdom of men but in the *power* of God."

We must therefore be endued with, and trust in, not our own ability, but rather - *the ability of God.*

It is important to note also that when Paul wrote the Ephesian believers, exhorting them to put on the armor of God, and thus measure up to true discipleship, he said -"Be strong in the Lord and in the *power* of His might." (Ephesians 6:10)

This time the word *power* is translated from yet another Greek word *kratos* which means *strength*.

In light of all these facts, we can truthfully say that if we are *true disciples*, we have received strength, ability, and authority from God...divine strength, divine ability and divine authority. These three things spell power - *dynamite power*.

We have the God-given *authority* to destroy the works of the devil...power to win the lost, power to heal the sick, power to cast out devils, power to repeat the works of Jesus.

We have the *ability* to do these things successfully and gloriously...in Jesus' name.

We have the God-given *strength* to take a stand in this world for truth and to make it all the way to heaven.

This is all much more than just a blessed opportunity; this is a sacred *privilege (exousia)*...the *power-privilege* of becoming the sons of God...mature, effective and fruitful...His *disciples*.

• When Jesus was making His triumphant entry into Jerusalem the *disciples* shouted with a loud voice - "Blessed be the King that cometh in the name of the Lord." (Luke 19:29-40)

The frustrated Pharisees tried their best to subdue the press, but Jesus said - "If these should hold their peace, the stones would immediately cry out."

If they could not hold their peace on that day, when Jesus was drawing nigh on a colt, the foal of an ass, then how much more is it impossible for us to hold our peace now.

We know that He is drawing nigh.

We know that He will soon come with ten thousands of His saints and all His holy angels, riding this time on a glorious, white, heavenly steed. Therefore, we are constrained to herald His soon coming by filling up more than just the status of being *believers*.

• WE ARE CALLED TO BE HIS **DISCIPLES**...A CLOSE-KNIT FAMILY OF WORLD-FORSAKING, FRUITBEARING, LOVE-GIVING, WORD-FOLLOWING, PERSECUTED, CROSS-CARRYING, POWER-PRODUCING COPIES OF JESUS CHRIST.

We are each called to possess the ear and the tongue of a disciple...to hear as the learned and to speak as the learned...oracles of God.

This is the perfect product of the New Will.

This is the peak potential of the new birth.

This is the pleasant promotion of new dedication to God and to His purpose.

And this is a grand portion of the "**milk and honey Land of Promise Inheritance**" that we seek for and long after.

•   Jesus Himself summed up this line of thought with such simplicity and such plainness, such a long time ago.

On a dusty wayside, this former carpenter turned around to a band of twelve rugged-looking, common men and presented them with a challenge.

> *"He that findeth his life shall lose it: and He that loseth his life for My sake shall find it."*

(Matthew 10:39)

They absorbed His teaching.
They accepted the challenge.
They dared to try.
They became true disciples.
They shook the world.

Now...the torch is being handed to us.
We must accept it!
We must hold it high...in the name of our God!

---

*1 The phrases or words within brackets in this essay were inserted by the author of **Our Glorious Inheritance.**

· FRIENDS ·

COMPANIONS

THE HOUSE OF HIS FRIENDS

THE BRIDEGROOM'S FRIENDS

"Henceforth I call you not servants; for the servant knoweth not what his lord doeth: but I have called you FRIENDS..."

(John 15:15)

*"Thou that dwellest in the gardens, the **COMPANIONS** hearken to Thy voice..."*

(Song of Solomon 8:13)

*"And one shall say unto Him, What are these wounds in Thine hands? Then He shall answer, Those with which I was wounded in **THE HOUSE OF MY FRIENDS.** "*

(Zechariah 13:6)

*"Jesus replied, Can you expect **THE BRIDEGROOM'S FRIENDS** to go mourning while the bridegroom is with them? The time will come when the bridegroom will be taken away from them; that will be the time for them to fast."*

(Matthew 9:15 NEB)

FRIENDS

"Henceforth I call you not servants; for the servant knoweth not what his lord doeth: but I have called you FRIENDS..."

(John 15:15)

• There are many levels of relationship that we as believers can have with this Lord of lords and King of kings, some of them being:

A Bridegroom/bride relationship.
A Father/son relationship.
An Elder Brother/brother-sister relationship.
A Master/disciple relationship.
A Lord/servant relationship...and finally...
A Friend/friend relationship.

In some ways this last relationship is the most peculiar - peculiar in the sense that we are compelled to question how the holy King of all creation, the Author of life Himself, could actually come down from heaven and befriend lowly men.

We are filled with wonder when we realize that He has promised to forgive men of their sin and joyfully live in their hearts.

This is deity condescending to come into contact with humanity...and this is Jesus, a most compassionate, tender and unselfish friend, promising to share the fullness of His glory with those who believe.

• It would do us all good, every now and then, to remind ourselves of this reality by confessing:

Jesus is not only Maker
Not only Lord Supreme,
He is Captain - He is Bridegroom
He is everlasting King.

He is Master - He is Saviour
He'll preserve us 'till the end.
But most curious of all,
He lives in our hearts...
An ever constant Friend.

And how true it is that Jesus would rather spend a few moments communing with the simplest son or daughter in His family than to spend hours in the company of the most rich, famous, influential and intelligent members of society who are not born again.

He is not attracted to men simply because they are well-known philosophers, actors, poets, writers or other notable personalities that the people of this world tend to idolize. But He is highly attracted to those who humbly and sincerely love Him and call upon His name.

We are His chosen comrades...His earthly companions. He took upon Himself the form of human flesh, sharing our grievous plight, simply because we are exceedingly precious to Him.

He is extremely involved in the most minute details of our lives.

His tender thoughts toward us every day are simply innumerable.

He rejoices even more than we over the fact that truly...we are called to be *friends*.

THE EVERLASTING INVITATION

Our God has powerfully confirmed the potentiality of this relationship by giving us His Word as an outward testimony, and His Spirit as a living, inward witness. God has done His part well.

- He has presented to us the everlasting and sure invitation:

> *"Behold, I stand at the door, and knock: if any man
> hear My voice, and open the door, I will come in to him,
> and sup with him, and he with Me."*
>
> (Revelation 3:20)

When taken in context, it is clear that this is not just a general salvation-promise extended to the world; this is a personal covenant-commitment presented by Jesus to every individual member of the church. Opening the door to Him simply involves opening our hearts entirely to His gracious, yet commanding influence.

If we will so abandon ourselves to this relationship that we throw the door open unreservedly, He has promised to come in to us, and sup with us. This speaks of a relaxed, mature and fulfilling relationship with God.

This speaks of sweet communion with the Creator Himself...hidden secrets and veiled mysteries shared, revealed and understood (dipping the sop together...sharing heavenly bread and spiritual drink through the anointing).

Supping with Jesus...yes, this speaks of the nourishment of the soul...the one thing that we really long for and the only thing we desperately need. But, to sum it up, this speaks of the blessed availability of divine friendship...being one of God's favored and choice companions, hearts intermingling and emotions intertwined.

This is already the heart-cry of the Saviour. Jesus is always there...knocking patiently, waiting for the loving response He deserves.

Now the rest is up to us.

ENTERING THE RELATIONSHIP

The Word of God is definitely an expertly written roadmap leading us to the goal of right relationships with God and with our fellowman.

O, what comfort we feel when Jesus' words never-failing are gently inscribed on the pages of our hearts, ever-hungry for the sure way of acquiring His love.

• We read His everlasting wisdom and we find tender communications from the past that still echo in the present, full of divine life and spiritual vitality. We discover keys to obtaining, maintaining and developing our "friendship relationship" in passages such as the following:

> *"And I say unto you My friends, Be not afraid of them that kill the body, and after that have no more that they can do.*
> *But I will forewarn you whom ye shall fear: Fear Him, which after He hath killed hath power to cast into hell; yea, I say unto you, Fear Him."*

(Luke 12:4-5)

This is an enigma...a divine mystery.

• Here, in one breath, Jesus refers to His disciples as friends and counsels us *never to fear* earthly foes or satanic powers, yet at the same time He cautions us *definitely to fear* the God who controls our destiny.

Initially, it may seem strange that Jesus would lay this down as a prerequisite to obtaining His friendship, but then upon reflection understanding comes.

Jesus is speaking of two totally different kinds of fear.

The person who fears Satan or adverse circumstance is constantly being intimidated, hindered and even paralyzed spiritually. But the person who fears God is never hindered in this way, for he recognizes and reveres the absolute purity and sovereignty of the Almighty God. A believer with such spiritual sensitivity feels God's utter abhorrence of sin and then acts consequentially.

That person who fears God can be assured of His favor and protection, for - "The secret of the Lord is with them that fear Him; and He will shew them His covenant" and also "The angel of the Lord encampeth round about them that fear him, and delivereth them." (Psalm 25:14; 34:7)

• **Therefore, the man or woman who fears God has nothing else to fear.**

When we fear, respect and reverence the Almighty we truly obtain God's friendship. It is then that the power of fear is crushed.

It is then that we can boldly say - "The Lord is my light and my salvation; whom shall I *fear*? the Lord is the strength of my life; of whom shall I be *afraid*?" (Psalm 27:1)

By this, we see that the fear of God is not an end; it is a means, a path that leads to something better. It is not a barrier between God and man; quite the contrary, it is a door...for those who fear God, God can trust.

• They are men and women "after God's heart" and to them Jesus gives a blessed assurance, revealed in the next two verses of the same passage:

> *"Are not five sparrows sold for two farthings, and not one of them is forgotten before God?*
> *But even the very hairs of your head are all numbered. Fear not therefore: ye are of more value than many sparrows."*

(Luke 12:6-7)

So we see...those who truly fear God are welcomed into His heart and discover in Him that perfect and mature revelation of divine love that ultimately "casteth out fear". (I John 4:18)

This is the first key - a very necessary key. But there are at least four other key attitudes that must also be discovered and implemented if we are to successfully reach this "friendship goal".

They are: obedience, submission, opposing the spirit of the world, and maintaining a passion to give all the glory to our heavenly Bridegroom.

OBEDIENCE AND SUBMISSION

• Jesus qualified who would be included in this *title-inheritance* when He said, - *"Ye are My friends, if ye do whatsoever I command you."* (John 15:14)

This involves obedience to the written Word and submission to the living Word (God's expressed will for us at any moment).

We are even exhorted to bring into "captivity every thought to the obedience of Christ." (II Corinthians 10:5)

This must be our New Covenant passion...for "to obey is better than sacrifice, and to hearken than the fat of rams." (I Samuel 15:22)

Even if men scorn us and call our actions extreme or ridiculous, still, we must purpose in our hearts to "obey God rather than men." (Acts 5:29)

We know that our Father pledged through Isaiah, the prophet - "If ye be willing and *obedient*, ye shall eat the good of the land." (the abundant fruitfulness of the **"Promised Land Inheritance"** available to us as sons of God). (Isaiah 1:19)

Moreover, Jesus Himself promised:

> *"If a man love Me, he will keep My words: and My Father will love him, and We will come unto him, and make Our abode with him."*

(John 14:23)

- We know also that the Bible emphatically declares -"know ye not that the friendship of the world is enmity with God? whosoever therefore will be a *friend* of the world is the enemy of God." (James 4:4)

If this be true, and it is, then certainly the opposite is true also. If we count ourselves enemies of the "spirit of the world" and set ourselves in variance against that which is carnal and displeasing to God, then again we can truthfully declare that we are *"the friends of God!"*

GIVING ALL GLORY TO THE BRIDEGROOM

- Finally, we find in John 3:29 that John, the Baptist, referred to himself as *"the friend of the bridegroom."*

To understand the hidden meaning behind this statement, it is important to know the following: in the Jewish culture, at that time, *"the friend of the bridegroom"* would often involve himself in the preliminary negotiations between the bride, the groom, and their respective families.

Thus, if the proposed marriage became a reality, "the friend" would find great satisfaction, knowing that he had played such an important role in the whole affair.

The "friend's" sense of satisfaction would obviously reach a peak upon hearing the voice of the bridegroom uttering his marriage vows.

In a similar manner, John the Baptist, *"the friend of the bridegroom"*, worked diligently to "prepare the way of the Lord" by readying a portion of the bride to receive Him at His first coming.

This was John's ordination from the foundation and certainly his whole purpose for living while on this earth.

Thus, when Jesus began His preaching ministry, announcing certain New Covenant vows, John *"rejoiced greatly"* to hear the heavenly Bridegroom's voice.

Even as Jonathan rejoiced to see David anointed as King instead of himself, the rightful heir (because their spirits were knitted together and he loved David as his own soul) so also, John the Baptist, "the friend of the bridegroom", rejoiced over Jesus.

John knew that his own ministry and influence were going to be diminished. John knew that the attention of the people was going to be shifted to the Messiah. John knew that he was going to decrease and Jesus was going to increase. But John declared - *"this my joy therefore is fulfilled."*

John's greatest joy was to give all honor, all praise and all dominion to Jesus - the Lord of glory. He rejoiced to be able to say - "Behold the Lamb of God, which taketh away the sin of the world..." (John 1:29)

In like manner, when we fully die to the desire for glory and recognition, when we *"rejoice greatly"* to cast all of our crowns at Jesus' feet, and

111

when we live to attend unto His every command, then we too can be called "**THE BRIDEGROOM'S FRIENDS**" (as the NEB translation of Matthew 9:15 reveals).

When this transpires, we will also be able to say - *"This our great joy is therefore fulfilled!"*

THE VALUE AND RESULT OF THE RELATIONSHIP

Friends confide in one another...they are transparent in each other's presence. They share deep secrets...in absolute trust.

• In one of our *title-scriptures*, the Song of Solomon 8:13, the bride speaks of the heavenly Bridegroom saying - *"Thou that dwellest in the gardens, the COMPANIONS hearken to Thy voice..."*

From time to time, through the centuries, God has chosen certain individuals to fill this *title-position* and thus be sensitive in *hearkening* to His living Word.

Exodus 33:11 declared that - "the Lord spake unto Moses face to face, as a man speaketh unto his *friend"* - and surely, much of the reason for this was Moses' meekness, obedience and self-sacrificing spirit.

Also we find that Abraham was called "the *friend* of God"...and because of this, God confided in Him and revealed to him some of His deepest mysteries. God even refused to destroy Sodom without first discussing it with this father of the Jewish race. (Isaiah 41:8, James 2:23)

We ask ourselves why this man, Abraham, was chosen out of all the world to hear God's voice, to know God's secrets, and to father the nation that would ultimately bring forth the promised Messiah.

Why Abraham? What made him special?

Certainly, when we survey his life, we can all agree that there is one righteous deed that outshines all the other events of his earthly existence. He was willing to sacrifice one of the very things he loved the most in life, his own beloved son, Isaac, in order to fulfill the perfect will of God.

The love of God and the very attitudes of God filled his heart to such degree that he acted as God would act - because by offering Isaac, Abraham foreshadowed Calvary, where God would eventually offer up His only begotten Son.

Thus, by this act of obedience, Abraham captured God's heart and their friendship was established forever, sealed eternally!

• In like manner, when we show ourselves willing to deny self and to sacrifice some of the very things in life we may love the most, God discovers in us a kindred spirit that He loves.

He expresses that love by revealing and unveiling the mysteries of His Word and of His eternal plan. The following are precious words.

"Henceforth I call you not servants; for the servant knoweth not what his lord doeth: but I have called you friends; for all things that I have heard of My Father I have made known unto you."

(John 15:15)

O, what a grand privilege this is - to actually hear from Jesus all that He has heard from the Father! To be allowed entrance into the heart of God, to know His secrets!

And we have discovered one of the greatest secrets of all - that the more we yield to the character and personality of Jesus, the more this revelation knowledge will come.

• One of the most essential Christlike attitudes that we should yield to and emulate is **grace**...*the ability to love those who are undeserving.*

In Matthew 11:19, Jesus was called "a *friend* of publicans and sinners" (and it is significant to note that the normal definition of *a friend* is...*one who is attached to another by affection or esteem, a favored companion).* How amazing it is that Jesus affectionately attached Himself to those who were considered by others to be the "offscouring of the earth" and esteemed them more important than even His own life!

• Now, He has commanded us to walk in His footsteps and do likewise...to love as He loved. He has given us an often unheeded charge:

"When thou makest a dinner..call not thy friends, nor thy brethren, neither thy kinsmen, nor thy rich neighbors; lest they also bid thee again, and a recompense be made thee.

But when thou makest a feast, call the poor, the maimed, the lame, the blind:

And thou shalt be blessed; for they cannot recompense thee: for thou shalt be recompensed at the resurrection of the just."

(Luke 14:12-14)

In other words, Jesus was entreating us to be friends to the friendless, to give hope to the hopeless, and help to the helpless. By doing so, we reflect the nature of the firstborn Son, and our friendship with Him blossoms...for we prove that we value the things that He values most.

HOW SURE IS THIS RELATIONSHIP?

• A true friend will continue to love despite surface faults or failures, for through constant contact he has grown to see the deeper side, the hidden side...the "true self" of his companion.

Proverbs 17:17 declares that - *"A friend loveth at all times."* This is especially true of Jesus, for He is spoken of as being a - *"friend that sticketh closer than a brother."* (Proverbs 18:24)

Once He becomes convinced of a person's sincerity, He pledges - "I will never leave thee, nor forsake thee." (Hebrews 13:5)

Jesus is committed to us. He will surely guard this relationship, for He paid such a dear price to make it possible.

•   In a vision from God, long before the crucifixion actually took place, Zechariah saw and heard a strange question being posed to the Lord - *"What are these wounds in Thine hands?"* And He answered - *"those with which I was wounded in the house of My friends."* (Zechariah 13:6)

What a heart-gripping statement this is! What a chord of pathos it strikes in our spirits! That Jesus would actually be wounded in *"the house of His friends."*

This term refers not only to Israel, but also to the entire family of God, for it was not merely the Roman soldiers or the Jewish nation who crucified Him.

We all crucified Him. Our very sins nailed Him to the cross - yet He still calls us *friends,* because He did it all for us.

Surely this is a love that surpasses knowledge!

Surely this is a love that will carry us all the way to heaven.

Surely - "Greater love hath no man than this, that a man lay down his life for his *friends."* (John 15:13)

•   No wonder the bride in the Song of Solomon uttered her praise of the Bridegroom saying - "My beloved is white and ruddy, the chiefest among ten thousand...His head is as the most fine gold [everlastingly unchangeable]...His eyes are as the eyes of doves by the rivers of waters [gentle, forgiving, merciful and kind]...His hands are as gold rings set with beryl [strong in gripping tightly those He counts His own]...His legs are as pillars of marble [steadfastly taking a stand in our behalf]...His mouth is most sweet [full of comforting words]."

"Yea, He is altogether lovely. This is my beloved, and this is *my friend,* O daughters of Jerusalem." (Song of Solomon 5:10-16)

How amazing it is that He who is called "altogether lovely" would draw into sweet communion with Himself those who within themselves, at their best state, are said to be "altogether vanity"!

But this is His generous choice. This is the beauty of His nature.

And this is just another "milk and honey" blessing of the lovely **"Land of Promise"** in which we live...the unutterable privilege of walking with Jesus, *"a friend* that sticketh closer than a brother" - our eternal companion throughout the ceaseless ages.

Let us therefore, honor one another with the very honor God has freely bestowed...uniting our hearts in a "covenant of friendship" that will ever grow and never end.

Let us purpose to be personal, warm, loving and openhearted with both the Saviour and every other child of God. And as John, the beloved, so aptly put it - "Greet **THE FRIENDS** by name." (II John 12)

114

HEBREWS

JEWS

ISRAELITES

"Thus saith the Lord God of the ***HEBREWS****, Let My people go, that they may serve Me."*

(Exodus 9:1)

"For he is not ***JEW****, which is one outwardly; neither is that circumcision, which is outward in the flesh:*

But he is a ***JEW****, which is one inwardly..."*

(Romans 2:28-29)

"Who are ***ISRAELITES****; to whom pertaineth the adoption, and the glory, and the covenants, and the giving of the law, and the service of God, and the promises."*

(Romans 9:4)

*"When **ISRAEL** went out of Egypt,
THE HOUSE OF JACOB from a
people of a strange language;*
*Judah was His sanctuary, and Israel
HIS DOMINION."*

(Psalm 114:1-2)

*"And as many as walk according to
this rule, peace be on them, and mercy,
and upon **THE ISRAEL OF GOD.**"*

(Galatians 6:16)

*"I bring near My righteousness: it
shall not be far off, and My salvation
shall not tarry: and I will place salvation in Zion for **ISRAEL MY
GLORY.**"*

(Isaiah 46:13)

*"Bless ye God in the congregations,
even the Lord, from **THE FOUNTAIN
OF ISRAEL.**"*

(Psalm 68:26)

· ISRAEL ·

HIS SERVANT ISRAEL

THE ISRAEL OF GOD

ISRAEL HIS INHERITANCE

ISRAEL HIS GLORY

ISRAEL HIS ELECT

THE FAMILIES OF ISRAEL

THE HOUSE OF ISRAEL

BOTH THE HOUSES OF ISRAEL

THE WHOLE HOUSE OF ISRAEL

THE FOUNTAIN OF ISRAEL

THE CHILDREN OF ISRAEL

· HIS DOMINION ·

*"Sing, O ye heavens...for the Lord hath redeemed **JACOB**, and glorified Himself in **ISRAEL**."*

(Isaiah 44:23)

*"**ISRAEL** shall then dwell in safety alone: **THE FOUNTAIN OF JACOB** shall be upon a land of corn and wine: also his heavens shall drop down dew."*

(Deuteronomy 33:28)

*"Verily, I say unto you, That ye which have followed Me, in the regeneration when the Son of man shall sit in the throne of His glory, ye also shall sit upon twelve thrones, judging **THE TWELVES TRIBES OF ISRAEL**."*

(Matthew 19:28)

*"The portion of Jacob is not like them; for He is the former of all things: and Israel is **THE ROD OF HIS INHERITANCE**: the Lord of hosts is His name."*

(Jeremiah 51:19)

· JACOB ·

JACOB HIS PEOPLE

THE SONS OF JACOB AND OF JOSEPH

THE CHILDREN OF JACOB

THE FOUNTAIN OF JACOB

THE TRIBES OF JACOB

THE TRIBES OF ISRAEL

THE TWELVE TRIBES OF ISRAEL

THE TRIBES OF THE LORD

THE TRIBES OF HIS INHERITANCE

THE TWELVE TRIBES SCATTERED ABROAD

THE ROD OF HIS INHERITANCE

"...Now will I bring again the captivity of JACOB, and have mercy upon THE WHOLE HOUSE OF ISRAEL, and will be jealous for My holy name."
(Ezekiel 39:25)

"From following the ewes great with young He brought him to feed JACOB HIS PEOPLE, and ISRAEL HIS INHERITANCE..."
(Psalm 78:71)

"...But the Lord will be the hope of His people, and the strength of THE CHILDREN OF ISRAEL."
(Joel 3:16)

"Thou hast with Thine arm redeemed Thy people, THE SONS OF JACOB AND JOSEPH. Selah."
(Psalm 77:15)

"Whither the tribes go up, THE TRIBES OF THE LORD, unto the testimony of Israel, to give thanks unto the name of the Lord."
(Psalm 122:4)

· JUDAH ·

THE CHILDREN OF JUDAH

THE HOUSE OF JUDAH

THE WHOLE HOUSE OF JUDAH

THE TRIBE OF JUDAH

· HIS LAWGIVER ·

A PEOPLE NEAR UNTO HIM

"In JUDAH is God known: His name is great in Israel."

(Psalm 76:1)

*"Behold, the days come, saith the Lord, that I will make a new covenant with the house of Israel, and with **THE HOUSE OF JUDAH.**"*

(Jeremiah 31:31)

*"For as the girdle cleaveth to the loins of a man, so have I caused to cleave unto Me...**THE WHOLE HOUSE OF JUDAH,** saith the Lord; that they might be unto Me for a people, and for a name, and for a praise, and for a glory..."*

(Jeremiah 13:11)

*"...Judah is **MY LAWGIVER.**"*

(Psalm 60:7)

*"He also exalteth the horn of His people, the praise of all His saints; even of **THE CHILDREN OF ISRAEL, A PEOPLE NEAR UNTO HIM.**"*

(Psalm 148:14)

HEBREWS
JEWS
ISRAELITES

"Then the Lord said unto Moses, Go in unto Pharaoh, and tell him, Thus saith the Lord God of the HEBREWS, Let My people go, that they may serve Me."

(Exodus 9:1)

- The offspring of Abraham were originally known as *Hebrews.*
They inherited this entitlement from Abraham himself, for he was traditionally referred to as *Abram, the Hebrew.* (Genesis 14:13)

There is diverse opinion concerning the meaning and origin of this peculiar surname.
Some theologians say that it was passed down to Abraham from an ancient Semitic forefather named **Eber**, the same person referred to as **Heber** in Luke 3:35. (Refer to Genesis 11:10-32)

This one called **Heber** was the son of Salah and the father of Peleg; his great-great-grandfather was Shem, the son of Noah.
It is definitely possible that his name - **Heber** - could have been passed on to his descendents, eventually to be pronounced and spelled in a slightly different way **(Hebrews).**
This would be a logical explanation.

- But some Bible authorities feel quite strongly that in its initial use, this *title* referred directly and exclusively to Abraham, for the actual meaning of the word is - *the one who crossed over.* (UBD)
This is also a very reasonable assumption, for in order to obey the revelation and calling given to him by Jehovah, Abraham had to *cross over* the river Euphrates on his journey to the Land of Promise.

He had to leave behind a country and a family that was steeped in polytheism and idolatry and *cross over*, in a spiritual sense, into the true concept of monotheism (the doctrine or belief that there is but one God). (Joshua 24:2)
By doing so, Abraham passed from death into life, for he entered into a lasting relationship and covenant with the Almighty.
Thus, in an even greater sense, he is rightfully to be called - *Abram, the Hebrew* - for by faith he crossed over from the gross darkness of spiritual blindness and ignorance into the brilliant light of revealed truth.

The living Word that came to this great patriarch was, therefore, a

123

great bridge, compassionately built by God Himself, spanning the terrible rift existing between Jehovah and all of mankind.

Surely at the very moment of Eve's deception and Adam's transgression, peaceful Eden was suddenly invaded by the ominous rumblings of divine justice and divine anger.

The recompense that was meet erupted with the fury of an earthquake, violently rending that initial beauteous union of heaven and earth, thus opening up a terrible and treacherous fissure that no man could span.

At the bottom of this "spiritual gulf" the flames of hell were heard from then on, cracking and popping with deafening roar, reaching up without respect of persons to greedily devour and destroy every future victim of Adam's original sin.

The situation could have easily remained utterly hopeless.

But the heart of God overflowed with mercy toward man, for the plan of redemption and restoration welled up within His inner being.

Part of that plan involved His revelation to Abraham - "Get thee out of thy country, and from thy kindred, and from thy father's house, unto a land that I will shew thee." (Genesis 12:1)

These were the very words that manifestly began the construction of a supernatural bridge ordained of God to eventually rescue multiplied millions.

Abram, the Hebrew, *crossed over* almost four thousand years ago.

Now he beckons from the pages of history, challenging all who hear his voice to *cross over* in like manner.

The ability , the privilege, and the right to cross over are all a part of the legacy that Abram left to his heirs, both natural and spiritual.

• Therefore, in a very logical and true sense, because we are *the children of Abraham* we can also claim the spiritual status of being *Hebrews.*

We have *crossed over* from an Egypt-like land of bondage - the dominion of sin - into a more excellent, more glorious "Land of Promise" - the spiritual land of abundant life "in Christ".

(And all because our Messiah, in Moses-like manner, rebuked that harsh tyrant, Satan, demanding in an even more profound way - "Thus saith the Lord God of the **HEBREWS,** Let My people go that they may serve Me.") (Exodus 9:1)

At the moment of salvation we *crossed over* from hate into love, from depression into joy, from uncleanness into holiness, and from bondage into liberty.

Presently, "we know that we have passed from death unto life", and we know this is a glorious part of **OUR GLORIOUS INHERITANCE.** (I John 3:14)

But we also know that eventually every true *Hebrew* will actually *cross over* from time into eternity...forever to dwell in the manifest presence of the great and gracious God of Abraham...in that heavenly and

124

ultimate "Land of Oil Olive" that not only flows, but overflows, with the oil-like anointing of the Most High.

A confirmation of this truth is found in the very epistle written to the Hebrews: the statement - "here we have no continuing city, but we seek one to come." (Hebrews 13:14)

Ultimately crossing over to such a spectacular heavenly dwelling place is truly our wondrous future and our glorious destiny. It will be the highest fulfillment of an ancient *title*, lovingly and purposefully bestowed upon a man the Bible described as being - *"the father of all them that believe"*.

ISRAEL - PRINCE OF GOD

• The name - **Israel** - comes from the union of two foundational Hebrew words...*sar* which means *prince,* and *El* which means *God.*

Therefore it is quite clear to see that the term **Israel** foundationally means *prince of God.*

Other sources give this word slightly different shades of meaning, such as...*ruling with God, having power with God, God's fighter and God's soldier.* (YC, UBD, DARB)

This beautiful and meaningful appellation was first given by God to a singular man and then to an entire nation. Later, it was applied also to the very land that the nation eventually inhabited.

The man was Jacob, the son of Isaac, the grandson of Abraham.

The nation is comprised of the multitude of descendants who have since sprung forth from Jacob's loins.

The land is that territory which was biblically called "the Land of Canaan", situated between the Mediterranean Sea on the west, and the Jordan River and Syria on the east.

The Old Testament is primarily an historical account of this blessed nation: their beginnings, the four hundred and thirty years spent in Egypt's bondage, the nearly forty-one years spent wandering in the wilderness, the conquest of Canaan; the experiences they had under sixteen judges and forty-two kings; their time spent in captivity, and their subsequent restoration under Ezra and Nehemiah.

Through it all, the Old Testament also records, in great detail, the revelation of God's nature, God's law and God's plan - delivered to Israel at the will of God over a period of hundreds of years.

It is significant to note that even though Israel was "the fewest of all people", God still said, in tones of predetermination, - "I have loved thee with an everlasting love." (Deuteronomy 7;7, Jeremiah 31:3)

• In fact, God's love for Israel was at the start so deeply personal that at least once He referred to the entire nation as one person, saying - *"Israel is My son, even My firstborn."* (Exodus 4:22)

To prove and display His fatherly concern for His "firstborn son", Jehovah gave the Israelites an amazingly detailed system of laws and ordinances that dealt quite often with even the most common day-to-day endeavors and necessities.

This set the **ISRAELITES** apart from the rest of the world as God's peculiar people...His peculiar treasure, uniquely special to Him...for they inherited "the adoption, and the glory and the covenants, and the giving of the law, and the service of God, and the promises." (Romans 9:4)

ISRAEL - HIS DOMINION
THE ROD OF GOD'S AUTHORITY

To understand the intricacies of this God-given *title* **Israel**, it is also significant to see that, after having freed Israel from the bondage of Egypt, Jehovah called the wandering offspring of Abraham **"His dominion."** (Psalm 114:2)

This word - **dominion** - means *a domain...that over which a ruler has sovereignty (supreme authority).*

And it is so very true that as long as Israel remained in submission to Jehovah, as long as they were **"His dominion"**, they were able to successfully **"take dominion"** in His name.

The Jordan River could not block their path, the walls of Jericho could not stop them, and all the Canaanite tribes could not prevent them from possessing their God-bequeathed heritage.

Thus, they lived up to their royal name and enjoyed the living reality of their *title-right* inheritance...for they were Israelites, *"ruling with God."*

This is probably why, in the beginning, God only allowed the Jews to have judges, not kings..for Israel was to be a theocracy, a kingdom ruled directly by God, ordained to be a channel of His power.

God Himself directed the "affairs of state" by means of certain tribal heads that were entrusted to occupy seats of authority. The priesthood mediated between Jehovah and the people of Israel, the high priest even obtaining direct orders from God through the Urim and Thummim.

Finally, the prophets kept the priesthood and judicial leaders from overstepping the boundaries of their authority by acting as God's oracular voices to the nation.

This was so vastly different from any other governmental system in this world, and so effective, that God even called Israel - **"THE ROD OF HIS INHERITANCE."** (Jeremiah 51:19)

In other words, He was proclaiming Israel to be the symbol and proof of His authority in this world. Even as the shepherd's rod in Moses' hand represented his authority, for by it he worked wonders, so also Israel, in the hand of God, represented His authority.

126

For by this chosen nation, Jehovah, at least in the Old Will, worked the greater majority of all His supernatural miracles, signs and wonders in this world.

THE TWELVE TRIBES OF ISRAEL

• The nation of Israel was initially divided into twelve tribes, named after the twelve sons of Jacob - Reuben, Simeon, Levi, Judah, Zebulun, Issachar, Dan, Gad, Asher, Naphtali, Joseph and Benjamin.

Later on, Jacob, on his deathbed, adopted the two sons of Joseph - Ephraim and Manasseh - and thus divided the tribe of Joseph into two tribes, bringing the total number of tribes, strictly speaking, to thirteen.

This number was then reduced back to twelve because the Levites, being the priestly tribe, were never allowed an inheritance in the land of Israel. God did this for two reasons: first, the Lord was to be "their portion" and they were to concentrate on service to Him; and second, the Levites were scattered at the command of God all over the land of Israel that they might effectively minister to all the other tribes in the mediatorial position for which they were ordained.

It is interesting to note that the two main Hebrew words translated **tribe** are *matteh* and *shebet,* both meaning branch, for the twelve tribes were truly *branches* that grew out from Jacob, thus inheriting the covenant promises given to him.

Both of these Hebrew words are also translated into the word *rod* in the Scripture.

The first word, translated **tribe** - *matteh* - refers primarily to the genealogical branch, but the second term - *shebet* - is more of a reference to the fact that each tribe was under one scepter, one rod. (UBD)

This tribal organization remained relatively strong until the great rift that took place in 975 B.C., when ten tribes rebelled against the rule of Rehoboam, Solomon's ill-advised son. (I Kings 12)

From the time of the breach onward, the ten tribes that made up the Northern Kingdom retained the name **Israel.**

At times they were also referred to as **Ephraim,** after the primary tribe, and **Samaria**, after the capital city.

This Northern Kingdom was dissolved around 721 B.C. when it fell to the Assyrians. The Southern Kingdom endured until around 587 B.C. when they were finally brought under Chaldean rule and enslaved for seventy years in Babylon before being restored.

This Southern Kingdom was comprised of two tribes, Judah and Benjamin, and they were known as **Jews.**

WHAT DOES IT MEAN TO BE A JEW?

• It is evident that the word **Jew** evolved from the tribal name of **Judah,** which itself means *praise.*

To obtain the full revelation of this particular *title-name*, though, we must trace it all the way back to its source.

• In Genesis 49, we find where Jacob gave his final prophetic words over his sons, just before "he gathered up his feet into the bed, and yielded up the ghost, and was gathered unto his people".

During that final, oracular, death-bed statement Jacob said:

> *"Judah, thou art he whom thy brethren shall praise: thy hand shall be in the neck of thine enemies...*
> *Judah is a lion's whelp: from the prey, My son, thou art gone up: he stooped down, he couched as a lion, and as an old lion; who shall [dare] rouse him up?*
> *The scepter shall not depart from Judah, nor a lawgiver from between his feet, until Shiloh come; and unto Him shall the gathering of the people be."*
>
> (Genesis 49:8-10 AV, NIV)

• **We see by this passage of Scripture that Judah was to be praised because of three main reasons.**

First - because of the ultimate triumph God promised to give them.

Second - because of the fierce tribal character that would mark Judah as a near-invincible foe: somewhat akin to the fearless and furious, regal-like nature of a lion.

And third - Judah was to be praised because it was chosen of God to be the tribe that would bring forth kings in Israel, ultimately the King of all kings Himself, called *Shiloh* in Jacob's prophecy.

This threefold prophetic heritage and blessing is, to one degree or another, the God-given possession of all who can legally and rightfully refer to themselves as *Jews* (members of *the tribe of Judah*).

• In this present covenant, the born again, blood-washed offspring of the Most High have as much or more of a right than any to claim the benefits of this *title* for the following reasons.

We know that Jesus came forth from the tribe of Judah, and that "spiritually speaking" we have come forth from Him, so we conclude that "spiritually speaking" we are a part of *Judah* as well.

Moreover, in the epistle to the Romans, we have also discovered the irrefutable promise:

> *"For he is not a Jew, which is one outwardly;*
> *neither is that circumcision, which is outward in*
> *the flesh:*
> *But he is a Jew, which is one inwardly; and*
> *circumcision is that of the heart, in the spirit, and not in*
> *the letter; whose praise is not of men, but of God."*

(Romans 2:28-29, See also Revelation 3:9)

Both of these are logical, scriptural proofs that we can rightfully claim the status of being *Jews,* and that we, too, can legally claim the resulting threefold inheritance (reiterated now in a greatly enhanced sense).

First - God has promised that we, as Jews, can truly be victorious during this earthly sojourn, placing our hands on the necks of our enemies. For us this means subduing satanic forces, dominating sin, and conquering self: the most deceitful, seductive and illusive enemy of all.

It is certain that this portion of God's pledge to Judah will be fulfilled perfectly at the end of the Millenial Kingdom, when Jesus, the King of the *Jews,* will cast Satan and all his evil spirits into the lake that burns with fire and brimstone forever. It is then that sin's power will be irreparably broken. But on the way that direction, we must daily take authority over the powers of hell and over the carnal side of our nature. Thus we spiritually "tread on serpents and scorpions" and thus we "crucify the flesh with the affections and lusts," conquering our enemies even now. (Galatians 5:24)

Second - God has promised that our "tribal character" should be similar to the fearsome authority, the undaunted courage, the fearless fury and the regal-like nature of a lion.

This is quite simply and evidently the way it should be, for we are *Judah* - *"a lion's whelp"* - begotten of the very *"lion of the tribe of Judah"* who lives in our hearts and manifests His nature within us. If we have yielded to the strong, sanctifying influence of this indwelling Christ, this perfected Jew, then we can dare to walk in bold authority as He did...for "the wicked flee when no man pursueth: but *the righteous are bold as a lion."* (Proverbs 28:1, See also Revelation 5:5))

Finally - as spiritual *Jews,* we are also called to reign as spiritual kings...for *Shiloh* has come to us, bringing to birth His kingdom and the perpetuation of His royal character, calling and commission deep within our hearts.

He is the Ancient of Days, the Lawgiver of old, who visited Moses on Mt. Sinai and supernaturally wrote the ten commandments of the law with a fiery finger on tablets of stone. In this present age, His fiery finger is writing still...but in a new and more profound way.

For now, especially through the word of our testimony, He is burning, carving, and chiseling the law, and love for the law, not merely into tablets

129

of stone, but rather into the stony hearts of men.

In Psalm 60:7 God announces - "Judah is **MY LAWGIVER**" - and this is still true in a New Covenant sense. We, the children of the New Covenant, are now **His anointed lawgivers,** for the great **Lawgiver** of the tribe of **Judah** lives in our hearts and in us He perpetuates His work.

Through our testimony the laws of the kingdom of God are evidenced in this world. We become the revelation of God's expectations, God's demands, and God's provisions for those who come to Him.

Especially in this era, His lawgivers are called to promote "**the law of the Spirit of life in Christ Jesus**" - revealing the present dispensation of grace and its lifegiving properties.

Psalm 76:1 declares that - "In **Judah** God is known". It is also true that through Judah, God is revealed.

The body of Christ, from Pentecost onward, inherited the *"scepter of Judah"* (a scepter of righteousness and authority) and will bear it in this world until Shiloh comes again the second time. (See Hebrews 1:8)

Spiritually speaking we are *the children of Judah, the house of Judah, the whole house of Judah,* and *the tribe of Judah.* (Jeremiah 13:1; 31:31; 32:30, Psalm 78:68) More simply said, we are *Jews...*God's regal family: those who reign as kings in this life.

We understand now what God meant when He said that He would exalt us *"high above all nations, in praise, and in name, and in honour."* (Deuteronomy 26:19)

And we understand more fully now why the tribal name - **Judah** - actually means *praise,* for we have discovered the *praiseworthy* parts of the transcendental legacy with which we have been enriched.

Because God has poured forth such abundant honor on us, you might say that we have become recipients of the kind of *praise* that proceeds from Him alone.

But not only have we had heaven-born *praise* heaped on us. As a part of *the tribe of Judah* even more so we are called to be channels of praise - *the high praises of God* - more than willing, and always ready, to return all the *praise,* the honor, and the glory back to the very God who has so graciously given it to us.

"*Judah* shall dwell for ever" to fulfill this calling, for part of *the blessing of Judah* is the promise that Jehovah will hear our voices when we worship, and answer when we pray! (Joel 3:20, Deuteronomy 33:7)

ISRAEL - THE UNFORGETTABLE NAME CHANGE

• To fully comprehend the biblical and the prophetic significance of the name - **Israel** - we must also go back to its source.

This divinely authored *title* was first revealed and imparted around the year 1739 B.C. Jacob, the grandson of Abraham, was somewhere on the southern bank of a brook called *Jabbok* (a stream sixty-five miles long that begins in the Hauran mountains and empties into the East side of Jordan, approximately forty-five miles south of the Sea of Galilee).

Jacob was returning to the land of Canaan after spending twenty years with Laban, his uncle, in the land of Haran.

Confirming Jacob's fears, word arrived that his twin brother, Esau, was swiftly approaching with four hundred men.

Jacob envisioned a bloodbath, certain that his brother was coming to finally take vengeance on him for the shrewd, opportunistic way Jacob had "snatched" the birthright from Esau many years before and the heartless, crafty way he had even lied to his dying father, Isaac, in order to "snatch" the inheritance blessing as well.

• (But these were just two of the ways that Jacob succeeded in living up to his first name...a name pronounced *Yaaqob* in the Hebrew, and meaning - *supplanter, cheater, defrauder and deceiver).*

But now craftiness had lost its power and disaster seemed almost inevitable.

The "supplanter" that "took hold" of his brother's heel when they came out of the womb, now desperately tries to "take hold" of his brother's heart. Across the waters of Jabbok he sends many generous gifts and congenial servants, as well as all of his wives and children, to encounter Esau first.

Having once provoked him to anger, now Jacob seeks to provoke his brother to sympathy.

"Will it all be useless?" he must have thought, "Will my estranged brother rejoice at the opportunity to murder them all and then set out after me as well?"

As the darkness began settling thick and moist around Jacob a sense of helplessness must have gripped him as well. He paces apprehensively, barely able to see by the moonlight reflecting off the brook. Jacob is alone...really alone. He realizes that all his dreams and aspirations could be shattered in one night.

He is afraid.

But deep in his spirit he keeps hearing the echo of the words he first heard at Bethel some twenty years before: "I am the Lord God of Abraham thy father...the land whereon thou liest, to thee will I give it, and to thy seed...I will not leave thee until I have done that which I have spoken to thee of." (Genesis 28:13-15)

Fear and faith are struggling in Jacob's heart now, even as he and Esau struggled in the womb of Rebekkah their mother so many years before .

We can imagine what might have happened:

Jacob buries his face in his hands, falls to his knees and pleads - "God you promised! You have got to make a way! Without your help we will surely perish..."

A startling noise interrupts his prayer. Jacob's heart is racing. He jumps to his feet. It's the noise of someone swiftly approaching.

131

Who could it be? One of his servants? Friend or foe? Abraham's heir peers into the night, bracing himself for the worst.

Then, suddenly...almost before Jacob has time to react...strong arms reach out of the darkness pulling him to the ground.

The Bible tells the rest in vivid detail.

> *"...and there wrestled a man with him until the breaking of the day.*
>
> *And when he saw that he prevailed not against him, he touched the hollow of his thigh; and the hollow of Jacob's thigh was out of joint, as he wrestled with him.*
>
> *And he said, Let me go, for the day breaketh, And he said, I will not let Thee go, except Thou bless me.*
>
> *And he said unto him, What is thy name? And he said, Jacob.*
>
> *AND HE SAID, THY NAME SHALL BE CALLED NO MORE JACOB, BUT ISRAEL: FOR AS A PRINCE HAST THOU POWER WITH GOD AND WITH MEN, AND HAST PREVAILED."*

(Genesis 32:24-28)

IDENTIFYING THE "MAN"
COMPREHENDING THE REASON

• We know that this was no ordinary man that challenged the patriarch, Jacob, to an all-night wrestling match.

This was an epiphany - a bodily appearance of the Most High God (and there are several arguments that prove such an astounding statement).

First - the word that was translated *man* in verse twenty-four of this passage is the Hebrew word *ish* and it has clearly been used other times in reference to God (as when Moses and all of Israel sang, "The Lord is a *man* of war" Exodus 15:3 - or when Joshua had the vision of a *man* standing before him who revealed Himself as "the Captain of the Lord's host" Joshua 5:13).

Second - according to Hosea 12:3-4, Jacob wrestled with *"the angel"* *of the Lord* - an Old Testament term often employed in describing the preincarnate Christ. (See Genesis 22:11; Exodus 3:2, 13:20-23, 14:19)

Third - after having had such a profound spiritual experience, Jacob called the name of the place **Peniel,** meaning *face of God*, for he said - *"I have seen God face to face, and my life is preserved."* (Genesis 32:30)

• To fully understand the significance of this event and the symbolism it contains, it is important to reemphasize that this visitation transpired at the precise time when Jacob was coming back to take possession of his "Promised Land Inheritance."

• It is also quite evident that Jacob personified the great struggle that all of God's chosen and elect people go through in finally possessing the fullness of their God-given rights and privileges.

Jacob represents both natural Israel and spiritual Israel, for all can trace their heritage either naturally or spiritually back to him.

How natural Israel alone has "wrestled with God" through the centuries, rebelling against the revelation of God's covenants over and over again, suffering the consequences, and then oftentimes rending their hearts in repentance and seeing the restoration power of God come to their rescue!

And how every individual in spiritual Israel has "wrestled with God" as well, the flesh lusting and striving against the Spirit, and the Spirit striving against the flesh! How often we have pled for a new nature, and how very often the carnal part has tried to compel us to take the easier route and let the Lord go.

How many times God also Himself has "loosened the reins" to test our hearts, saying - *"Will you go also?"*

The night has been dreadfully long, woefully dark, and critically intense. We would have yielded to the pressure long ago had not the ordination of God gripped us tightly, subduing the flesh and giving us the unction to cry aloud in a Jacob-like manner:

"I will not let Thee go except Thou bless me."

Even as the Angel of the Lord *touched* the hollow of Jacob's thigh, so God has also in a sense *touched* us...convicting, constraining, conquering, and even, in a sense, crippling the Jacob part of us.

This conquered part is the flesh part, the human heart that is "deceitful above all things and desperately wicked"...the part that must be conquered. (Jeremiah 17:9)

To undergo such a necessary, spiritual subjugation-process is at times quite painful, but in the end highly rewarding - for the "inward man" is transformed and given the preeminence.

• Jacob received *a change of name,* because when he prevailed by his faith, God simultaneously gave him *a change of nature.*

No longer was he to be the *"defrauder and deceiver."*

No longer was he to be the *"supplanter"* meaning *one who deceitfully takes that which is not his own.*

He was to be **Israel** - *prince of God, God's fighter, ruling with God.*

• In the same way, if we persist in faith, and if we refuse to *let go* of the God we love and serve, surely He will *change our name* and manifestly, progressively *change our nature.*

In a very evident way, we will inherit the name **Israel** - *ruling with God* by ruling over the flesh and over the powers of hell that beset us.

The royal Spirit of the King of kings will take up residence in our hearts, raising us up to occupy a position of princely excellence "in Christ".

When this happens, we become "**His dominion**" and "**the rod of His inheritance**", for we become the proof of God's power and authority in this world, and the channel of such authority in this world and the world to come.

• In this New Covenant era, the entire body of Christ has inherited from God the *title-positions* of being "**His dominion**" and "**the rod of His inheritance**" for through us He has worked, and will yet work, the vast majority of all His signs and wonders in the earth.

These *title-positions,* as so many others, will be greatly enhanced and magnified at the resurrection.

And incidentally, this grand event, this ultimate *change,* cannot be too far away...*"for the day breaketh."*

These words that the angel spoke to Jacob, announcing the dawn, seem even more relevant to us now...for "the kingdom of heaven is at hand." We can see the first filtering rays of prophetic light streaming across the horizon.

We know that Jesus is coming again...the Dayspring from on high will soon bring the dawning of a brand new day.

The dark night of separation will be over.

And "we know that, when He shall appear, we shall be like Him; for we shall see Him as He is." (I John 3:2)

On that wonderful day, it is quite possible that we will hear the echo of what the Angel of the Lord spoke originally to the patriarch Jacob:

> *"Thy name shall be called no more Jacob, but*
> ***Israel:*** *for as a prince hast thou power with God and*
> *with men, and hast prevailed."*

For on that day of resurrection we will be delivered forever from the deceitful Jacob-flesh in which we are encaged, and thrust into our royal inheritance as glorified kings reigning with Christ forevermore.

As this New Covenant Age comes to completion, the Jacob/Israel symbol will likewise reach a peak of completion...for we will finally reach our "Penial". We will see God "face to face" and our lives will be eternally preserved.

THE ULTIMATE SALVATION OF ISRAEL

• When the kingdom of heaven fully comes to earth, the Bible boldly declares that - *"all Israel shall be saved."* (Romans 11:26)

This does not necessarily mean that every natural-born Hebrew will be able to claim ultimate salvation - *"for they are not all Israel, which are of Israel."* (Romans 9:6)

It rather means that every Israelite or proselyted Gentile under the Old Covenant, who sincerely served Jehovah-God and refused to *"let go"* of their commitment to Him, will be saved in the end.

And all the born again offspring of the New Covenant, who have known the God of Jacob and who have also refused to *"let go"* of their relationship with Him, will be saved in the ultimate outcome.

Matthew 24:13 declares - "He that shall endure unto the end [wrestling, fighting, striving and believing] the same shall be SAVED."

• In the time of the restitution of all things, the faithful of both covenants will fully and finally merge together into one eternal nation, called **"the house of Israel"** in Jeremiah 31:31.

This oft-used Old Testament phrase reveals the fact that all who are a part of Israel are not only citizens of the same eternal nation; they are members of the same eternal family.

Forevermore we are "the house of Israel", a family so large that it can be called a nation, but still a nation/family begotten of just one heavenly Father: brothers and sisters of just one spiritual household.

But, in a sense, this is a family made up of families - many individual church and fellowship units blending together into one.

> *"At the same time, saith the Lord, will I be the God of all THE FAMILIES OF ISRAEL, and they shall be My people."*
>
> (Jeremiah 31:1)

O, what a grand reunion it will be on the day of resurrection when all the families making up this one eternal family gather for the final homecoming celebration!

No wonder the Psalmist prayed for this joyous future event, saying:

> *"Oh that the salvation of Israel were come out of Zion! When God bringeth back the captivity of His people, JACOB SHALL REJOICE, AND ISRAEL SHALL BE GLAD."*
>
> (Psalm 53:6)

On that blessed day, in a more perfected sense than ever, Israel will again be both the name of a man and the name of the very nation that sprang forth from the man.

• For according to Isaiah 49:3, the name **Israel** is also one of Jesus' *titles.*

We know that His flesh "wrestled" with the Father in Gethsemane, but we also know that He cried - "Father...not My will, but Thine, be done."

135

Moreover, on the third day, after "wrestling" with sin, Satan, death, hell and the grave, Jesus prevailed and came forth declaring - "all power is given unto Me in heaven and in earth." (Matthew 28:18)

So in the highest prophetic sense, He fulfilled all the intricate, symbolic meanings of the *title,* for He was and is and ever will be **Israel**...*ruling with God, God's fighter, God's soldier, God's prince.*

Now, because we are begotten of the Lord, we have inherited the right to be called by this prophetic name as well. Isaiah declared that this Messiah, called **Israel,** would - "raise up **the tribes of Jacob** and...restore **the preserved of Israel.**" God also promised to Him in the same verse - "I will also give Thee for a light to the Gentiles, that Thou mayest be My salvation unto the end of the earth." (Isaiah 49:6)

Jesus has truly fulfilled this prophecy for He has enlightened our lives.

He is worshipfully entitled *the glory of Israel, the hope of Israel, the consolation of Israel, the King of Israel, the Governor of Israel, the Lord of Israel, the God of Israel, the Creator of Israel,* and *the ruler of Israel "whose goings forth have been from of old, from everlasting."* (Micah 5:2)

• But we are His offspring, ordained of God to inherit both the Israel-name and the Israel-nature. Jesus won the right to be called by this name Himself and then transferred the trophy to us.

First, we are **"the house of Jacob"**...for though we are chosen and ordained, the flesh part of us still "wrestles" against powers of hell and against the will of God and must be continually brought under subjection. (Luke 1:33)

But secondly, we are also **"THE HOUSE OF ISRAEL"**, fighting in an intense spiritual war now, but destined to "rule with God" in the perpetual perfection of celestial glory.

ISRAEL - A FOUNTAIN OF LIFE

Though "natural Israel" of the Old Covenant involved themselves in many God-authored rituals and ceremonies that the "spiritual Israelites" of the New Covenant have since discarded, still, in the culmination of all things, we will reckon our inheritance as one and our salvation as coming from the same source.

We can truthfully say - *"In the Lord shall all THE SEED OF ISRAEL be justified, and shall glory."* (Isaiah 45:25)

The God that inhabited their praises in the Old Covenant is still inhabiting ours in the New. (Psalm 22:3)

In fact, we have an even greater right to claim this portion of the Israelite heritage for "rivers of living water" have taken up their abode within our grateful hearts.

• How very right it is, therefore, for both Jewish and Gentile "saved" persons to claim the highest fulfillment of a lovely promise and command given in Psalm 68:26:

> *"Bless ye God in the congregations, even the Lord,*
> *from THE FOUNTAIN OF ISRAEL."*

Having become a part of Israel we have also become part of a *fountain.* This was first a natural fountain of offspring who traced their heritage back to the patriarch Israel. But now, under the New Will, this is a spiritual and eternal fountain filled with unending praise. This great and living fount of life, positioned presently in both heaven and earth, is ordained to ultimately quench the deep thirst of God for true, spiritual communion and fellowship with divine offspring.

This "fountain" will eventually enliven the earth.

For the glorified saints dwelling in this earth will joyfully participate in its restoration...bringing Eden-like harmony, life, fruitfulness and beauty back to a place that has been filled for hundreds of years with chaos, discord, confusion, and death.

Moses, in his final blessing, foretold that:

> *"Israel shall then dwell in safety alone: THE*
> *FOUNTAIN OF JACOB shall be upon a land of corn*
> *and wine: also his heaven shall drop down dew."*
> (Deuteronomy 33:28)

O, what a blessed era it will be when the dew of heaven's glistening Shekinah falls in this realm like a perpetual, gentle rain! *The land of red-purple* will then reach a level of glory never known before.

In the very last verse of Moses' prophetic farewell address, this stalwart prophet announced to Israel that in that day - "thine enemies shall be found liars unto thee; and thou shalt tread upon their high places". (Deuteronomy 33:29)

In an ultimate sense this refers to the utter privilege and joy of finally subjugating all the principalities and powers of Satan who ever opposed us during our earthly sojourn.

All things will then be reinstated to flawlessness and righteousness.

We know that in the beginning, Israel was "holiness unto the Lord...the firstfruits of His increase". (Jeremiah 2:3)

In the end, in a far more perfect sense, we will be "holiness unto the Lord" again.

For we will spend eternity pouring out our souls in sacred, holy, worship of the King, "the Holy One of Israel," who has so graciously imparted His flawless and holy Israel-nature to us.

In that day, we will not only arrive at the fullness of **OUR**

GLORIOUS INHERITANCE, we will more fully BECOME AN IN-HERITANCE to the Mighty One of Jacob as well.

This is only to be expected, for even now we are called **JACOB HIS PEOPLE, ISRAEL HIS INHERITANCE, ISRAEL HIS ELECT** and **ISRAEL HIS GLORY.** (Psalm 78:71, Isaiah 45:4; 46:13)

We know that our deliverance will be for His glory; our eternal existence will be for His pleasure; our election is His choice.

Therefore, we petition the Messiah as did Isaiah of old:

> *"Return for Thy servants' sake, THE TRIBES OF*
> *THINE INHERITANCE."*

(Isaiah 63:17)

JACOB REDEEMED
ISRAEL GLORIFIED

• This highly symbolic entitlement - **ISRAEL** - occurs 2,540 times in the Scripture. Most Bible scholars would agree that foundationally, it almost always refers to just the natural offspring of Abraham.

Often, the promises and commands given can only be applied to them.

But having received the deeper revelation contained in this chapter, we will surely be bold from now on in assimilating many of the promises into our "Promised Land Inheritance" as well (yet often on a higher, more spiritual level.)

Prophetic pledges such as the following, instead of being written on the pages of history will rather be written on the pages of our hearts:

> *"O Israel, thou shalt not be forgotten of Me.*
> *I have blotted out, as a thick cloud, thy*
> *transgressions, and, as a cloud, thy sins...I have*
> *redeemed thee.*
> *Sing, O ye heavens; for the Lord hath done it: shout,*
> *ye lower parts of the earth: break forth into singing ye*
> *mountains, O forest, and every tree therein:*
> *FOR THE LORD HATH REDEEMED JACOB,*
> *AND GLORIFIED HIMSELF IN ISRAEL!"*

(Isaiah 44:21-23)

Undoubtedly, this glorification is soon to take place and when it does, we will surely come to a more full revelation and realization of "who we are" in God's great and infinite plan.

We will ever be "**THE CHILDREN OF ISRAEL**" - THE CHILDREN OF "THE PRINCE OF GOD" - "**A PEOPLE NEAR UNTO HIM.**" (Psalm 148:14)

We will be the true "**SONS OF JACOB AND JOSEPH**", "**THE CHILDREN OF JACOB, THE TRIBES OF JACOB,** and the fullness of "THE HOUSE OF JACOB" - and Jesus, the Christ, the Anointed One, will reign over us in the majesty of His never-ending kingdom. (Psalm 77:15, Luke 1:33, See Isaiah 29:22-23; 44:5; 49:6)

• In that day, we will have a perfect right to eternally claim the *title-position* of being **Hebrews**...for we will have permanently *crossed over* from a grievous time of earthly exile into the joyous freedom of absolute oneness with the Almighty God.

• We will joyously confess the inheritance of being **Jews** ...for when we rise in royal, supernal and infinite splendor, our enemies will permanently be made our footstool and the victory will be irreversibly sealed.

• Finally, we will declare ourselves to be **Israel** in a never-ending way...for we will ultimately prevail and emerge as God's princely people..."ruling with God" over all His vast domain.

As everlasting **ISRAELITES** we will fully reap the benefits of "the adoption, and the glory and the covenants." (Romans 9:4)

We will enjoy the fulfillment of every one of His good promises and continue in the "service of God" in His holy and eternal city.

AN ETERNAL CITY
THE EVERLASTING TRIBES

We are told that in the walls of New Jerusalem, the capital city of the New Creation, there will be "twelve gates, and at the gates twelve angels, and names written thereon...the names of **THE TWELVE TRIBES OF THE CHILDREN OF ISRAEL.**" (Revelation 21:12)

So apparently, these designations will be perpetual.

In an eternal sense, Jerusalem will be the spiritual center "whither the tribes go up, **THE TRIBES OF THE LORD**, unto the testimony of Israel, to give thanks unto the name of the Lord." (Psalm 122:4)

In that coming era, on the highest level of interpretation, **BOTH THE HOUSES OF ISRAEL** (the redeemed of both the Old and New Covenants) will become **THE WHOLE HOUSE OF ISRAEL.** (See Isaiah 8:14, Ezekiel 39:25)

We will no longer be **THE TWELVE TRIBES...SCATTERED ABROAD** (DISPERSED AMONG THE NATIONS), we will be, in a perfected sense, **HIS SERVANT ISRAEL** and **THE ISRAEL OF GOD**...serving Him with heartfelt adoration in the splendor of the kingdom...heirs to a princely status. (James 1:1, Luke 1:54, Galatians 6:16)

Unspeakable mercy and boundless peace will rest upon us all.

Moreover, the pledge has been given:

"Then shalt thou delight thyself in the Lord; and I
will cause thee to ride upon the high places of the earth,

and feed thee with the heritage of Jacob thy father: for
the mouth of the Lord hath spoken it."

(Isaiah 58:14)

In an even deeper measure, we will then be **the fountain of Israel,**
increasingly and unceasingly returning back to God, in never-ending,
heavenly bliss, the depth of worship He deserves.

When Jesus came the first time, these words - *Hebrew, Jew, and
Israelite* - had blended together and become for the most part synonymous.
They referred to all those in a covenant relationship with God at that time.
(See John 3:1, 3:10)

• When Jesus comes again, these God-breathed terms will again blend,
yet in a deeper, more perfect and more profound way. (See Isaiah 44:5)

For these highly symbolic *titles* will simply be three more wonderful
surnames, stored from infinite ages past in the treasury of God's heart, to
be lovingly, purposefully and everlastingly bestowed on every child of
God.

"For as the New Heavens and the New Earth, which I will make, shall
remain before Me, saith the Lord, SO SHALL YOUR SEED AND YOUR
NAME REMAIN." (Isaiah 66:22)

As we meditate on such an irreversible heritage, we are compelled to
lift our hands upward in gratitude, echoing Psalm 106:48:

"Blessed be the Lord God of Israel from everlasting
to everlasting: and let all the people say, Amen." *1

---

*1 This **title-essay** has purposefully not dealt with those diverse and even conflicting
opinions concerning the future of the natural seed of Abraham during the Kingdom Age
and the New Creation beyond. Rather, we have focused on the future destiny of those
glorified saints who will ever be a part of **the Israel of God.**

• AN HOLY NATION •

THE HOLY PEOPLE

A NATION

THE NATION

HIS NATION

A DEDICATED NATION

AN HOLY PEOPLE UNTO THE LORD OUR GOD

THE MIGHTY AND HOLY PEOPLE

"But ye are a chosen generation, a royal priesthood, AN HOLY NATION, a peculiar people..."

(I Peter 2:9)

"And they shall call them **THE HOLY PEOPLE,** *The redeemed of the Lord..."*

(Isaiah 62:12)

"Thou hast multiplied **THE NATION,** *and [increased their joy]; they joy before Thee according to the joy in harvest, and as men rejoice when they divide the spoil."*

(Isaiah 9:3 AV, NIV)

"That I may see the good of Thy chosen, that I may rejoice in the gladness of **THY NATION,** *that I may glory with Thine inheritance."*

(Psalm 106:5)

"For thou art **AN HOLY PEOPLE UNTO THE LORD THY GOD:** *the Lord thy God hath chosen thee to be a special people above all people that are upon the face of the earth."*

(Deuteronomy 7:6)

AN HOLY NATION

AN HOLY PEOPLE UNTO THE LORD OUR GOD

"...ye are a chosen generation, a royal priesthood,
AN HOLY NATION, a peculiar people."

(I Peter 2:9)

• The main Hebrew and Greek words in the Bible that are translated into the English word *holy* also mean - *to be separated or set apart.*

God's original desire, purpose and plea to all of Israel was that they be *separated and set apart* from the rest of the world as His peculiar treasure, a kingdom of priests and *an holy nation.* (Exodus 19:5-6)

He gave no reasoning behind this demand, and really no explanatory arguments, except to say - "Be ye holy, for I am holy." (I Peter 1:16, Leviticus 11:44-45)

In other words, God was saying - "If you want to walk in fellowship with Me, you will have to love what I love and hate what I hate - so be ye separate and set apart from the world, for I am separate and set apart from the world."

This was then, and still is now, one of God's fundamental requirements if we are to effectually approach Him.

HOLINESS - GOD'S NATURE, GOD'S DEMAND

• God is the absolute of holiness.

Holiness is such an essential part of His nature, He cannot even be tempted with evil.

It is utterly impossible for Him to sin!

He is the epitome of righteousness, the ideal example of sanctity, purity and perfection.

Not only is He separate from that which is immoral and evil...He is the ultimate expression of that which is moral and good.

God is holiness itself.

Apart from Him, this divine character trait would have no existence.

Everything about Him simply exudes holiness, and everything associated with Him must necessarily reflect holiness.

His Spirit is called a Holy Spirit.

His Word is referred to as the Holy Bible, the holy Scriptures and the holy Word of God.

Psalm 105:42 speaks of His holy promise.

Romans 7:12 even states that "the law is holy and the commandment holy."

143

Under the Old Will, different parts of his tabernacle dwelling place were referred to as: the courts of His holiness, the holy place, the holy of holies, and the holy oracle.

The sacrifices offered up in this place were designated holy gifts, holy offerings, and holy oblations.

Certain items used in religious ceremonies were called holy vessels and holy things. The ointment used for consecration was termed holy anointing oil.

The high priest was clothed with holy garments and adorned with a holy crown.

The Sabbath was called holy, feast days were holy days, and all mass gatherings to worship Jehovah were said to be holy convocations.

Certain dedicated instruments of music were named holy instruments. (Numbers 31:6)

Even the tithe is described as being holy. (Leviticus 27:30)

Jerusalem is called the holy city and the hill in Jerusalem on which David's tabernacle was erected in days of old bore the entitlement, the holy hill.

The mountains surrounding Jerusalem, as well as the mountains on which significant spiritual events transpired (Sinai, Moriah, Calvary etc.) are termed the holy mountains. (Psalm 87:1)

God's true prophets and oracles, both then and now, are respectfully called holy men of God; some are entitled holy apostles.

The salvation "contract" that presently exists between God and man is labeled His holy covenant. (Luke 1:72)

• And Jesus, our divine example in all things, bears numerous names of holiness: **the Holy One, the Holy One of God, the Holy One of Israel, the Holy Child, that Holy Thing, the Most Holy** and **God's Holy Arm,** who was "made bare" by the Father before all nations and who has "gotten Him the victory." (Ps. 98:1, Is. 43:14; 52:10, Dan. 9:24, Lk. 1:35, 4:34, Acts 3:14, 4:30)

Moreover, the present heavenly abode of the Almighty is called "the habitation of His holiness" and "the high and holy place" where "the Holy Father" dwells with those who are "of a contrite and humble spirit" - those who tremble at His Word. (Is. 57:15; 66:2; 63:15, John 17:11)

This glorious Lord of all is surrounded by an innumerable host of holy angels. And when we praise Him, we are even commanded to lift up "holy hands, without wrath and doubting", and build up ourselves on our "most holy faith, praying in the Holy Ghost." (I Tim. 2:8. Jude 20)

All of this is simply the way it should be, for our God is "the high and lofty One that inhabiteth eternity, **whose name is Holy**." (Isaiah 57:15)

Yes, holiness is such a part of the nature of God that it has become His name.

Furthermore, God has emphasized His great love for holiness by creating four heavenly creatures that adore Him unceasingly saying - *"Holy, holy, holy, Lord God Almighty, which was, and is, and is to come."* (Revelation 4:8)

These celestial beings do not rest from this ministry day nor night.

Apparently, for all eternity... continually, perpetually, from them and from ten thousand times ten thousand others, the cry *"Holy, holy, holy"* will ascend like incense before the throne of His Majesty, the King of kings.

Therefore, this blessed and holy nature of God, magnificent yet fearful, always ultimately redounds to His praise, for once it is beheld, we are compelled to reverence Him, to stand in awe of Him...and to fall prostrate before Him in utter worship.

When we sense His absolute hatred and abhorrence of that which is evil, we feel all the more the depravity of the flesh, and we are constrained to - "serve the Lord with fear, and rejoice with trembling." (Psalm 2:11)

We are changed inwardly as a result, for when we truly see Him, we become like Him.

• We manifestly become His holy brethren, an holy priesthood, the holy seed, an holy temple in the Lord, and **AN HOLY PEOPLE UNTO THE LORD OUR GOD**. (Heb. 3:1, I Pe. 2:5, Is. 6:13, Eph. 2:21, Deut. 7:6)

This progressive transformation is the "holy calling" with which we have been called...and this is the great challenge that has been set before every member of the body of Christ...especially in these present perilous times. (II Timothy 1:9)

THE FEARFULNESS OF HIS HOLINESS

• When Israel beheld the Egyptian army destroyed with one sweep of God's hand, they certainly rejoiced, but they must have done so with trembling.

As the bloated bodies of the charioteers of the sun floated downstream, the Jews began singing - "Who is like unto Thee, O Lord, among the gods? Who is like Thee, *glorious in holiness*, fearful in praises..." (Exodus 15:11)

They worshipped, they adored, they praised the holiness of the mighty Jehovah - but at the same time their hearts were gripped with fear, for they had just witnessed the righteous indignation of a holy God bringing judgment on an evil nation. And surely they felt all the more convicted over the condition of their own hearts by just being there in His presence.

• I Samuel 2:2 says - "There is none holy as the Lord."

The closer we draw nigh to Him, the more we feel our actual distance from Him.

When Daniel entered into a vision of the Holy One of Israel, he said -

"my comeliness was turned in me into corruption, and I retained no strength." (Daniel 10:1-12)

When Isaiah was caught up to view the Lord, sitting on a throne, high and lifted up, he cried - "Woe is me! for I am undone; because I am a man of unclean lips..." (Isaiah 6:1-8)

Just one glimpse of the utter sanctity and purity of this blessed King of all creation was enough to bring these two righteous prophets to their knees in humility and contrition.

And as it was with them, so it must be with us.

If we are to be accepted in God's presence and cleansed by His power, receiving His imparted holiness, we must first humbly recognize our own inherent unholiness.

But simultaneously we must prove that our most deep-rooted desire is to be clean and to walk softly before the Lord.

We must keep the fire of conviction continually burning on the altar of our hearts that we might stay melted before Him, yet at the same time we must never attribute the resulting strength to the power of our own will.

It is a sobering fact that, in a sense, we forfeit our standing of imparted holiness and spiritually default, if we ever become steeped in pride and self-assurance.

These two deadly attitudes, if given free rein, quickly stamp the words - *null* and *void* - on this part of the spiritual contract that we have with the Almighty God.

• In Numbers 16, we read of Dathan, Korah and Abiram arrogantly and enviously challenging Moses' leadership by saying to him - "ye take too much upon you seeing all the congregation are *holy*..."

Moses answered - "Even tomorrow the Lord will shew who are His, and who is *holy*..."

When the congregation gathered the next day, God clearly revealed His feelings.

Judgment fell, the ground opened up, and the leaders of the rebellious uprising went down quickly into the pit.

Two hundred and fifty priests were consumed and instantly killed by the devouring fire of God's wrath.

And all these things took place simply because haughty men, who thought they were holy, pridefully insulted and outraged the holiness of God.

The Bible also clearly states that - "these things happened to them as examples - as object lessons to us - to warn us against doing the same things." (I Corinthians 10:11 LB)

• I Samuel 6 relates to us the story of what happened to the men of Bethshemesh when they looked into the ark of the covenant which the Philistines had sent back to Jerusalem.

146

The Bethshemites must have known the unlawfulness of such a deed, but their curiosity overtook and bypassed their wisdom.

They desecrated the ark (the golden box containing the tablets of stone that God gave to Moses) when they opened the door and gazed within. Over fifty thousand men died as a result.

The remaining Bethshemites lamented over the terrible tragedy, woefully crying - *"Who is able to stand before this holy Lord God."*

This is surely the same cry that will rend the hearts of men in the last days as well, for men are again desecrating that which is holy by curiously gazing into the things of God with no intention of repenting and dealing with their sin. By doing so they are exalting themselves above "all that is called God, or that is worshipped". (II Thessalonians 2:4)

This is the spirit of Antichrist in one area of manifestation.

We know that the severe final judgments of God are soon to fall, causing the earth to reel to and fro like a drunkard. The sun will become black as sackcloth of hair and the moon will become as blood. The stars of heaven will fall to the earth - "even as a fig tree casteth her untimely figs, when she is shaken of a mighty wind." The heaven will depart as a scroll, and every mountain and island will be moved out of their places.

At the height of this disastrous sixth-seal cataclysm the Bible declared that the kings of the earth, and the great men, and the rich men, and the chief captains, and the mighty men, and every bondman, and every free man will hide themselves in the dens and in the rocks of the mountains and say to the mountains and rocks..."Fall on us, and hide us from the face of Him that sitteth on the throne, and from the wrath of the Lamb: for the great day of His wrath is come; and *who shall be able to stand?*" (Revelation 6:12-17)

It appears that this age-old query will burn in the hearts and minds of men until the very end.

As the surface of the earth boils with caustic calamity and the wicked become as ashes scattered by the whipping winds of tribulation, surely the echoing question will ring louder than ever...*"Who is able to stand before such a holy Lord God?"*

THE ONLY ANSWER

•   There is only one response to this recurring question, for there is only one place of spiritual safety, one position of spiritual acceptability.

In Psalm 130 David admitted - "If Thou, Lord, shouldest mark iniquities, O Lord, *who shall stand?*" - then he added - "But there is forgiveness with Thee, that Thou mayest be feared." (Psalm 130:3)

The true and full source of this forgiveness is quite evident now though it was veiled in symbolism under the Old Will.

147

For instance, when the death angel passed over the land of Egypt, Jehovah declared to His chosen people of that era - "When I see the blood, I will pass over you." (Exodus 12:13)

The mere blood of an animal - a lamb - applied to the doorposts of their houses kept the Jews from physical death during those intense hours of divine visitation that preceded their exodus from the land of Pharaoh's bondage.

We can easily conclude, therefore, that the far more precious blood of the Son of God, the true Lamb of God, applied to our hearts, will yet preserve us from the far greater jeopardy that exists in this hour.

This New Testament atonement covering is our only refuge from the overflowing scourge to come and our only place of protection from the death-dealing sin and the satanic forces that war against us constantly.

In this blessed place of security we are kept from spiritual death...for through the precious blood of Jesus, we can legally and rightfully claim a standing of holiness in the presence of the Almighty.

• **In fact, we can legally and rightfully claim to be just as holy as the firstborn Son...**"because as He is, so are we in this world." (I John 4:17)

This is the miracle of the new birth...the proof that our sins have truly been blotted out!

This is the beauteous result of a divine union and a sacred conception!

This is the garment of salvation, the covering that we must wear as we prepare for another great exodus...the deliverance of God's people from the bondage of the natural into the glorified liberty of the supernatural.

This is the precious salvation-gift that has finally enabled us to stand unafraid and unashamed - *"holy and without blame before Him in love."* (Ephesians 1:4)

This is the everlasting answer to the perpetual question.

THE ACQUISITION OF GOD'S HOLINESS
PUTTING ON "THE NEW MAN"

• Ephesians 4:22-24 presents God's New Covenant people with the following charge:

> *"That ye put off concerning the former conversation the old man, which is corrupt according to the deceitful lusts;*
> *And be renewed in the spirit of your mind;*
> *And that ye put on **the new man**, which after God is created in righteousness and true holiness."*

• **The old man** - this is a phrase referring to the unregenerated and carnally ruled person that we once were. In that state of being, most of our desires, goals, attitudes, and motives were all to one degree or another corrupt - for they were tainted by pride, depression, fear, unbelief, self-will, self-condemnation, covetousness, selfishness or lust. This "old man" - this unholy fallen nature - still seeks to control our attitudes and actions now, even though we have been born again. Therefore, we must continually keep the flesh under subjection and thus - *"put off the old man"*.

• **Be renewed in the spirit of your mind** - we can only succeed in living in our "Promised Land Inheritance" as sons of God if our thoughts, desires, goals and motives are reshaped into that which is pleasing to God.

For this cause Paul also urged in Romans 12:2 - "be not conformed to this world: but be ye transformed by the *renewing of your mind,* that ye may prove what is that good, and acceptable, and perfect will of God." The process is primarily effected by the Word and the Spirit. The more time we spend under the influence of the Word or in the atmosphere of the manifestation of the Holy Spirit, the more we are going to "think like God thinks", for the "pure mind", the "mind of Christ", will be stirred up within. (II Peter 3:1, I Corinthians 2:16)

Only then can we properly and easily discern God's will for our lives - rejecting any wrong standards, or any lesser inheritance than He would have us to enjoy or attain. Therefore, the mind can either be a dam blocking the progress of the river of life in us, or a gateway leading us into "the land of red-purple" - the glory of our New Covenant heritage.

• **Put on the new man** - *"the new man"* is the "inward man", the "hidden man of the heart" - the born again part of every child of God. This "new man" does not strive to become holy; it is holy! It is in the image of Christ - "created in righteousness and *true holiness*".

We conclude, therefore, that the possession of holiness is undoubtedly our birthright...in this spiritual part of our being.

False holiness is something attained purely by self-effort and works.

True holiness is the result of the inward change of nature.

First, we become holy through the new birth, then, as we die to self and grow in God, this inherited holiness is automatically released into the actions and attitudes that fill our lives. As we choose to surrender to the influence of the Word and the Spirit, "the new man" gains the predominance in us...for yieldedness begets blessedness.

This is the God-given key to the conquest of the fallen Adam-nature and this is the fulfilling of the Law. For the prophecies have been given of old:

> *"But this shall be the covenant that I will make with the house of Israel; After those days, saith the Lord, I will put My law in their inward parts and write it in their hearts..."*

> (Jeremiah 31:33)

"And they shall call them THE HOLY PEOPLE,
The redeemed of the Lord..."

(Isaiah 62:12)

THE CONSTANT BATTLE

In theory, this acquisition of holiness sounds like a relatively simple and easy-to-enact process.

In reality, it is an all-out battle - "For the flesh lusteth against the Spirit, and the Spirit against the flesh: and these are contrary the one to the other: so that ye cannot do the things that ye would." (Galatians 5:17)

Just because we are under grace does not mean the struggle is over; neither does it give us a license to give in to the battle, claim God's mercy, and hope for the best.

No, quite the contrary, we must never allow our striving for perfection to be inhibited or restrained in any way - for the acquisition of holiness, by the pattern, plan and revelation given in the New Testament, is one of the most important goals that any Christian can pursue.

• Moreover, it is so important that if we fail to seek it on our own, God has promised to send chastisements if necessary for this very purpose - "that we might be partakers of His *holiness*". (Hebrews 12:10)

"For God hath not called us unto uncleanness, but
unto holiness. He therefore that despiseth, despiseth not
man, but God, who hath also given unto us His Holy
Spirit."

(I Thessalonians 4:7-8)

THE WORD EMPHASIS

• Even though scriptures such as the last two are sprinkled throughout the New Testament, it is evident that in the Old Testament the words *holiness* and *holy* were used much more often.

This shift in the emphasis of certain words, though, does not mean a shift in God's attitudes, neither does it mean that the manifestation of holiness is any less important in the eyes of God now!

It simply means that what God presented before in the spirit of a stern demand, He now desires to be a heartfelt response of worshipful gratitude.

This is exactly what Isaiah was referring to when he prophesied that Jesus would - "magnify the law, and make it honourable." (Isaiah 42:21)

For now, more than ever, holiness has become a means of worship. (See Psalm 29:2. 96:9)

150

SEPARATION FROM THE WORLD

• It is important that we repeat: the word **holy** means *separated unto God.*

God has charged us through His Word to - "come out from among them, and be ye *separate,* saith the Lord, and touch not the unclean thing; and I will receive you". (II Corinthians 6:17)

It is a wonderful thing that we have received Him into our hearts; but how much more wonderful it is when He receives us into His heart!

This is the purchased privilege of obtaining intimate fellowship with God.

To receive Him costs us nothing, for it is a free gift of grace. To be received by Him may well cost us everything, for it is the reward of true discipleship.

Yet truly communing with Him and being used by Him are well worth any sacrifice we must make.

• To this end, Hebrews 12:14 exhorts believers to..."follow peace with all men, and *holiness,* without which no man shall see the Lord."

For we will never see the Lord in that future revelation of all His celestial glory and beauty, neither will we see the Lord overflow our lives presently in a full manifestation of His precious promises and supernatural power unless we cultivate this essential quality of character.

No wonder Paul said - "I beseech you therefore, brethren, by the mercies of God, that ye present your bodies a living sacrifice, *holy,* acceptable unto God, which is your reasonable service." (Romans 12:1)

And II Corinthians 7:1 cautions - "Having therefore these promises, dearly beloved, let us cleanse ourselves from all filthiness of the flesh and spirit, perfecting *holiness* in the fear of God."

We that dare to make a difference between the holy and profane must dissect our own characters and scrutinize our own hearts - daily - until we purge out all that contaminates the flesh and the spirit. (See Ezekiel 22:26)

Every weakness of the Adam man must be brought under control...even some that are often overlooked like slothfulness, obesity, backbiting, self-pity, or a tendency to exaggerate or stretch the truth.

Negative habits must be conquered.

Unruly thoughts and imaginations of the mind and heart must also be brought into captivity and nailed to the cross.

• Even our reasons for striving toward the goal of holiness must be constantly under the surveillance of our conscience...for our motives must remain just as pure and perfect as the purity and perfection for which we seek.

THE LAST DAYS CHURCH

Surely the church will once again seek after holiness in the latter days for the urgency of the hour and the great need of humanity will constrain us to do so.

Daniel 8:24 declares that we will be a "**MIGHTY AND A HOLY PEOPLE.**"

• Moreover, Psalm 110:3 prophesies - *"Thy people shall be willing in the day of Thy power, in the beauties of holiness from the womb of the morning..."*

Surely this prophecy can on one level refer to us, for we are definitely in *"the womb of the morning."*

We are dwelling in the *dark womb* of the end of this age with all of its impending judgments. We can be comforted, though, for we know that this time of great travail and tribulation will undoubtedly, eventually bring to birth the kingdom of God in this world and increase the same to perfection in us.

But just prior to this time of great revelation and restoration, God's people as a whole must reach a place of unprecedented *willingness* and surrender. When our lives and our hearts overflow in this manner, with the *beauties of holiness,* automatically *"the day of His power"* will be ushered in, a prophetic hour when the Spirit of God will manifest through His people in marvellous and miraculous ways.

This key to revival has been implemented successfully in times past: therefore it can easily happen again, and will happen according to this prophecy.

Therefore, let us enter zealously into the arena of battle. Let us purpose to "die daily", ever crucifying the flesh with its affections and lusts.

For if we stubbornly try to live like the world, act like the world, and in an idolatrous way pursue the pleasure trends and goals that the world sets upon a pedestal, we will forfeit the "milk and honey" heritage God desires us to have.

If we allow rebellion to take hold of our hearts, in a Moses-like manner we may well die and be buried by God in the plains of Moab, never entering into our "**Promised Land Inheritance**".

If we allow fear or unbelief to grip us, like the children of Israel, we will spend our lives wandering in a wilderness of sin.

"But He giveth more grace." (James 4:6)

• Concerning the Messiah - our Elder Brother and divine forerunner - Romans 1:4 states that He was "declared to be the Son of God with power, according to the *spirit of holiness,* by the resurrection from the dead."

In other words, sin could not penetrate Him, neither could "death by sin" engulf Him...because He was *holy*, He was innocent. Therefore the Holy Ghost, the *spirit of holiness*, confirmed His "sonship status" by raising Him from the dead.

And so will the *spirit of holiness* do for every yielded member of the family of God. He will verify our position as sons of God by "resurrecting" us out of every "death-trap" Satan sets in our path.

He will make us unreproveable and unrebukeable in the sight of the Father by the application of the blood of the Son...both now and forevermore.

THE BLOSSOMING WILDERNESS

• With respect to the covenant people who passionately and devotedly strive for this goal of sanctity, purity and self-denial, Isaiah prophesied:

> *"The wilderness and the solitary place shall be glad for them; and the desert shall rejoice and blossom as the rose...*
> *And the parched ground shall become a pool, and the thirsty land springs of water..."*
>
> (Isaiah 35: 1,7)

O, how beautifully the prophet depicted the flourishing of the kingdom of God that comes even in the most desert dry lives when we accept the challenge to walk through the "parched land" of temptations and trials consecrated to God. Isaiah went on to say:

> *"And an highway shall be there, and a way, and it shall be called **The way of holiness**; the unclean shall not pass over it; but it shall be for those: the wayfaring men, though fools, shall not err therein."*
>
> (Isaiah 35:8)

It is on this *righteous road* that - "sorrow and sighing flee away" - for God pours out the reward of everlasting joy upon our heads. (See entire chapter, Isaiah 35)

It is on this *road of consecration* that we find courage, stability, and strength, for He commanded concerning those who walk there - "Strengthen ye the weak hands and confirm the feeble knees. Say to them that are of a fearful heart, Be strong, fear not."

It is also in this *highway of holiness* that "the eyes of the blind shall be opened, and the ears of the deaf shall be unstopped...then shall the lame man leap as an hart, and the tongue of the dumb sing..."

This passage can, of course, be interpreted literally.

But in a figurative sense, it speaks of our spiritual eyes and ears being opened...as well as the surplus of strength and the ecstatic kind of victory that God's *holy* offspring can rightfully claim and expect. Those who

153

receive this blessing sing out the praises of the One who set them free, for their tongue has been loosed to give glory to God.

On the highest level, this passage foretells the glory, liberty, and utter joy of the future resurrected state when we will be delivered forever from "blinding, deafening, and crippling effects" of the fallen Adam nature.

O, what ecstatic victory will be ours in that day when the Lord will establish our hearts "unblameable in *holiness* before God, even our Father, at the coming of our Lord Jesus Christ with all His saints." (I Thessalonians 3:13)

THE JOY OF HOLINESS

• It must be said that this ecstatic kind of joy, just described, is not only a future hope for God's sanctified ones; it is very much a present tense possession!

In yet another chapter Isaiah foretold the wonderful effects of the "righteousness imparting New Covenant" and said:

> *"Thou hast multiplied* **THE NATION***, and [increased their joy]; they joy before Thee according to the joy in harvest, and as men rejoice when they divide the spoil."*
> (Isaiah 9:3, AV NIV)

This joyous prophecy has been fulfilled four major ways:

First, God's holy nation has been enlarged and multiplied primarily because of the door of salvation opening to the Gentiles.

Second, the joy has been increased because we are partakers of a better covenant. Our joy is no longer just the product of human emotion for it is supernatural and spiritual - "joy in the Holy Ghost" as Paul so aptly put it.

Third, this unspeakable joy is likened to the joy in harvest for we are reaping the spiritual fruit that has resulted from the implantation of the seed of the Word within our hearts.

Fourth, we can rejoicingly divide the spoil...for the wicked one was defeated and plundered almost two thousand years ago, and all that he stole from Adam is now being freely returned to those who believe.

• In light of these precious truths we are all the more compelled to pray Psalm 106:4-5 every day:

> *"Remember me, O Lord, with the favour that Thou bearest unto Thy people: O visit me with Thy salvation; That I may see the good of Thy chosen, that I may rejoice in the gladness of* **THY NATION***, that I may glory with Thine Inheritance."*
> (See also Isaiah 51:4)

THE TRUE IDENTITY OF "THE NATION"
BOTH NOW AND FOREVERMORE

Jesus warned the rebellious and hypocritical Jewish leaders of His day that:

> *"...the kingdom of God shall be taken from you, and given to A NATION bringing forth the fruits thereof."*
> (Matthew 21:43)

This new and fruitful covenant nation is presently comprised of both Jews and Gentiles who accept "the stone which the builders rejected" and build their lives upon Him. (See Matthew 21:42-44)

By His indwelling presence, we bear the fruit of the kingdom in this present evil world.

Ultimately and eternally this covenant nation - this *holy nation* - will be made up of the redeemed of both the Old Will and the New Will.

This union under one *title* will take place fully at the resurrection of the dead in Christ and the translation of the living believers.

For at that spectacular climax of the Old and New Will "**A NATION** shall be born at once" and "the earth shall be made to bring forth in one day!" (Isaiah 66:8)

As we come back with the Lord to this earth-plane to fully and victoriously establish the kingdom of God, we will rejoice to behold the "restitution of all things".

For "the earth and the fulness thereof" will also be restored back to holiness and sanctity by the transforming fire of God's manifest presence.

• In that day, instead of spiritually being called Sodom and Egypt (because of recurring accounts of rebellion and foreign occupation) **"Jerusalem shall be called holy, and there shall no strangers pass through her any more.** (Revelation 11:8, Joel 3:17)

"And it shall come to pass in that day that the mountains shall drop down new wine, and the hills shall flow with milk" - for the land will be drenched with the richness of the Spirit and the Word.

God Himself will dwell in Zion.

And we will gather there every year to "worship the King, the Lord of hosts, and to keep the feast of tabernacles".

In that blessed era even the bells on the horses will bear the inscription *"holiness unto the Lord"* - for both the creation and the creature will be in submission to the Holy One who reigns as King. (See Zechariah 14:16-20)

And as the multiplied thousands of saints congregate, to participate in those annual holy convocations, certainly more than ever before, we will be quick to affirm Psalm 111:1 - "I will praise the Lord with my whole heart, in the assembly of the upright, and in the congregation."

• Then shall the angel of the Lord decree the decree over us - "he that is *holy,* let him be *holy* still." (Revelation 22:11)

How wonderful it will be when weakness and frailty take their flight, never to drag our wayward souls into the mirey clay again! Jehovah God will set our feet on the "solid rock" of an unchanging and perfected character, and an unchanging relationship with Himself.

In that day we will worship God in the *beauty of holiness*...in a depth and measure never previously known.

And as the high priest under the Old Will wore a holy crown, a miter, bearing the inscription *holiness unto the Lord*, so Jesus, our great High Priest, will be crowned with the splendor of absolute holiness...radiating the indescribable beauty of Shekinah unveiled.

As the Most Holy, He will "sit on the throne of His holiness" in the "mountain of His holiness" and rejoice over His **HOLY PEOPLE** with everlasting and ever-increasing joy. (Palm 47:8; 48:1)

We, in return, will ever "give thanks at the remembrance of his holiness". (Psalm 97:12)

We will ceaselessly adore the chosen One who was "in all points tempted like as we are, yet without sin." (Hebrews 4:15)

By the seal of His Holy Spirit, we will be eternally secure in our inheritance and exalted above all nations, kindreds and tongues. FOREVER WE WILL BE...**HIS HOLY NATION, HIS DEDICATED NATION** and **AN HOLY PEOPLE UNTO THE LORD OUR GOD**... (I Peter 2:9 NEB)

Defiled once...but never to be defiled again; yes, never to be defiled again.

We are compelled to bow before Him even now in reverential awe.

THE LILY AMONG THORNS

_____

"As **THE LILY AMONG THORNS,** *so is My love among the daughters."*

(Song of Solomon 2:2)

THE LILY AMONG THORNS

*"As **THE LILY AMONG THORNS,** so
is My love among the daughters."*

(Song of Solomon 2:2)

• The first man Adam must have trembled with fear as he heard the pronouncement of God's judgment:

*"Cursed is the ground for thy sake; in sorrow shalt
thou eat of it all the days of thy life;
Thorns also and thistles shall it bring forth to thee."*

(Genesis 3:17-18)

It is certain that this curse fell initially on the earth and certain parts that had been an Eden paradise gradually became a wilderness wasteland in comparison.

But it is also certain that this divinely authored curse fell on Adam's body - the very flesh and bone structure that had been formed originally out of the dust of the earth.

From that day forward nature was cursed and fruitless, useless, *thorny* plants and pricking *thistles* began to grow wild everywhere.

• Adam's nature was also cursed, and in a different though related sense, his flesh also began to bring forth *thorns and thistles...*thorny, lustful temptations and painful, pricking attitudes that would never cease to tear at his soul.

All sons of Adam have inherited this same curse...*thorns and thistles.*

We have been compelled to *eat of "the ground"* - to partake of the fallen Adam nature in *sorrow* all the days of our lives.

No human being is exempt from this sore travail.

Even Jesus, the firstborn Son - "suffered, being tempted." (Hebrews 2:18)

"He was oppressed and He was afflicted."

He was - " a Man of sorrows and acquainted with grief." (Isaiah 53:3-7)

We conclude therefore, that if the spotless Lamb of God had to walk this difficult road, then we should not be surprised when the slashing, slicing seductions of Satan make their attempt to lacerate us mentally, emotionally and spiritually.

This is a necessary and inescapable part of walking through the valley of the shadow of death.

Thorns and thistles grow in this valley, and we must forge our way through them in order to reach our final destiny.

We are not afraid though, for He is with us.

We have a sure source of great comfort in times of tribulation.

We know the compassionate One who promised to give power to the faint and increase the strength of those who have no might.

We are in intimate contact with this pure and irreproachable One, whose image we reflect.

* We are called **the lily among thorns**...something very protected in the midst of lurking danger, something very pure in the midst of dark, entangling evil.

* But Jesus is called **the Lily of the valleys**...(and not just one valley, but every valley we go through).

His abiding presence transforms this place of ugliness and chaos into a place of beauty and purpose.

He has determined from the foundation to use this extremely painful experience as a means of propelling us forward to an extremely blissful and pleasurable experience...the utter joy of emerging totally into His likeness.

We are of a kindred spirit even now.

Our souls have been knit together.

We realize that He became like us, that we might become like Him.

In the Bible we are told that - "He **feedeth** among **the lilies**." (Song of Solomon 2:16)

In other words, as we cry out to Jesus because of the piercing thorns that seem to prevail against us, He feeds on our prayers and petitions.

We are His garden of lilies.

He thirsts to see real faith growing in us, therefore, He thrives on the trust that we lovingly generate toward His throne.

He hungers for intimate fellowship with us, therefore, He is nourished by our laughter when we praise Him, and even by our tears when we weep before His throne.

We fill His heart!

He deeply desires our adoration.

He truly feeds among us.

He is nurtured by our worship, as we are by His loving care and His gentle understanding nature.

We can endure this valley together...growing side by side.

We know that we will both come forth from it, far better off in the end.

We will finally obtain beauty for ashes.

When all things are ultimately brought to perfection we will surely be able to look back and confidently affirm - "He hath made everything beautiful in His time." (Ecclesiastes 3:11)

THE VALLEY OF THORNS
GOD'S PROVING GROUND

What is the purpose for this earthly sojourn?
How could a God of love create a place of such torment and despair?
Why do even the righteous suffer here?

These and other related questions have plagued the minds of men for centuries...and most of the answers given, and conclusions reached, are really only partially satisfactory.
We do know this.
God allowed the Jews to wander in the Wilderness of Sin for forty years...*to humble them, to prove them, and to see what was in their hearts.* (Deuteronomy 8:2)
We, too, are wandering through a wilderness - a spiritual "wilderness of sin", covered with a thick and seemingly impenetrable growth of brambles and nettles.

• It is quite possible that the same threefold reason is a major part of God's purpose in allowing our treacherous trek through time...*to humble us, to prove us, and to see what we are really made of...deep inside.*

Apparently the authority that we will possess in the kingdom to come is so great that we could be a possible threat to the New Creation if there was any potential for rebellion still remaining in our spirits.
This earthly pressure chamber will kill that potential, destroying it forever, if we sincerely and successfully yield to God.
Therefore, this intermediate step is absolutely necessary and critically important for the sake of the plan of God and for our sakes as well.

We conclude therefore that this world is **God's proving ground**...a place where God **proves** us, and yet at the same time, a place where we **prove** Him. For thistle-like circumstances continually force us to test the faithfulness of God, and the veracity and integrity of His Word.

The resulting revelation of the personality of deity will be our prized possession forever...one of the very few treasures that we can take with us when we leave this world.
The essence and value of God's purpose in His sons is surely not reserved to the span of time from Adam to the resurrection...for it was birthed in the infinite past and it will yet expand and enlarge itself with perpetual, flowerful glory throughout the infinite future.
We are presently caught in the middle, suspended in time, captivated within the limiting walls of sense-consciousness. We are bound in the confining, temporary form that Paul called - *"the body of our humiliation."* (Philippians 3:21 RV)

161

Though we have been born again and spiritually lifted into heavenly places, still the outer man is full of *thorns* and *thistles* and always will be - that is, until the resurrection.

As we wait for that day, we have the charge and the challenge to bring this flesh under subjection, but even as we attempt to do so, we recognize that the sin-nature is like an untamed, caged lion, pacing to and fro, continually roaring out its threatenings.

As *the lily among thorns* we are reminded of the vulnerability of our position every day.

On our own, we are helpless; we are defenseless.

But the gracious Gardener is watching over us intently.

If we trust in Him, we will not be put to shame.

OUR ONLY SOURCE OF FRUITFULNESS

We know that our human part can never, of itself, produce the perfected personality and flawless, moral makeup required of those candidates seeking heavenly acceptance.

Though the flesh can attain righteousness and morality to a certain degree, still the flesh cannot produce the true fruit of the Spirit.

We must first have the indwelling presence of the Lord for this to take place.

• Jesus Himself asked the pointed question -

> *"Do men gather grapes of thorns, or figs of thistles?*
> *Even so...a good tree cannot bring forth evil fruit,*
> *neither can a corrupt tree bring forth good fruit."*
>
> (Matthew 7:16-18)

The fallen Adam flesh, full of *thorns* and *thistles*, cannot produce a person good enough to earn eternal life.

But, thank God, we are new creatures in Christ - born of the Spirit.

The *life-sap* of the Holy Spirit, the inward flow of the personality of deity, is ever seeking to produce good fruit in us...that which is valuable, lasting and Godlike.

THE EVER-PRESENT STRUGGLE

Even though we have received a new heart, and have the potential for true fruitfulness, still the human part, the old man, is unfortunately always there, "deceitful above all things and desperately wicked." (Jeremiah 17:9)

This is the ever-present struggle!

• Paul was quite possibly the greatest apostle of all time, yet he too experienced this struggle, for he too had to walk through this valley.

162

He confessed the nature of his battle to the Corinthian church:

> *"And lest I should be exalted above measure through the abundance of the revelations, there was given to me a thorn in the flesh, the messenger of Satan to buffet me...*
> *For this thing I besought the Lord thrice, that it might depart from me. "*

(II Corinthians 12:7-8)

We do not know for certain what Paul's *thorn in the flesh* was, for he did not elaborate on the subject much further.

But we do know that it was a messenger from Satan and we do know that it was purposefully sent to buffet him.

We conclude that this *messenger* must have been an evil spirit bearing some evil *message* to Paul and not a sickness or a disease as some theologians have assumed.

It seems apparent that this terrible trial consisted of some kind of recurring mental pressure or temptation - something that refused to stop hammering on Paul's mind.

Could it have been the overwhelming guilt that Paul surely suffered for having tortured and killed so many who believed in the name of Jesus?

Could it have been a satanic force driving him to gratify the sinful, sensual demands of the weak, carnal side of his nature?

Or maybe it was just a powerful principality out of hell that would stir up opposition against Paul in the different cities where he preached.

• Whatever it was, we know that it was far more than just a pricking, probing annoyance, for the Greek word that was translated *thorn* in this passage is *skolops* and actually means - *a sharp stake.*

This was something that lanced Paul's soul and cut him to the very core of his being, over and over again.

Regardless of the true character of the problem we find that, through it all, Paul received an invaluable revelation from on high.

He discovered two infinite truths that transformed his life and can transform ours as well.

We do not know how long this battle persisted.

But we do know the answer the apostle received.

THE DUAL DIVINE PROMISE

• When the pressure of the battle reached a peak in Paul, Jesus gave to His chosen vessel a wonderful pledge:

> *"My grace is sufficient for thee: for My strength is made perfect in weakness. "*

Listen to Paul's reaction to this dual divine promise:

> *"Most gladly therefore will I rather glory in my infirmities, that the power of Christ may rest upon me.*
> *Therefore I take pleasure in infirmities, in reproaches, in necessities, in persecutions, in distresses for Christ's sake: for when I am weak, then am I strong."*

(II Corinthians 12:9-10)

What a marvellous unveiling of the wisdom of God!

* Paul suffered through the experience of being *a lily among thorns* on an individual level, and behold what spiritual insight he received and passed on to us as a result.

Now we understand.

Now we know.

As long as we are trusting in our own strength, our own abilities, and our own will, we are weak...for in a moment's time these things can fail us.

But if we reach a place where we cast all of our cares on the Lord, trusting only in His mercy and grace, then we become utterly strong.

Our strength becomes stable and unchanging, for it equals the strength and stability of the everlasting promises on which we hope and believe.

Our faith is no longer in the flesh; our faith is focused on the God of all power and might...therefore, in a certain sense, we become just as unconquerably strong as He!

Of course, this God-given strength does not reside in the flesh, it rather resides in the born again part of us...the hidden man of the heart.

Therefore, possessing such a hidden resource does not insure freedom from all failure; it just means that if we fail, we are not bound to that failure, for our strength is "in the Spirit."

THE CHOKING THORNS

Knowing these truths, concerning the sufficiency of grace and the availability of strength "in Christ", should never make us drop our guard or give in to the advance of the enemy.

* Quite the contrary, those who please God never cease to war against *"the cares of this world, and the deceitfulness of riches, and the lusts of other things."* (Mark 4:19)

In **The Parable of the Sower and His Seed** (Matthew 13:1-23, Mark 4:1-20) we are cautioned by Jesus, the Heavenly Sower, to beware of these three *thorn-like,* worldly enticements that will make a concerted attempt to choke the Word in us, and to render us unfruitful.

All inhabitants of this earth are constantly beset with *lust*...that treacherous thorn-covered vine of selfish desire.

Egocentric cravings continuously seek to coil themselves around the heart, in serpentine fashion, enticing us to focus on and indulge in that which is pleasurable, transitory and oftentimes forbidden.

So often human beings are wooed as well by the false allurement of the "high life" - the deceitful, softly penetrating voice that jabs and digs, whispering over and over to the searching soul that true happiness and fulfillment will only come when possessions and *riches* are acquired. Such a horrendous lie! And such a perilous trap, that can easily drown the souls of men in "destruction and perdition." (I Timothy 6:9)

But if these two types of thorny projections are too obviously evil, or too easily ignored or rejected, there is yet a third that will often entwine itself around the mind of even the most consecrated person and drain its unfortunate victim of all spiritual impetus....*"the cares of this life."* (Luke 21:34)

None of us can escape either the subtle or the forcible assault of these thorny branches that with insatiable desire, daily seek to overtake and overcome new prey. So without question, we must never ease up on our resistance.

We must tirelessly beat these persistent branches back and hew them down with the sword of the Word, lest we be duped and brought under their insidious control.

O, it is true, the pressure often seems unbearable...but to give in to the battle only makes things worse.

To be pricked, penetrated, or at times, even thrashed with thorns is difficult to endure, but it is far better than being overtaken, overwhelmed and finally strangled by the constricting, suffocating undergrowth of the fallen Adam nature.

• Concerning certain rebellious, idolatrous men of Israel, God warned - *"nettles* shall possess them...*the thorn and the thistle* shall come up on their altars; and they shall say to the mountains, Cover us; and to the hills, Fall on us."* (Hosea 9:6, 10:8)

Because these men had become possessed by the sin-nature - given over to *thorns and thistles* - they lost their sincere love for God and even their religious observances reeked of carnality.

Thorns came up on their altars, making them quite unacceptable in the presence of God.

They were crushed beneath the very mountains that they could have moved, and should have moved, through faith and obedience.

The same dreadful and damnable thing could easily happen to us unless we maintain a diligent watch over our souls and over our lives.

We must forcefully, even violently, drive out the corrupting influence of sin, lest it contaminate our hearts and destroy us spiritually.

We must build a wall of separation and consecration between the iniquity-laden part of our old nature and the born-again, sanctified, new creation part.

There must be no attempt to form any kind of compromising union between the two, or sensuality and carnality ultimately will blind us spiritually, and we will not be able to perceive the deep things of God.

• Joshua warned the Israelites that if they intermarried with the Canaanites, those heathen unbelievers would be *scourges in their sides and thorns in their eyes* until they perished from off the land. (Joshua 23:13)

The same thing will happen to us in a spiritual sense if we allow our will to be married to the will of the flesh.

We will perish right in the very land of our inheritance, when instead we should be prospering there above measure in the abundant life promises given to us through the New Covenant.

OUR ONLY KEY TO SURVIVAL

There is only one answer...one key to survival.

We must go to Calvary and be willing to die there - sharing the pain of self-denial and crucifixion with the One who cared enough to share with us the pain of separation.

He died for the ungodly.

He was crowned with thorns!

• The very *thorns* that greedily sprang forth to possess the earth, at the pronouncement of God's curse, finally were made to encircle *the pure Lily of all ages*...four thousand years later.

He purposefully brought it on Himself.

He willed it to be so.

As the soldiers platted that diadem of death and cruelly pressed it upon the head of the sinless Saviour of the world, their intentions were only to royally mock and torture this Holy One who claimed to be the King of all creation.

They treated Him with great indignities and sought to brand Him as an imposter.

They considered Him worthy of execution, so they adorned Him with the kind of crown that in their eyes befitted His terrible fate.

Little did they know the depth of what was actually taking place, though the prophetic symbol had already been given in the Law of Moses.

166

THE SCAPEGOAT SYMBOL

• During the Old Testament era, God instituted a very unique ritual to be performed one time a year, on the Day of Atonement (which fell on the tenth day of the Jews' seventh month - around the beginning of October according to our calendar). (Leviticus 16)

On this somber and momentous feast day, when the sins of the whole nation of Israel were to be atoned for, the high priest would take two goats...one as a blood sacrifice for Jehovah and the other for a scapegoat.

The **scapegoat** was called *Azazel.*

Apparently, this name comes from two Hebrew root words - *aze* which means *goat* and *azal* which means *to remove completely.*

• So clearly, the interpretation of the word **Azazel** is *"a goat which removes completely"*...for he represented the yearly *"carrying away"* of Israel's sin.

The high priest would lay both hands on the head of *the scapegoat* (something that never happened in any other sacrifice ritual) "and confess over him all the iniquities of the children of Israel, and all their transgressions in all their sins, putting them upon the head of the goat."(Lev. 6:21)

Then by the hand of a "fit man" *the scapegoat* was led away into the wilderness, into a "land not inhabited", and let go.

Something very similar to all of this happened on the dark day of Jesus' demise.

All the sins of humanity were somehow transferred to this heaven-sent *Scapegoat* (though it was ruthless Roman soldiers and not the high priest who laid their hands on His head, crowning Him with thorns).

But it was during those hours that Jesus "bare our sins in His own body on the tree, that we, being dead to sins, should live into righteousness." (I Peter 2:24)

Though the divine part was never contaminated, mysteriously, God "made Him to be sin for us, who knew no sin; that we might be made the righteousness of God in Him." (II Corinthians 5:21)

Isaiah, viewing the crucifixion in advance, cried - "Surely He hath borne our griefs, and carried our sorrows." (Isaiah 53:3-4)

So evidently, the agony of the cross went far beyond the mere physical pain that Jesus suffered, for He bore not only our sin and our shame, but our sorrow as well.

• In fact, it seems quite significant that the name of that horrid place of execution was **Calvary**, which actually means *the place of a skull.*

And it is no coincidence that such a lonely, barren hill - that became the focus of eternity and the hinge of humanity - should actually bear the somewhat dreadful and morbid shape of *a human skull.*

But such was nature's premonition and the Creator's subtle and symbolic forewarning.

For Jesus surely tasted of extreme mental and emotional pain as well as physical death, when He was suspended above those cruel, jagged, unsightly rocks.

It is possible that the sum total of all the mental anguish of the human race somehow penetrated Jesus' mind, when the piercing, slender, yet unyielding thorns penetrated his skull.

He was the Scapegoat.

As the rivulets of blood ran down the battered face of the Messiah, His mind like a sponge must have soaked in all the crippling confusion and all the debilitating fear that ever had, or ever would, plague the inhabitants of this world. Surely it all raged through His inner being like a windswept fire (for He was "in all points tempted like as we are" and "in all things it behooved Him to be made like unto His brethren"). (Hebrews 4:15; 2:17)

All of our sin, and all of the agonizing result of our sin, viciously descended on this heaven-sent Saviour.

He was the substitute.

• He was crowned with the very grief that plowed the first deep-rutted furrows on Adam's brow.

He wrestled with it.

He struggled against it.

He strove unto blood.

He sank under the load.

Like the four walls of a condemned building suddenly collapsing inward, the boundaries of time, and all the sorrow contained within its walls, suddenly fell inward with swift severity on the Son of God.

He was buried beneath the rubble.

But the foreshadowed miracle of atonement was only beginning.

For there were two goats: the sacrificed goat of the Old Testament ceremony represented Jesus in His substitutionary death for us. But the scapegoat represented the living Saviour, quickened by the Spirit, conquering death and carrying our sin away.

Again, it was stated that a "fit man" was to lead the scapegoat into a wilderness area, into a land not inhabited, and there let him go.

• In like manner, Jesus was led by the Holy Ghost, the only fit and suitable guide, through the very portals of death, to mysteriously and potentially transport our sins to a "land not inhabited", - a land of emptiness and nothingness.

Because for those who would eventually claim His precious blood, transgressions would quite effectively be blotted out.

• There would be an *utter removal,* as well as an *everlasting removal* of sin, for God promised:

> *"Their sins and iniquities will I remember no more."*
>
> (Hebrews 10:17)

• Psalm 103:12 says it in a way that is quite unique and quite beautiful:

> *"As far as the east is from the west, so far hath He removed our transgressions from us."*   ·

There is a valuable truth hidden in this thrilling verse of Scripture.

If a person begins traveling north in a straight line, eventually, at the north pole, they will always encounter the south again and begin traveling that direction, only to encounter the north again at the south pole, repeating the process over and over.

But if a person begins traveling east in a straight line, in a sense, they will never encounter the west again. Symbolically speaking, they could potentially keep going east for all eternity.

The only way to face the west again would be to turn around and look back.

It works the same for us, with regard to our past sins.

God did not say, *"As far as the north is from the south."* Quite the opposite, He said - *"As far as the east is from the west, so far hath He removed our transgressions from us."*

The only way sincerely repentant children of God can encounter their sins again is to erroneously submit to   guilt and self-condemnation and thereby gaze defeatedly into the past.

To do so is to unnecessarily review such mistakes and relive the pain time and time again.

This is definitely not the will of God for His own.

• If the God who cannot forget has forced Himself to forget the very stains of our past, then who are we to remember them again.

Our blessed scapegoat, our heaven-sent *Azazel,* carried our sins away into a "land of nothingness" - "a land not inhabited" - a "land" that we will never inhabit or visit again.

After having accomplished such an awesome redemption, Jesus was then *set free* after the pattern of the Old Testament scapegoat.

He was *set free* from the pangs of death and from the burden of His commission...and He came back from the gates of death to set us free as well.

He gave the precious promise well in advance - "Ye shall know the truth and the truth shall make you free." (John 8:32)

Therefore, having obtained this valuable insight, we must purpose to always look forward to the resurrection, fully persuaded that our past is under the blood.

- It is also interesting to note that the generally accepted definition of the word **scapegoat** is - *one who bears the blame for others, or one who is the object of irrational hostility.*

Such definitions are perfectly descriptive of Jesus, for He was continously the object of irrational hostility and He bore all this blame for us. But He went through it so that He, in a Samson-like manner, could place his hands firmly against the pillars of sin and succeed in bringing "the kingdom of Satan" toppling to the ground.

THE CURSE FOREVER LIFTED

At Calvary, Jesus won quite valiantly...He triumphed quite gloriously...so that now, it is only a matter of time until the kingdom of God is fully established in this world.

The Son of man became "the curse" and conquered "the curse" so that eventually He could utterly remove "the curse".

This glorious end result will be manifested completely at the second coming of the Lord when the *thorns and briers* will be burned in one day. (See Isaiah 10:17; 27:4)

Such a mighty transformation will take place, not only in the creature, but in creation as well.

For, it is a prophetic fact that during this Kingdom Age to come, not only will we be raised in the likeness of the Lord, but -"the whole of created life will be rescued from the tyranny of change and decay, and have its share in that magnificent liberty which can only belong to the children of God." (Romans 8:21 PME)

- Isaiah foretold that in that day -

> *"Instead of the thorn shall come up the fir tree, and instead of the brier shall come up the myrtle tree: and it shall be to the Lord for a name, for an everlasting sign that shall not be cut off."*

> (Isaiah 55:13)

The myrtle and the fir tree are both plants which are noted as being evergreen, so they speak of that which is ever-living, never-failing and ever-lasting.

So again, it must be emphasized: *the curse* that filled the earth with *thorns and thistles*, and imprisoned the sons of Adam behind bars of bones, will finally be lifted forever.

In this soon-to-come Age of Restoration, when the lovely myrtle blossoms with its tender-petaled white flowers, never to wither or wilt, surely it will be *an everlasting sign* of the infinite purity, serenity, and tranquility that will reign once again in the minds of men.

And also - *"it shall be to the Lord for a name"* - or as another translation put it - *"this will be for the Lord's renown."* (NIV)

Delivering creation from the devouring and death-dealing debacle, brought on by Eve's desire to be wise, will surely cause the greatness of the Lord to be royally acclaimed throughout the universe.

His glory will be all the more celebrated in heaven because of this, His great conquest!

• And for those who have chosen to be crucified with Christ, suffering the awesome mental, emotional, and spiritual pressure that results from such a decision, He has reserved an exceeding great reward!

For those who have dared to bear His reproach and share His thorny crown, He has promised the splendid privilege of a final and marvellous exchange.

James 1:12 declares - "Blessed is the man that endureth temptation: for when He is tried, He shall receive **the crown of life,** which the Lord hath promised to them that love Him."

I Peter 5:4 announces that - "when the chief Shepherd shall appear, ye shall receive **a crown of glory** that fadeth not away."

And having fought a good fight and kept the faith, Paul made the proclamation in II Timothy 4:8 - "Henceforth there is laid up for me **a crown of righteousness,** which the Lord, the righteous judge, shall give me at that day: and not to me only, but unto all them also that love His appearing."

O, hallelujah! This is our promise too!

We will soon be crowned with the very life of God, clothed with His immortality and endued with His majesty and authority!

We will be resurrected in His great power - gloriously adorned with His supernal beauty and divinity.

We will be crowned with the royal diadem of His imparted righteousness...a spectacular and infinite trophy testifying that corruption is conquered forever!

We will be led forth with peace. The mountains and hills will break forth before us into singing and all the trees of the field will clap their hands.

What a reward of victory!

What a dramatic display of climactic success...and all in exchange for the temporary hurt of **a crown of thorns,** lovingly shared and willfully borne.

• O, how true, how very true it is...*Blessed are those who endure temptation.*

Blessed are those heaven-bound pilgrims who pass through this fear-gripped valley of unbelief - *this valley of thorns and thistles* - yet still keep their hearts brimming with faith, integrity and child-like trust.

Blessed is that *lily in God's garden* who illuminates this dark vale of tears with persistent, radiant, blossoming beauty, as if to silently, yet confidently, defy the danger of those outstretched thorny branches that grope through the darkness with murderous intent.

O, how blessed, how very blessed is that *lily among thorns* who, though constantly beset by weakness and adversity, still nods knowingly in the gentle breath-wind of God's sent-forth presence as if to say:

> *"He is with me. When I am weak, then I am strong. He will never leave me. His grace is sufficient. He is the Dayspring from on high. He will bring the dawning of a new day...All the days of my appointed time will I wait until my change comes."*

MORE THAN CONQUERORS

"Who shall separate us from the love of Christ? shall tribulation or distress, or persecution, or famine, or nakedness, or peril, or sword?

As it is written, For Thy sake we are killed all the day long; we are accounted as sheep for the slaughter.

Nay, in all these things we are *MORE THAN CONQUERORS* through Him that loved us."

(Romans 8:35-37)

MORE THAN CONQUERORS

*"Who shall separate us from the love of Christ?
shall tribulation or distress, or persecution, or famine, or
nakedness, or peril, or sword?*

*As it is written, For Thy sake we are killed all the
day long; we are accounted as sheep for the slaughter.*

*Nay, in all these things we are MORE THAN
CONQUERORS through Him that loved us."*

(Romans 8:35-37)

This particular descriptive phrase - *more than conquerors* - is definitely one of the most powerful and glorious *titles* given to the sons of God.

There are a number of strength-imparting revelations associated with this divinely ordered appellation that are potent enough to totally transform our thinking and propel us to sure, constant and absolute victory.

• First, let us define the word *conqueror.*

A conqueror is simply an individual who gains the victory...a winner.

To conquer is to beat, to subdue, to defeat, and to master.

To conquer is to discomfit, to subjugate, to vanquish and to rout.

*To conquer is to prevail over, to overthrow, to overwhelm, to over-
power and to overcome.*

This word - *over* - is constantly being joined to other words, to form conjugate words, that become synonyms of the word *conquer.*

Therefore, *to conquer* always means to rise above or to be *over* something, bringing it into subjection.

In light of this, it is clear to see, that according to the accepted, usual standard, it is necessary to win - outwardly, evidently and apparently - in order to be classified as a *conqueror.*

It is also very clear that we do not always win our battles - outwardly and evidently.

Sometimes they loom over us, and seem to swallow us up, like the darkness of night engulfing the day.

Sometimes we are weak; sometimes we err.

Sometimes we fail miserably.

• **At times such as these, we cease to be conquerors outwardly, but not inwardly, if we are truly born again.**

For though we suffer temporary setbacks, we never lose our status as winners...if we keep our hearts melted in humility and sincerity before the

Lord, and if we dare to believe our God-given privileges and rights as sons of God.

- **In fact, this is exactly what makes us *more than conquerors.***

Because our standing, our position as victors, is not contingent on whether or not we win or lose individual battles.

Our faith is firmly and boldly set in the finished work of Calvary...where there is a perpetual, blood-bought victory available to those who believe.

OVERCOMING THROUGH FAITH

Because of the victory available at Calvary sin can no longer have dominion over us...whether we are weak or whether we are strong.

Circumstances can no longer have dominion over us.

The flesh can no longer have dominion over us.

Failure can no longer gain the supremacy over us, for we have centered our trust in the One who is supreme and sovereign over all things.

We are seated with Christ spiritually, in heavenly places.

We are enthroned with Him who is "the head of all principality and power." (Colossians 2:10)

The will of God has placed us in this position of rest, privilege and authority in Christ. His Spirit in us is brimming with dominion...a quality of character, and a spiritual possession, that He gladly imparts to those who dare to yield.

He has commanded us to be **strong in faith,** and then warned us that - "without faith it is impossible to please Him." (Hebrews 11:6)

- We may at times be weak emotionally, mentally and even spiritually, but we must purpose in our hearts never to be **weak in faith.**

We must never stagger at the promises of God through unbelief..."for whatsoever is born of God overcometh the world: and this is the victory that overcometh the world, **even our faith.**" (I John 5:4)

This kind of victorious overcoming spirit and experience of life is not based on works; it is founded on the cross and faith in the shed blood of Jesus.

This kind of simple trust and persistent faith is the spiritual substance, the elixir from heaven, that can turn even habitual losers into *conquerors* and *overcomers.*

- Furthermore, it is important to note that throughout the Scripture, the word *overcome* and the word *conquer* are translated quite often from the very same foundational Greek word...*nikao.*

In Revelation 6:2, when the first seal was opened, the rider on the white horse - "went forth conquering, and to conquer."

176

The Greek word here is *nikao* (translated *conquer*).

In John 16:33 Jesus said - "These things I have spoken unto you, that in Me ye might have peace. In the world ye shall have tribulation: but be of good cheer; I have *overcome* the world."

Again, the Greek word in this passage is *nikao* (translated *overcome*).

Jesus conquered the world. He overpowered sin. He overthrew the kingdom of the devil and discomfited hell itself. He successfully and valiantly overcame death, the greatest foe of the human race. He was, and is, and shall always be, the supreme Conqueror, Overcomer and Victor of all ages!

But what redounds to His praise even more is the wondrous truth that He has exalted His redeemed to a position and granted them a *title* that even exceeds His own.

He ran the race and then gave us the prize.

He endured the heat of the battle and then gave us the trophy. He emerged as the conqueror and overcomer of death, hell and the grave, but then He compassionately made a way for us to assume the exalted position of being *more than conquerors.*

This three-word entitlement - *more than conquerors* - is translated from just one Greek word - *hupernikao.*

Again, this is the familiar word *nikao*, joined to and preceded by another word, *huper* (which means *over, above, and beyond*). The Scripture clearly reveals, therefore, that we have arisen *over, above and beyond* the status of being overcomers and *conquerors.*

We are more than overcomers!

WE ARE **MORE THAN CONQUERORS!**

We can "be of good cheer" and enjoy the supernatural peace that passes understanding because of our inherited position "in Christ".

We did nothing to defeat the enemy, yet we have been invited to partake of the spoil.

We have been birthed into that supernatural victory which is already "forever settled in the heavens" - a spiritual gift of dominion that has already been established for the elect from the foundation of the world.

Listen closely now to Jesus' words.

Even before He went to Calvary, He announced to His disciples - *"Be of good cheer; I have overcome the world."* (John 16:33)

Foundationally and simply this meant that Jesus had walked for thirty-three-and-a-half years through this sin drenched world without once being contaminated Himself. But this bold declaration reached into and embraced Jesus' future as well, for the reverberation of His words went far beyond His position in time!

177

It is imperative to emphasize that the Son of God spoke this strong assertation in *the past tense.*

The eternal Word could legally do this, for it was already the predetermined purpose of the Father that Jesus would rout the hellish forces that would oppose Him, and that He would utterly vanquish the prince of darkness, ultimately to subdue and restore all things back to Eden-perfection.

It is possible, therefore, that when Jesus proclaimed Himself to be triumphant in advance, He was not necessarily speaking from His natural vantage point at that precise moment; He was rather speaking from an eternal perspective.

He was speaking as "the great I Am" would speak.

He was talking in *the prophetic tense,* speaking of something yet to transpire as if it had already been done.

He knew the sovereignty of the plan of God, so He also knew that He could rest in total confidence that it would all come to pass, because He was a yielded vessel.

Though He had not yet gone to Golgotha, as far as the plan of God was concerned, He had already won...so He could rightfully proclaim - *"I have overcome the world."*

• In like manner, I John 2:14 makes the announcement to every truly committed child of God that - *"ye have overcome the wicked one!"*

Again, this bold statement is placed in the past tense - *the prophetic tense* - for the conquest is over.

We are God's occupational forces, going forth to occupy a spiritual "Promised Land" territory already captured and secured by the Captain of our salvation.

Three other translations of the very same passage declare in unison that - *"ye have mastered the evil one", "you have defeated the Evil One"* and *"you have won your struggle against Satan".* (NEB,TEV,LB)

• No wonder the prophet Isaiah joyously predicted the blessedness and strength of the New Covenant by saying:

> *"Comfort ye, comfort ye My people, saith your God.*
> *Speak ye comfortably to Jerusalem, and cry unto her,*
> *that her warfare is accomplished, that her iniquity is*
> *pardoned..."*

(Isaiah 40:1-2)

The price of redemption has already been paid, iniquity has already been atoned for, and reconciliation is now an eternally established fact and a perpetually available gift.

Satan is a defeated foe even before He makes His futile and vain attempts to furiously lash out against us!

The first epistle of John doubly emphasizes this prophetic fact of faith by declaring in yet another passage that - "*ye are of God, little children, and have overcome...because greater is He that is in you, than he that is in the world.*" (I John 4:4)

• This scripture compels us to believe that before we even face tomorrow's battles, in a sense we have already won! We have already overcome, for God in us is bigger and greater than any opposition that Satan can muster!

Thank God, we have discovered a spiritual mother lode - one of the primary veins of gold running through the New Testament gold mine of "exceeding great and precious promises." (II Peter 1:4)

We have already achieved success and triumph by faith in the right-now inheritance that belongs to us.

Our God is greater than even our defeats, so we simply refuse to be defeated any longer.

• John even said that "if our heart condemn us, God is greater than our heart, and knoweth all things." (I John 3:20)

The revelation of this, **OUR GLORIOUS INHERITANCE,** has made us all the more determined to scrape off the barnacles of depression, discouragement and self-condemnation that have encrusted the hull of this "ship of Zion"...this heaven-bound family of God.

We know that on the cross Jesus was at His weakest moment, and Satan was at his strongest moment...yet Jesus still came forth totally victorious. Therefore, when we arrive at our weakest moments in life, Jesus Christ in us is still stronger than the devil at His strongest point.

• Revelation 12 speaks of a dreadful time coming soon when the accuser of the brethren, Satan, will be cast down to the earth "having great wrath, because he knoweth that he hath but a short time."

He will make war against the remnant of believers in this world that - "keep the commandments of God, and have the testimony of Jesus Christ."

But we need not fear.

John prophesied our sure victory by declaring in *the past tense - the prophetic tense* - that the saints of God "*overcame* [Satan] by the blood of the Lamb, and by the word of their testimony, and they loved not their lives unto the death."

These are weapons that are mighty through God, and in them we have absolute confidence.

Our confidence is in the blood of Jesus.

Our confidence is in the Word of God.

Our confidence is in His everlasting love toward us...a love that compels us to gratefully submit ourselves to Him, loving not our lives unto death.

Making all other weapons potent and powerful, this yieldedness, coupled with faith, keeps us in close and constant contact with the cleansing, sanctifying *agape-love* of the Almighty God.

This love-contact with deity makes us unshakeable - for our confidence is not in the flesh but in God's everlasting promise toward us.

Though the flesh is changeable, this divine love-factor is unchangeable...for in our God there is "no variableness, neither shadow of turning." (James 1:17)

We may go through grave disappointments and terrible tragedies in life, and should not be surprised when we do so.

• But Romans 8:36-37 reveals that although we are accounted as sheep for the slaughter, we are still *"more than conquerors through Him that loved us."*

Notice that this statement is also given in the past tense, for this love motive was settled in the heart of God a long time ago.

He declared to Israel, and to us, through Jeremiah the prophet - *"I have loved thee with an everlasting love."* (Jerermiah 31:3)

An *everlasting love* is an undying, unchanging, irreversible, invincible, sin-forgiving, sickness-healing, soul-delivering and righteousness-restoring kind of love.

It has no beginning and no end...it is eternally settled.

• Paul enhanced this love-revelation even more in Romans 8:38-39 by saying:

> *"For I am persuaded, that neither death, nor life, nor angels, nor principalities, nor powers, nor things present, nor things to come.*
> *Nor height, nor depth, nor any other creature, shall be able to separate us from the love of God, which is in Christ Jesus our Lord."*

We remain *more than conquerors*, more than victors, when we realize that no defeat or spiritual upset can separate us from this great love of God as long as we stay melted, yielded and repentant before His throne... again, *loving not our lives unto death.*

This is the key to the unveiling of the mystery!

There is an infinite bond of divine love between the heart of the Creator and the heart of every son of God and this bond gives us victory in every circumstance.

Under the constant spiritual influence of this redemptive love we are continually kept pure, justified and sanctified in the sight of His majesty, the King of kings.

KEEPING OURSELVES
IN THE LOVE OF GOD

•   For the very reasons mentioned thus far, Jude 21 commands -*"Keep yourselves in the love of God, looking for the mercy of our Lord Jesus Christ unto eternal life."*

This action is not an option. This is a responsibility given by God to every believer.

Another translation interprets this passage a unique way - *"Stay always within the boundaries where God's love can reach and bless you."* (Jude 21 LB)

This *boundary* could be compared to a three-slat fence.

The slats in the fence are **humility, sincerity** (a sincere desire and striving for obedience and righteousness) and **faith.**

Inside of this "fence", these three qualities of the spirit, God's love can always reach us and bless us.

Outside this fence, His love cannot reach us.

All three are complementary and all three are necessary.

We may seem to possess humility and sincerity and yet, if lacking in faith, we end up pushing ourselves out of the victory-imparting flow of the love of God.

The opposite is also true.

We may appear to have a great deal of faith, but lack humility or a sincere desire for holiness, and this too will make us quite unacceptable in God's sight.

But when these three attitudes are married together, they position us unshakably in Christ, where we are constantly being washed in the precious blood of Jesus and in the everlasting river of His grace.

GOD'S ONE-WAY-OR-THE-OTHER PLAN

•   Grace is God's *one-way-or-the-other-plan,* given, as already stated, to the humble, the sincere, and to those who have faith in God.

Grace is *divinely imparted ability,* giving us the supernatural strength to stand and to live above all sin. (I Corinthians 15:10)

But if by chance we falter and fail, grace changes its face, and becomes unmerited love from God, sent to forgive us, restore us and lift us up again.

Grace is therefore an integral part of God's plan to make us *"more than conquerors",* for *one-way-or-the-other* God intends to get us to heaven.

One-way-or-the-other God intends to keep us abiding in the victory until we arrive at our eternal goal!

So, whether grace manifests as divinely imparted ability or as unmerited love, through it our spiritual needs will surely be supplied abundantly...for God did pledge - "My grace is sufficient for thee..."

THE SECRET TO CONSTANT VICTORY

Paul never did say, in Romans 8:35-39, that we would be totally free from distresses, tribulations, persecutions or times of peril; he just let us know that when they come, these things cannot conquer us, for they cannot separate us from the unceasing flow of God's love and grace.

Daniel did not escape from going into the lions' den, but the lions could not conquer him.

Meshach, Shadrach, and Abednego did not escape having to go into the furnace of fire, heated seven times above normal by Nebuchadnezzar, but the fire could not conquer them.

By the world's standard, if you conquer poverty, you are not poor anymore.

If you conquer sickness, you are not sick anymore.

If you conquer depression, you are not depressed anymore.

But we are a different breed of people.

• Whether or not we get our desired answer or miracle does not change the fact that we are *more than conquerors.*

We expect to win every battle.

We expect to always rise above temptation.

We expect to prosper, we expect to be healed, and we expect to have prevailing joy. But if, by chance, these things do not happen, we are still winners...for our God is an expert in making all things work together for our good!

• No wonder the Bible said - *"Now thanks be unto God, which always causeth us to triumph in Christ."* (II Corinthians 2:14)

Again, it is this inherited spiritual position "in Christ" that makes us constant in our winning - for "in Him" we are righteous, "in Him" we are blameless, and "in Him" we have eternal life.

"In Him", and through Him, we have "access by faith into this grace wherein we stand, and rejoice in hope of the glory of God." (Romans 5:2)

Yes, we can really rejoice all the way through any disappointment for we have discovered our true source.

Job was *more than a conqueror* even when he lost everything - his possessions, his sons and daughters, and even his own health - because he was still in contact with God through trust and His great loss could not conquer Him !

He was not depending on anything of the natural to maintain his spirit of victory. His source was Jehovah God!

He was so bold in saying -

> "Naked came I out of my mother's womb, and naked shall I return thither: the Lord gave, and the Lord hath taken away: BLESSED BE THE NAME OF THE LORD."
>
> (Job 1:21)

This was not a statement showing lack of faith. Quite the contrary, Job was declaring in essence that irregardless of how circumstances changed outwardly...that his faith was unshakable.

He put his trust in an undefeatable source of power, and by doing so, he became undefeatable.

By the world's standard he was, for a season, defeated; but by God's standard he was a winner all the way through...yea, more than a winner.

This exemplary patriarch learned a valuable lesson and passed down his spiritual insight to us in the process.

Now we understand.

To *conquer* is to overcome by force (mere human will); but to be *more than a conqueror* is to overcome by faith.

To be a *conqueror* is merely to gain the victory by the power of our own might and goodness.

• But for a New Testament believer, to be **MORE THAN A CONQUEROR** is to accept the victory that has already been secured through Jesus' atoning death.

It is impossible for Satan to win against us now for we have been enlightened.

Experience has begotten this revelation in our hearts and given it life.

Zechariah, the prophet, summed it up quite well when he said - *"not by might, nor by power, but by My Spirit, saith the Lord."* (Zechariah 4:6)

Thank God! We know now where to find everlasting victory... trusting in an everlasting God whose everlasting arms reach out to us with everlasting love.

Through Him and through Him alone we are winners in the absolute sense of the Word...now and forevermore!

• PARTAKERS •

PARTAKERS OF THE AFFLICTIONS OF THE GOSPEL

PARTAKERS OF THE BENEFIT

PARTAKERS OF CHRIST

PARTAKERS OF CHRIST'S SUFFERING

PARTAKERS OF THE CONSOLATION

"And this I do for the gospel's sake, that I might be **PARTAKER** *thereof with you."*

(I Corinthians 9:23)

"But rejoice, inasmuch as ye are PARTAKERS OF CHRIST'S SUF- FERINGS; that, when His glory shall be revealed, ye may be glad also with exceeding joy."

(I Peter 4:13)

"Whereby are given unto us excee- ding great and precious promises: that by these ye might be PARTAKERS OF THE DIVINE NATURE, having es- caped the corruption that is in the world through lust."

(II Peter 1:4)

"Forasmuch then as the children are PARTAKERS OF FLESH AND BLOOD, He also Himself took part of the same.."

(Hebrews 2:14)

"The elders which are among you I exhort, who am also an elder, and a witness of the sufferings of Christ, and also a PARTAKER OF THE GLORY THAT SHALL BE REVEALED."

(I Peter 5:1)

PARTAKERS OF THE
DIVINE NATURE

PARTAKERS OF
FLESH AND BLOOD

PARTAKERS OF THE GLORY
THAT SHALL BE REVEALED

PARTAKERS OF THE
HEAVENLY CALLING

PARTAKERS OF HIS HOLINESS

PARTAKERS OF THE
HOLY GHOST

PARTAKERS OF THE
INHERITANCE

PARTAKERS OF
HIS PROMISE IN CHRIST

*"Wherefore, holy brethren, **PARTAKERS OF THE HEAVENLY CALLING,** consider the Apostle and High Priest of our profession, Christ Jesus..."*

(Hebrews 3:1)

*"For they verily for a few days chastened us after their own pleasure; but He for our profit, that we might be **PARTAKERS OF HIS HOLINESS."***

(Hebrews 12:10)

*"Giving thanks unto the Father, which hath made us meet to be **PARTAKERS OF THE INHERITANCE** of the saints in light."*

(Colossians 1:12)

*"That the Gentiles should be fellow-heirs, and of the same body, and **PARTAKERS OF HIS PROMISE IN CHRIST** by the gospel."*

(Ephesians 3:6)

PARTAKERS

*"And this I do for the gospel's sake, that I might be
PARTAKER thereof with you."*

(I Corinthians 9:23)

• To be a **partaker** is literally *to take part or to share in something, to be a participant or to possess some of the qualities or attributes of a certain person, place or thing.*

The perfect purpose and the perfect pleasure of God, from the very beginning, have centered around a glorious plan to share divinity with humanity.

God determined from the foundation of the world to raise up a family of divine offspring, sons and daughters who could and would *participate* in the activities of God and receive His very *attributes.*

As the planets revolve around the sun, so all of history from the dawn of creation until now, and all the circumstances of our individual lives, revolve around this central purpose of God.

PARTAKERS OF HIS GLORY

In His great intercessory prayer, Jesus declared that every individual member of the church would be a partaker of the same glory that He possessed.

This has always been His ordination for us...a heritage and destiny so sure that He prayed in the past tense when He said -"Father...the glory which Thou gavest Me I have given them." (John 17:1,22)

To fully understand this facet of **OUR GLORIOUS INHERI-TANCE,** we must first realize that the phrase - *the glory of the Lord* - refers to several different aspects of His existence, all of which will ultimately, to one degree or another, be transferred to us.

• *The glory of the Lord* **is primarily the manifestation of His divine personality...the flawless perfection of His character.**

This is *the glory of God* that is intangible in essence but easily seen by viewing the wonderful, the mighty, and the sometimes fearful way that He manifests Himself to the children of men.

In reference to this aspect, the Scripture declares that -"all have sinned, and come short of *the glory of God.*" (Romans 3:23)

In other words, our personalities have all been grossly tainted by the fall of Adam, and we could never, within ourselves, measure up to the absolute excellence of virtue found in the nature of the Creator.

But now, thank God, we are no longer confined within the imprisoning walls of the frailty and deficiency of the human frame.

"For God, who commanded the light to shine out of darkness, hath shined in our hearts, to give the light of the knowledge of *the glory of God* in the face of Jesus Christ." (II Corinthians 4:6)

God's glory now radiates from within, for Jesus now lives within. We have seen the beauty of His character and that beauteous character is now progressively manifesting out of us, for - "we all, with open [unveiled] face beholding as in a glass [a mirror] *the glory of the Lord*, are changed into the same image from glory to glory, even as by the Spirit of the Lord." (II Corinthians 3:18)

• **The glory of God is also descriptive of the anointing that flowed out of Jesus during His earthly sojourn,** for John said - "We beheld *His glory, the glory* as of the only begotten of the Father, full of grace and truth". (John 1:14)

Because Jesus was God manifested in the flesh, He was also the *glory of God* manifested in and through a human form...tangibly revealed in life-transforming words, deliverance power, wondrous works and miraculous creative acts.

Now we have been chosen of God to be vessels of the same...instruments of His divine ability, His grace, His truth and His deliverance power...channels of His creativity.

Our anointing is our *glory*; the terms are interchangeable. We can utilize our *glory* for the benefit of others, ministering grace according to the specific gift of God placed in our lives. Or we can return this *glory* back to the God who gave it...in praise, in prayer, in intercession, in adoration. David said - "O, God, my heart is fixed; I will sing and give praise, even with my *glory*." (Ps. 108:1; 30:12)

• **The glory of God is also the outward radiance of the Spirit, the Shekinah, with which He adorns Himself.**

Jesus, the eternal Dayspring from on high, is also referred to as "the brightness of [God's] *glory*." (Hebrews 1:3)

This descriptive *title* relates most of all to His present celestial state of existence. The Scripture declares that He is the sovereign "King of kings, and Lord of lords; who only hath immortality, dwelling in the light which no man can approach unto; whom no man hath seen, nor can see." (I Timothy 6:15-16)

He covers Himself with light as with a garment. (Psalm 104:2)

He clothes Himself with a resplendent kind of heavenly honor and majesty so glorious that only glorified eyes can behold it in its fullness.

This is *the glory of the Lord*...visibly expressed.

This is also His ultimate gift to every son of God, for it has been promised that the righteous will one day shine like the sun in the kingdom of their Father.

• **When Solomon dedicated the temple, the Scripture tells us that -** *"the glory of the Lord* filled the house." (II Chronicles 7:1)

190

This was the manifest and personal presence of God, the warmth of His love, the splendor of His beauty, breaking forth through the veil into the earthly sphere.

The huge edifice consecrated that day, though magnificent, was still only a temporary and inanimate dwelling place for deity, subject to eventual corruption.

On the contrary, God has reserved the body of Christ as His living and eternal dwelling place...incorruptible and imperishable.

It is only natural for us to conclude, therefore, that God will manifest, express and display His *great glory* in us...in a far more excellent way than He did in Solomon's temple...and He will do so both now and forevermore.

- **The glory of the Lord is also simply His greatness.**

In reference to this aspect the Psalmist wrote - "The heavens declare *the glory of God.*" (Psalm 19:1)

In other words, the greatness - the remarkable size, beauty, and nature - of the cosmos testifies to us continually of the far more transcendent greatness that must be attributed to the One who brought it all into existence to begin with.

- *The glory of the Lord* **is likewise His eminent position of incomparable honor and supreme authority in the universe.**

- *The glory of the Lord* **is furthermore the far-reaching dominion of His kingdom, a kingdom that is never-ending, ever-increasing and infinitely expanding.**

- **But** *the glory of God*, **most of all, is the splendid truth that He has selflessly and lovingly promised to share all of this glory with those who believe in Him and love His name!**

We have undoubtedly been called - "to the obtaining of *the glory* of our Lord Jesus Christ." (II Thessalonians 2:14)

This is - "the mystery which hath been   hid from ages and from generations" - Christ in us, the hope of *glory*. (Colossians 1:26-27)

This blessed *glory-hope* will surely be unveiled in its fullness in the resurrection, but just prior to that spectacular event it is undeniable that the *glory* of the latter house (the church of the last days) will exceed the *glory* of the former. (Haggai 2:9)

This is a solid, dependable and prophetic fact.

The church is presently and progressively emerging in a greater demonstration of supernatural influence and power than it has ever witnessed in all of its history.

Quite possibly, this "greater glory" may be referring to not so much the quality, but rather the quantity, of what God does in the last days.

Then again, the spiritual outpouring and depth may be unprecedented.

Irregardless of how it transpires, though, the fulfillment of this promise will surely be glorious!

• Isaiah revealed the condition of the world and the state of the body of Christ in this hour when he gave the following prophecy:

> *"Arise, shine; for thy light is come, and **the glory of the Lord** is risen upon thee.*
> *For, behold, the darkness shall cover the earth, and gross darkness the people: but the Lord shall arise upon thee, and **His glory** shall be seen upon thee."*
>
> (Isaiah 60:1-2)

On one level this prophecy is speaking of Jerusalem being exalted as the throne of the Lord, the city of the great King, the capital center of the government of God during the Millenium.

But on a lesser level, this is an additional verification that the church will reach a pinnacle of glory during the last few years of this present dispensation.

Though this glory-goal at times seems distant, we know that we are being drawn upward into the promise of the Father.

We will keep climbing, steadily and persistently, until Jesus' prayer is fully answered and God's intentions are fully executed...in every son of God.

• The *"Father of glory"* is totally involved in the process of bringing many sons unto *glory*. (Hebrews 2:10)

• He is also entitled *the Lord of glory, the King of glory,* and *the God of glory,* and He has joyously engendered a divinity-potential and a glory-potential in all His many offspring.

This unspeakable gift, this glory-nature, will manifest completely and irreversibly in us when the Son of man comes - "in the clouds of heaven with power and *great glory."* (Matthew 24:30)

In that day, the decree will be made - "Let the whole earth be filled with His *glory*!" (Psalm 72:19)

• And each one of us will certainly be just as bold as Peter in claiming to be - *"a partaker of the glory that shall be revealed"* - for the great glory He brings with Him will be transferred to us and generated in us forever! This is our birthright and this is our inherited blessing. (I Peter 5:1)

We are recipients of the greatest honor that God could have ever bestowed on any part of creation.

We can sum it up by simply saying - "We are *partakers*!"

ALL THINGS SERVE GOD'S CENTRAL PURPOSE

II Peter 1:4 reveals that we are given exceeding great and precious promises that we might be..."**partakers of the divine nature.**"

Hebrews 12:8-10 exposes the truth that even when we are chastised, of which "all are **partakers**", God chastens us that we might be..."**partakers of His holiness.**"

As we go through fiery trials, bear the burden of lost humanity, and seek daily to crucify the flesh with its affections and lusts, we become - "**partakers of Christ's sufferings**" (I Peter 4:13).

As we learn to trust in the promises of God and manifest the authority we have as God's offspring, we become - "**partakers of the inheritance of the saints in light.**" (Colossians 1:12)

• Therefore, both the negative and the positive aspects of living in this earthly "vale of tears" bring forth the same end result...that is, if we react correctly.

Severe pressures only serve to push us into arising as - "fellow-heirs...and **partakers of His promise in Christ** by the gospel"...if we refuse to become discouraged, defeated, embittered or hardened. (Ephesians 3:6)

Adverse circumstances merely force us into claiming the rights and privileges we have by virtue of our spiritual position "**in Christ**"...if we dare to be bold in "possessing our possessions".

When Satan comes in like a flood we rise, confident of our Word-rights, and lunge at him with the sword of the Lord, speaking the Word and shouting in faith;

"In Christ" we are redeemed - bought back from bondage!

"In Christ" we are pure - even as He is pure!

"In Christ" we are triumphant - for He secured the victory - "It is finished"!

"In Christ" we are justified - reckoned righteous, just as if we had never sinned!

"In Christ" we are blessed with all spiritual blessings in heavenly places - for this bounty has been stored up for us!

"In Christ" we live and move and have our being...partakers of the very life of El Shaddai, the Almighty God!

And this is only a small portion of "His promise in Christ by the gospel"...for the full list of benefits is just as endless as God Himself.

And what is so amazing, when we finally win in this battle of life, God will not just replace our sorrow with happiness...He will actually turn our sorrow into joy! For some of the very things that have created the greatest grief in this world will eventually become the means of knowing the joy of the Lord in its heavenly perfection.

This was and is the inheritance of the firstborn Son.

For Calvary, His greatest suffering, forged the path and paved the road leading to the resurrection of the righteous, the coming in of the kingdom, and the union of this heavenly Bridegroom with His eternal bride...events that will surely prove to be His greatest joy!!

Therefore, it is clear that suffering, sorrow, and, at times, unutterable agony can all end up giving birth to unspeakable joy and inexpressible, infinite ecstasy for those who are chosen.

"And our hope of you is steadfast, knowing, that as ye are **partakers of the suffering**, so shall ye be also of the **consolation**." (II Cor. 1:7)

This is one of the laws of recompense and blessing that God has freely bestowed upon His saints...His ordained, elect and chosen heirs.
This law worked for Jesus. It will also work for us.

PARTAKERS OF THE AFFLICTION, THE SUFFERING, AND THE CONSOLATION

Luke 2:25 states that Simeon was a just and devout man who was patiently waiting for "the consolation of Israel."
This was a unique Jewish term referring to the coming of the Messiah!
Hoping for this eventual appearance was a source of great comfort, a source of great consolation to Israel, even in times of devastating disaster, horrible oppression, and heartrending grief.
This was the light that persisted in their darkest nights.
Now we of the New Covenant era have even greater reason to claim being "**partakers of the consolation**." (II Corinthians 1:7)

Certainly "the God of all comfort" - "comforteth us in all our tribulations", by the Word and by the Spirit, but our greatest source of comfort is knowing that the Messiah will yet come again in splendor and that we will then be changed into His splendorous image.
Having this blessed assurance gives us the spiritual stamina to endure to the very end.

• Paul cautioned Timothy not to be fearful nor ashamed of the testimony of the Lord, but rather to willingly be a "**partaker of the afflictions of the gospel**." (II Timothy 1:8)
Another translation says - "accept your share of the hardship that faithfulness to the gospel entails." (PME)
This command is for us as well.
Though we do not "look" for persecution, opposition, or rejection, we must not be surprised, depressed, or defeated by these things when or if they come.
This "affliction" shared "with the people of God" is the "reproach of Christ" that Moses esteemed "greater riches than the treasures in Egypt." (Hebrews 11:25-26)

We are NOT called upon to endure sickness or the dominion of certain sins or weakness in the flesh, for God has given us power over these things.

But we can certainly expect a barrage of temptations and buffeting tribulations to be hurled our direction by the powers of hell that seek to destroy.

In all these things, though, we have joy unspeakable and a victorious faith that overcomes the world.

• We are more than conquerors for we are "**partakers of the Holy Ghost**" and "**partakers of the benefit.**" (Hebrews 6:4, I Timothy 6:2)

We do not spend our time complaining to the Lord about being "loaded down" with sorrows and pain for He "daily loadeth us with **benefits**" (those things which promote our well-being and are favorable, profitable and advantageous). (Psalm 68:19)

The Psalmist David gave us insight into this area of our heritage when he wrote:

> *"Bless the Lord, O my soul, and forget not all his benefits:*
> *Who forgiveth all thine iniquities; who healeth all thy diseases.*
> *Who redeemeth thy life from destruction; who crowneth thee with lovingkindness and tender mercies.*
> *Who satisfieth thy mouth with good things; so that thy youth is renewed like the eagles."*
>
> (Psalm 103:2-5)

• This too, is a beautiful way of describing *"the land of red-purple"* - *"the land of oil olive"* - the royal realm of the anointing in which we live as sons of God.

GOD DELIGHTS IN SHARING

• God could have easily accomplished all the supernatural works that He has manifested in the realm of time without the aid of human flesh.

He could have parted the Red Sea without Moses stretching forth his rod. He could have effortlessly slain Goliath without the help of David and his sling.

He could have easily conquered those thousand Philistines without Samson swinging the jawbone of an ass.

He could have caused the walls of Jericho to collapse, in a moment's time, without the aid of Joshua and the people of Israel shouting aloud.

But God wanted to include His people in the blessedness and rapture

195

of experiencing the supernatural. He did not choose to exclude them and reserve this delight only unto Himself.

Jehovah has always desired partakers, not spectators!

This omnipotent Lord of all rejoiced to see Moses, David, Samson, Joshua and an innumerable host of others feel that glorious surge of divine power and authority flowing through them as they yielded to His purpose and plan.

This is simply the great love of the heavenly Father generated toward the members of His eternal family...for any father, who truly loves his offspring, also longs to see them grow into maturity and develop their potential abilities.

By doing so, they walk in his footsteps, reflecting his likeness.

• In Acts, Chapter 10, we read of Cornelius, a devout, God-fearing man, receiving an angelic visitation during prayer.

The angel directed Cornelius to contact Peter and invite him to his home to preach the Word to them.

Surely God could have allowed this heaven-sent angel, who flawlessly started the work, to continue talking and give a full explanation of the gospel himself.

But God's greater desire and perfect will was to include His apostle, so that Peter might experience the ecstatic thrill of having the Holy Ghost confirm his words and fall on those who heard the message.

• Again, it must be reemphasized that God's great joy is to share with us that which He could easily do Himself, so that we might rejoice together with Him, and feel all the more accepted, included and loved.

And if this is true in this earthly realm, and it is, then we wonder what phenomenal, creative works God will use us to perform in heavenly realms above...for Jesus is the same yesterday, today and forever.

The pattern of His character remains unalterable.

If God has chosen to manifest His power through weak, erring human flesh to the glorious degree that He has, then what kind of spectacular authority will He manifest through the saints of God when they are glorified, perfected and immortal!

Only God knows...

But our spirits soar on the wings of worship as we speculate concerning the future, knowing that we have been forever lifted out of the commonplace and the ordinary.

We have been chosen and elected for the extraordinary, the exceptional, and the supernatural.

This is to be expected for the Bible declares that we are -"**partakers of the heavenly calling.**" (Hebrews 3:1)

THE GREAT MYSTERY OF SPIRITUAL
IDENTIFICATION

• According to Paul's writings, we as sons of God *partake -"of the root and fatness of the olive tree."* (Romans 11:17)

The *olive tree* is Israel.

The *root* of this olive tree is Jehovah-God and His ordination that "brought forth" each one of the patriarchs and has "brought us forth" as well.

The *fatness* of this olive tree is the blessing of God and the blessing of Abraham, (the bountiful outpouring of abundant provisions, spiritual and natural, that come when this rich oil of God's presence is poured into our lives).

We are definitely a part of Israel, if we have been born again.

And we are definitely children of Abraham by faith in Jesus Christ.

Therefore we have been made **partakers** "**of the root and the fatness of the olive tree.**"

We were chosen and elected of God before the foundation of the world and are therefore **partakers of the root.**

We presently have abundant life in the Spirit and we are therefore **partakers of the fatness.**

We know that we are **partakers** of all the blessings that Abraham purchased through his obedience, but even more so, we are **partakers** of all that Jesus obtained through His obedience and His submission to the will of the Father.

• This is the marvellous miracle of spiritual identification, and this is God's gift to us.

We identify with Abraham.

We identify with Israel.

But most wonderful of all, we identify with Jesus - who was "the seed of Abraham" - and become partakers of the **glorious inheritance** bestowed on Him.

• And it must be said, that this has all been made possible because Jesus was willing to become a partaker first.

He identified with us in our weakness that we, in turn, might identify with His great strength.

Hebrews 2:14 declares - "forasmuch then as the children are **partakers of flesh and blood,** He also Himself likewise took part [became a partaker] of the same."

He became one with us in temptation.

He became one with us in frailty and weakness.

He became a curse for us, that we might be blessed in Him.

He became a partaker of the Adam-nature that we might become **partakers of the divine nature.**

He was made to be sin for us "that we might be made the righteousness of God in Him." (II Corinthians 5:21)

In light of this great redemption-revelation, in gratitude, we must separate ourselves from this present, evil world.

• We have been invited to feast at a heavenly table, and we know for certain that we - "cannot be **partakers of the Lord's table** and of the table of devils." (I Corinthians 10:21)

• The Bible said that we will only be made -"**partakers of Christ**, if we hold the beginning of our confidence steadfast unto the end." (Hebrews 3:14)

Our *confidence* was not in the flesh at the outset of our relationship with God, neither can it be now.

We must keep our *confidence* in the finished work of Calvary and the promise that through the blood of Jesus we inherit a standing of righteousness in the presence of the Father.

We must keep our confidence in the mercy of God and the infallible truth of His Word.

We must maintain unwavering trust in His promise of everlasting love toward us.

We must realize that we will never win this great spiritual conflict through self-righteousness or humanistic success plans.

We identify with Jesus.

We sincerely devote ourselves to Him.

This was *the beginning of our confidence*...so this will surely be *the conclusion of the whole matter.*

This simple faith will carry us all the way through to eternity.

This child-like trust will ultimately cause us to *partake of all that God is and all that God has.*

THE SUPERNATURAL TRANSFER

• We know that everything God has done in the past, in and through the anointed of the Lord, has simply served to build a bridge of promise, leading the church of the last days to a glorious culmination.

All that God did in and through Abraham, Isaac, Israel, the prophets, the early church, the apostles, Peter, James and John, and all his other vessels, has a profound influence and effect on us - right now!

• Paul unveiled this mystery when he said - *"ye all are partakers of my grace."* (Philippians 1:7)

The grace of God is the unmerited love and unearned favor of God.

The grace of God is also divinely imparted ability and the activity of God in a person's life.

• So, when Paul said that we are *partakers of his grace*...he was really saying that all the activity of God in his life and all the divine ability given to him is being spiritually transferred to us now.

We read of the depth of mercy bestowed on him, and faith is built in us to receive the same.

We read of the miracles he received, and we believe God can do it again.

We read the epistles and his revelation-wisdom is imparted to us.

The same life-giving, infinite river of wisdom that flowed into Paul has continued its journey, flowing out from Paul into those his ministry touches.

Truth that took Paul years to uncover becomes ours in only a few moments.

We become *partakers* of all that God did in His life.

This grace is passed on to us through the Word and through the Spirit.

• If this be true, then it is also logical to assume in like manner that...

We are *partakers* of Abraham's faith.

We are *partakers* of Jacob's perseverance.

We are *partakers* of Joseph's faithfulness.

We are *partakers* of Moses' meekness.

We are *partakers* of Joshua's boldness.

We are *partakers* of Gideon's courage.

We are *partakers* of David's humility and the sure mercies he received (a man after God's heart)!

We are *partakers* of Samson's strength and the high level of faith for restoration to which he attained!

We are *partakers* of the patience of Job and the wisdom of Solomon.

We are *partakers* of the miracles of Elijah, the revelations of Daniel, and the uncompromising spirit of Meshach, Shadrach and Abednego.

In fact, we are *partakers* of ALL that God did in the Old Covenant and we are *partakers* of ALL that Jesus has done in the church during the past two thousand years.

• We are presently sharing in, identifying with, receiving from, and *partaking* of, all the gifts, anointings, and callings that God has bestowed upon His elect of every age.

The grace of God applied to the lives of all those gone before us, and those anointed around us now, has been heaped together and literally poured out on us now.

Beloved, seeing that we know these things, what manner of men and women ought we to be!

No wonder the latter day church will reach a summit of glory - for the sum total of all the divine activity given to the people of God throughout the ages will blossom in us now, in ever-unfolding perfections.

Glory to God in the highest!

What a wonderful day it is in which to live!

O, let us arise and shine, for we are blessed beyond measure!

WE ARE GOD'S FAMILY OF **PARTAKERS**...NOW AND FOREVERMORE!

THE RANSOMED

THE RANSOMED
OF THE LORD

"*Was it not Thou who dried up the sea, the waters of the great deep; who made the depths of the sea a pathway [for* **THE RANSOMED** *to pass over].*"

(Isaiah 51:10 NAS, AV)

"*And* **THE RANSOMED OF THE LORD** *shall return, and come to Zion with songs and everlasting joy upon their heads: they shall obtain joy and gladness, and sorrow and sighing shall flee away.*"

(Isaiah 35:10)

THE RANSOMED

THE RANSOMED OF THE LORD

> *"Was it not Thou who dried up the sea, the waters of the great deep; who made the depths of the sea a pathway [for **THE RANSOMED** to pass over]."*
>
> (Isaiah 51:10 NAS, AV)

The term *redeemed* and the term *ransomed* are somewhat the same scripturally and normally interchangeable.

In fact, two Hebrew words - *gaal* and *padah* - are translated both ways in different scriptures.

But there is a unique and profound revelation that runs through the Scripture, like a vein of silver, using the word - *ransom.*

It is this rich and enriching concept that we now intend to explore.

THE FOUNDATION OF THE REVELATION

•   *A **ransom** is a price paid to recover a captured person or thing out of imprisoning hands. In simple terms, it is the cost of redemption.*

The first biblical reference to the word *ransom* is found in Exodus 30:11-16. In this Scripture passage God gave explicit directions to Moses, saying:

> *"When thou takest the sum of the children of Israel after their number, then shall they give every man **a ransom for his soul** unto the Lord, when thou numberest them; that there be no plague among them, when thou numberest them."*
>
> (Exodus 30:12)

The ransom price was to be "half a shekel after the shekel of the sanctuary" (about 32 cents in modern day currency). (Exodus 30:13)

It was only demanded of able-bodied men, twenty years and upward, not women, minors or the elderly. Moreover, God said - "The rich shall not give more, and the poor shall not give less than half a shekel, when they give an offering unto the Lord, to make atonement for your souls." (Exodus 30:15)

This "atonement money" was to be used for the "service of the tabernacle of the congregation; that it may be a memorial unto the children of Israel." (Exodus 30:16) Some say this became a yearly ordinance.

•   **Certain significant New Covenant realities are hidden in this Old**

Covenant symbol.

To be *"numbered"* among the everlasting sons of God - to be included in the everlasting family of God - we must be *ransomed* from the *plaguing* effects of sin.

Those included in this elite group, once glorified, will all be eternally *mature* in God - neither aged nor undeveloped, but fully perfected in Christ.

Also significant is the point that all men, whether rich or poor, intellectual or illiterate, good or bad, require *the same ransom price*...for God is no respector of persons.

Furthermore, the "price" paid for our *ransom* also, in a spiritual sense, provides for the upkeep or maintenance of "God's tabernacle". For we are that *living tabernacle* and we depend on the purchase price of the blood of Jesus to preserve us both now and forevermore.

Whenever we claim that precious blood we *memorialize* what Jesus did years ago. In a far more perfect way, we celebrate, over and over, the availability of the *"atonement for our souls"* - meaning *the covering for sin and the cancelling out of sin that provides that blessed state of being reconciled to God.*

• Even under the Old Will, some of those who participated in that covenant realized the insufficiency of the various rituals and ordinances it contained.

In Psalm 49, we find David admitting that -

> *"No man can redeem the life of another or give to God a ransom for him - the ransom for a life is costly, no payment is ever enough - that he should live on forever and not see decay.*

(Psalm 49:7-9 NIV)

But thank God! We need not stop at such a pessimistic declaration.

For we are no longer living under the shadowy veil of Old Testament symbolism. We are basking in the brilliant and excellent light of New Covenant realities.

We can be forthright in announcing that:

> *"...there is one God, and one mediator between God and men, the man Christ Jesus; who gave Himself a **ransom** for all, to be testified in **due time**."*

(I Timothy 2:5-6)

This *ransom price* is much more than just sufficient; this *ransom* is abundantly glorious....for through it we shall *live on forever*.

Therefore, let us lift our voices...for it is definitely *due time*.

Let us boldly *testify* to this enslaved and needy generation that there is endless hope in Jesus!

THE PECULIAR RANSOM FOR ISRAEL

Isaiah 43:3-4 makes a strange and moving assertation about the *ransoming* of Israel from the threat of opposing Gentile nations:

> *"For I am the Lord thy God, the Holy One of Israel,*
> *thy Saviour: I gave Egypt for thy ransom, Ethopia and*
> *Seba for thee.*
> *Since thou wast precious in My sight, thou hast been*
> *honourable and I have loved thee: therefore will I give*
> *men for thee, and people for thy life."*

(Isaiah 43:3-4)

This passage is quite possibly a reference to Sennacherib's attempted invasion of Judea and Jerusalem, for right at the critical moment his attention was apparently diverted to Egypt, Ethiopia and Seba. The Assyrians under his command were compelled to turn from the holy city in order to crush these other nations they considered a greater threat. Thus, the Egyptians, Ethiopians, and Sabeans who were destroyed became a *ransom* price paid for the rescue of God's people.

• Some Bibles scholars feel that this portion of Scripture serves as a general revelation-statement concerning all the many times God has supernaturally subdued the enemies of Israel in order to rescue His people. This is especially true concerning the original defeat of the Egyptians in the days of Moses.During that notable event, God revealed His willingness to actually sacrifice thousands of Egyptians for the sake of Abraham's offspring. (Again - *"Since thou wast precious in My sight...therefore will I give men for thee, and people for thy life."*)

And it is true that God did it, not only to free the Jews from the physical bondage they suffered as slaves under Egyptian taskmasters, but to progressively liberate them as well from the enslaving doubts, fears, and deceptions of the fallen Adam nature.

God set the stage well in advance; from the very foundation of the world He foresaw the opposition and ordained the necessary intervention that would bring about the deliverance of His chosen people.

A cloud of thick, choking, desert dust must have billowed high into the sky as Pharaoh's army of footmen and his "charioteers of the sun" moved swiftly across the sandy dunes and arid plains in furious pursuit of Abraham's seed.

Everything looked totally hopeless.

The Jews lifted their voices, wailing in despair.

They fearfully cried to Moses - "Because there were no graves in Egypt, hast thou taken us away to die in the wilderness?" (Exodus 14:11)

But God ignored their ignorance and unbelief. Centuries of fearfully recoiling at the crack of the Egyptian whip had broken their spirits and

205

God understood.

At the command of Jehovah, Moses stretched out his rod. The waters miraculously parted and God's people went through on dry ground.

The enemy still tried to pursue, but God marvelously spun their chariot wheels off and fought against them.

Moses stretched forth his hand and the waters came crashing in again. The helpless Egyptians were crushed and drowned under the frothing waves that seemed to churn themselves with the very indignation of God.

The women of Israel began jubilantly dancing before the Lord, singing - "The Lord is a man of war...He hath triumphed gloriously: the horse and his rider hath He thrown into the sea." (Exodus 15:1,3)

What a change in attitude! Through the death of the Egyptians, a spirit of victory and the ability to believe surged upward in the hearts of the Jews (and in our hearts too as we read the account).

• **In a very fearful and wonderful way, Egypt was amazingly a sacrifice unto the faith of all God's elect...both then and now.**

Through their death, we have all been benefited.

Through their destruction, we have all been edified.

God, therefore, sacrificed one group of people that others might be overtaken by His blessings.

Because we are *precious in the sight of the Almighty*, He has greatly honored us this way...that we might enter into life.

This is definitely part of the costly and heart-gripping *ransom price* that has been paid for the full redemption of our souls.

It almost seems that in the end result, Pharaoh and his army existed so that God might defeat them, proving the exceeding greatness of His power toward His elect.

"For the Scripture saith unto Pharaoh, Even for this same purpose have I raised thee up, that I might shew My power in thee, and that My name might be declared throughout all the earth." (Romans 9:17)

No wonder the Bible protested that "all things are for [our] sakes." (II Corinthians 4:15)

How thankful we should be and how very careful we should be never to draw back after the pattern of Israel's rebellion.

For after being rescued from Egypt, it was not long before they counted God's favor a small thing.

They stiffened their necks and hardened their hearts against His will.

"They rebelled, and vexed His Holy Spirit: therefore He was turned to be their enemy, and He fought against them." (Isaiah 63:10)

A journey that should have taken only two or three weeks lasted forty long years instead.

The Jews murmured and serpents destroyed them.

They complained about the manna, begging for flesh to eat, and grievous plagues came their way.

They denied the Holy One who bought them, compelling Aaron to make a golden calf for them to worship. In supposed worship of this false god, they indulged in orgies of lust, and twenty-three thousand died. Some were swallowed up by the earth; others were consumed by the fire of God falling from heaven. Their carcasses littered the desert sands.

Only two men, Joshua and Caleb, out of the original hundreds of thousands who were twenty years of age or older, made it into the Promised Land. The rest perished!

Our hearts burn within us at the remembrance of these disastrous events and we are compelled to question:

Why did they live?

But what is even more important - *Why did they die?*

What was the purpose of their existence?

Paul gave us an invaluable answer when he said - "all these things happened to them as examples - as object lessons to us - to warn us against doing the same things; they were written down so that we could read about them and learn from them in these last days, as the world nears its end." (I Corinthians 10:11 LB)

THE SAVOUR OF DEATH UNTO LIFE

• **Initially, Egypt was a sacrifice unto the faith of Israel, but that chosen generation, having rejected God's covenant of blessing, became a sacrifice unto the faith of all of God's elect who would come after them.**

Part of the reason that the God of all justice brought judgment on the rebellious Israelites was to save us from the same fate and to teach us the terribleness of sin. The thousands that perished also became *a ransom price, ransoming* God's people to come out from the influence of sin and the sting of rebellion. Proverbs 21:18 confirms this astonishing truth declaring:

> *"The wicked shall be a **ransom** for the righteous,*
> *and the transgressor for the upright."*

In a deep spiritual sense, the Israelites who were slain in the wilderness unwittingly and tragically became a living sacrifice unto us...*the savour of death unto life.*

They became a compelling, convicting and convincing witness from the pages of history that we should fear God enough to seek only those things which tend toward life.

(And it is a thought-provoking truth, that if we instead live a life of lustful rebellion, on the day of Judgment, not only will we be chargeable to God, but also to the twenty-three thousand who were destroyed to prove God's hatred of this type of sin).

And the list goes on and on.

• **When Goliath fell before David, the slain giant became a sacrifice to the service of the faith of God's elect.**

After beholding the defeat of the Philistine champion with just a slung-out stone, doubtful, cringing, cowardly Israelites were suddenly transformed into men of bold faith and resolute courage.

It is a wondrous thing that through one man's death their faith soared to greater heights than possibly they had ever known.

But not only were they edified - we are also. For every time we hear this glorious story preached we are lifted up to a higher realm of faith, and we believe more fully that our enemy Satan is an easily defeated foe.

We can definitely state, therefore, that in a certain sense, Goliath died for us. His blood was spilled for us. Yes, Goliath was a *ransom price* (for it is written - *"the wicked shall be a ransom for the righteous"*).

Through his death, we are greatly strengthened in the Lord.

• **Or take for example another instance when the Philistines came against Israel.** (I Samuel 14)

Saul and his army had been making relatively little progress in withstanding the enemy, but Jonathan, his son, dared to say - "there is no restraint to the Lord to save by many or by few."

Along with his faithful armorbearer, he walked right up to the Philistine garrison, though he was greatly outnumbered. About twenty Philistine sentries fell that day before Jonathan's sword.

This courageous prince of Israel did his part to the utmost, then God did the rest. An earthquake shook the whole area and the strangest thing happened.

The entire Philistine army seemed to melt away as they insanely began to attack one another, apparently under the influence of evil spirits released on them at the sovereign will of God.

Why did this great Philistine army exist? Why did they live and why did they die?

Think of all the human effort that it took (all the education and military training, all the natural provision, etc.) to get them to that one moment in time, and that one place of destiny.

Then, for the first time in their lives they came into a direct confrontation with the Almighty, only to be destroyed with one sweep of His hand.

They were a *ransom price* sacrificed on an altar of deliverance for God's people over three thousand years ago.

Yet even now we still receive great blessings from that startling event...for through such tragedy and triumph we behold the greatness of our God and His potential power toward us.

• **Before we go any further, it must be said that God did not create any of these individuals just for the sole purpose of destroying them.** Pharaoh could have repented. The Philistines could have repented. But they did not and the Creator knew their attitude would be such in advance. So from the beginning of creation God expertly planned to use all the opposition to further His divine purpose, even the demands of justice.

And this is still God's way of doing things!

• **Consider a New Testament example...Ananias and Sapphira** (Acts 5) who dropped dead at Peter's feet because they lied to the Holy Ghost? The Bible declared that as a result - *"great fear came on all the church."*

So we see that they too were made to be *a ransom* - a sacrificial example given to teach the church God's hatred of deceitfulness, lest any others fall into the same horrid trap.

• **Are not all of these examples perfect proof of an eternal truth?** Do they not affirm that God even uses the death and destruction of the wicked to produce life in His own?

In this area alone, the memory of the wicked becomes *the savour of death unto life* - ever attesting to the fact that our God can bring light out of darkness and reap good out of that which can seemingly yield no goodness at all.

THE SAVOUR OF LIFE UNTO LIFE

• If this ransom revelation can be viewed from a negative perspective, it can be observed working in a positive sense as well.

For instance, the prophets of old were living sacrifices unto our faith - but they were *the savour of life unto life* - "Unto whom it was revealed, that not unto themselves, but unto us they did minister the things, which are now reported unto you by them that have preached the gospel." (I Peter 1:12)

The memory of their message, their many sacrifices, and their exemplary lives has a profound effect on us now...challenging us to walk in their footsteps and measure up to their standard.

The patriarch Job became for all of time - "an example of suffering affliction and of patience." (James 5:10)

Abraham became an example of persevering faith.

Moses became an example of a once defeated man trying again at the will of God and attaining success.

Elijah became an example of uncompromising holiness.

Jonah became an example of the power of restoration grace.

And John the Baptist testifies to us all the passion and consecration that we should have in preparing the way of the Lord.

All of these things minister the life of God to us now.

Then, as we proceed into the New Covenant, we find the apostle Paul becoming a living sacrifice unto us, along with all the other apostles and disciples, *the savour of life unto life*, for he states... *"if I be offered upon the sacrifice and service of your faith, I joy, and rejoice with you all."* (Philippians 2:17)

209

And surely this is also true with respect to all the other early disciples and apostles who laid the foundation of the New Covenant Age.

Even later individuals like Francis of Assisi, Martin Luther, John Wesley, George Whitefield, Jonathen Edwards and countless others sacrificed their lives to promote the work of God in us, that we might be made stable and strong.

The work of faith in them is passed on to us.

The work of hope in them is passed on to us.

The work of love in them is passed on to us.

We are made partakers of all the victories, all the struggles, all the truth, all the consecration, and all the anointings of all the righteous men and women of God who have gone before us.

• AND IN THIS WONDERFUL SENSE, EVEN **THE RIGHTEOUS BECOME A RANSOM** FOR ALL THOSE RIGHTEOUS ONES WHO WALK IN THEIR FOOTSTEPS.

Even the positive and faith-building example of those who are obedient *ransoms* those who are presently upright from the possibility of ever erring or falling into disobedience again.

For we long to inherit a reward similar to theirs.

Again, this is not the savour of death - this is the savour of life unto life!

THE HEART-GRIPPING CONCLUSION

We are overwhelmed at the unveiling of such a breathtaking mystery.

We feel strangely surrounded...compassed about with a great cloud of witnesses.

Witnesses of life and witnesses of death.

• Witnesses of faith in God and witnesses of the fear of God...BUT ALL ARE WITNESSES OF THE POWER OF GOD.

Therefore, we dare not falter. We dare not even consider failing.

• Our position in the plan of God has been bought with much blood...and not only the precious, redeeming blood of Jesus, but also the blood of all who have died sacrificial deaths before us, both the wicked and the righteous.

Their very existence has played an important part, both negative and positive, in the plan and purpose of God concerning His elect.

In so many ways, their lives forged a way through this desolate wilderness of sin. Some were destroyed and some emerged triumphant, but all, in a certain spiritual sense, were servants unto this last generation - *sacrifices unto our faith.*

God forbid that we be slothful!

God forbid that we be unappreciative!

God forbid that we even think of backsliding or partaking of the evil of this world! How dare we be at ease in Zion! Woe unto us if we are! For too great a price has been paid to make us strong in faith and zealous in spirit!

We cannot fail those who have gone before us, nor those who will follow after.

• David would not drink of the water from the well of Bethlehem (water that his men of valor broke through enemy lines to secure). Rather, he gratefully and respectfully poured it on the ground saying -"Be it far from me, O Lord, that I should do this: is not this the blood of the men that went in jeopardy of their lives?" (II Samuel 23:17)

Even so we dare not take the promises of God lightly, nor drink in His blessings without regarding the awesome purchase price that has been paid. Over and over we must ask ourselves the pertinent question...How many have had to die to self spiritually, or how many have even had to die naturally, that the life of God might manifest in us now?

We must be mindful of the destruction of the wicked...who were destroyed not only for their sakes, but also for ours.

We must be true to the sacrifices of the righteous and the crosses they had to bear. Their existence in this world, and in some cases their very blood, became a *ransom price* for us.

We dare not trample their blood.

• **Above all, we dare not trample underfoot, nor lightly consider the precious blood of Jesus - that perfect and ultimate ransom price. (Be it far from us, O Lord, that we should do such a thing!)**

We know that Jesus has *ransomed* us - *bought us back* - from the power of sin, the authority of sickness, the dominion of self, and even the horror of death.

For long ago He promised:

> *"I will **ransom** them from the power of the grave; I will redeem them from death: O death, I will be thy plagues; O grave, I will be thy destruction: repentance shall be hid from Mine eyes."*

(Hosea 13:14)

• Hallelujah! Jesus never has and never will *repent* of fighting our battles for us. Neither will he show compassion to the enemies that war against our souls.

The victorious, risen Christ has succeeded in loosing us from the authority of fear, depression, rebellion, pride, lust, despair and all the other negative attributes of the fallen Adam-flesh and *He will not repent*!!

We may still fight battles in these areas, but we need not be enslaved to the same any longer.

• We are no longer under the harsh, oppressive rule of the wicked one - "For the Lord hath redeemed Jacob, and *ransomed* him from the hand of him that was stronger than he." (Jeremiah 31:11)

Because of the intervention of the "Messenger", "the Angel of the Lord", and "the One among a thousand" - when we die, the Father will graciously declare over each one of His redeemed:

> *"Deliver him from going down to the pit: I have found a* *ransom."*

(See Job 33:23-25)

This is the great victory that Jesus has wrought for us...a major part of the "milk and honey" inheritance available for us in this spiritual "Land of Promise".

We are now established as winners, not losers, and this is something that greatly pleases the heart of the Saviour.

For being a sacrifice to the service of our faith this way was the very reason for Jesus' incarnation, who "came not to be ministered unto, but to minister, AND TO GIVE HIS LIFE A **RANSOM** FOR MANY." (Matthew 20:28)

Moreover, without Jesus' ransom price being paid, all other "ransoms" would have been totally useless, totally futile, totally vain.

But thank God, this is not the case, for Jesus was faithful to His cause.

He did not fail those whose very existence utterly depended on his obedience to the plan of God.

He sanctified Himself that we might be sanctified as well.

He fought the good fight of faith that we might emerge triumphant.

Now God expects a similar selfless attitude on our part.

For as sons of God, we are called not only to be ransomed, but to present ourselves as a ransom for others.

I John 3:16 declares:

> *"Hereby perceive we the love of God, because He laid* *down His life for us: and we ought to lay down our lives for* *the brethren."*

This is the challenge and what a challenge it is!

This is the final conclusion and what a conclusion we have reached!!

For just knowing these things has worked a valuable work, an increase of awed respect deep within our hearts.

We feel more than ever the utter seriousness of our call.

We can no longer take our inheritance lightly, nor speak of it with the slightest lack of reverence.

How sacred, how very sacred, a gift it is from God, to be able to say...WE ARE **THE RANSOMED OF THE LORD**!!

SERVANTS

"And there shall be no more curse: but the throne of God and of the Lamb shall be in it; and His SERVANTS shall serve Him.

And they shall see His face; and His name shall be in their foreheads"

(Revelation 22:3-4)

"But now being made free from sin, and become SERVANTS TO GOD, ye have your fruit unto holiness, and the end everlasting life."

(Romans 6:22)

"...as ye have yielded your members servants to uncleanness and to iniquity unto iniquity; even so now yield your members SERVANTS TO RIGH-TEOUSNESS unto holiness."

(Romans 6:19)

"And I saw another angel ascending from the east, having the seal of the living God: and he cried with a loud voice to the four angels, to whom it was given to hurt the earth and the sea.

Saying, Hurt not the earth, neither the sea, nor the trees, till we have sealed THE SERVANTS OF OUR GOD in their foreheads."

(Revelation 7:2-3)

"Not with eyeservice, as menplea-sers; but as THE SERVANTS OF CHRIST, doing the will of God from the heart."

(Ephesians 6:6)

· SERVANTS TO GOD ·

SERVANTS TO
RIGHTEOUSNESS

THE SERVANTS OF GOD

THE SERVANTS OF CHRIST

THE SERVANTS OF
JESUS CHRIST

GOOD AND FAITHFUL
SERVANTS

FAITHFUL AND WISE
SERVANTS

ISRAEL HIS SERVANT

HIS SERVANT JACOB

THE SERVANTS OF THE LORD

· HIS SERVANT ·

*"Paul and Timotheus, **THE SERVANTS OF JESUS CHRIST,** to all the saints in Christ Jesus... "*
(Philippians 1:1)

*"...Well done, **GOOD AND FAITHFUL SERVANT;** thou hast been faithful over a few things, I will make thee ruler over many things..."*
(Matthew 25:23)

"No weapon that is formed against thee shall prosper; and every tongue that shall rise against thee in judgment, thou shalt condemn. This is the heritage of ***THE SERVANTS OF THE LORD,*** *and their righteousness is of Me, saith the Lord."*
(Isaiah 54:17)

*"Remember these, O Jacob and Israel; for thou art **MY SERVANT:** I have formed thee; thou art My servant: O Israel, thou shalt not be forgotten of Me."*
(Isaiah 44:21)

SERVANTS

"And there shall be no more curse: but the throne of God and of the Lamb shall be in it; and His SERVANTS shall serve Him.

And they shall see His face; and His name shall be in their foreheads."

(Revelation 22:3-4)

• A **servant** is defined as being...*one who serves others, one that performs duties about the person or home of a master, or a personal employer.*

It can also mean in a higher sense...*one who loses sight of self in order to aid, assist, help or promote a certain cause or the good of others.*

To the undeveloped, immature, or unspiritual child of God, this *title-position*, at first glance, may seem somewhat unattractive and unappealing.

Yet a thorough search of this calling and election will surely lead any heaven-bound pilgrim into the depths of what it means to follow Jesus and the heights of what it means to truly be like the firstborn Son of God, conformed to His wondrous image.

JESUS - THE EXEMPLARY SERVANT

• **In this particular calling, as usual, Jesus serves as our Forerunner, our prime example.**

He came for the purpose of filling up the inheritance position of a servant.

This was His ordination from the foundation.

In fact, the Old Testament often foretells the coming of the Messiah using this very terminology.

The Father spoke through Isaiah prophesying of the visitation of the Son of God, saying - "Behold My *servant,* whom I uphold; Mine elect, in whom My soul delighteth; I have put My spirit upon Him: He shall bring forth judgment to the Gentiles." (Isaiah 42:1, see also 49:3)

And in the New Testament Jesus questioned His disciples - "For whether is greater, he that sitteth at meat, or he that *serveth*? is not he that sitteth at meat? but I am among you as he that *serveth*." (Luke 22:27)

So we see clearly that this was a major part of Jesus' calling and character.

This heaven-sent Lord of lords was far different than the people expected Him to be...astoundingly and beautifully different, so much so that the Jewish traditionalists had a difficult time relating to Him.

He never lustily sought after earthly fame or fleshly glory, as men who aspire to be leaders almost always do.

Quite the contrary, He fled from it and strove hard to make Himself "of no reputation."

Jesus clearly did not come to dominate men in the brutish, steel-fisted way that the world considers normal.

Instead He simply came to serve.

Philippians 2:7 declares that "**He took upon Him THE FORM OF A SERVANT, and was made in the likeness of men.**"

Other translations of the same passage say that He "stripped Himself of every advantage", He "made Himself nothing" and He "emptied Himself, taking the form of a bond-servant" and "assuming the nature of a slave." (PME, NIV, NAS, NEB)

And as a slave He was bound with chains of compassion to the hurting and the needy, so that His only reason for existence was to give hope to the hopeless and help to the helpless.

In His own words, the Lord declared to His followers that - "the Son of Man came not to be ministered unto, but to *minister*..." (Matthew 20:28)

Though He was God incarnate, the King of all creation, He never regarded it an insult to His divinity to be born in a lowly stable or buried in a borrowed grave.

Though He was the flawless Holy One of Israel, He never reckoned it demeaning to His character to be surrounded with the drunks, harlots, publicans, and sinners, who came so hungry to hear His Word...for He came to administer grace to the lowest of the low.

Though He owned all things, He never considered it beneath His stature to sleep on the ground, and He was not complaining when He said - "The foxes have holes, and the birds of the air have nests; but the Son of Man hath not where to lay His head." (Matthew 8:20)

Though He alone could claim the *title* of being the *first* and the last, still, He never considered it a threat to His position to consistently put others *first.*

His was not a life of constantly grappling for advantage, possessions, or self-gratification.

He sincerely loved the joy of serving mankind and meeting needs was altogether and always the passion of His heart and the pleading of His prayer life.

Therefore, truer words could never be spoken than these...**Jesus did not come to take; He came to give.**

As the sun rises daily, never intending to *take* away, but always purposing to *give* light, warmth and life to the earth, so also Jesus, the Sun of

218

righteousness, arose almost two thousand years ago with healing in His wings, ready to freely shine forth deliverance and restoration on every believing heart.

He sacrificed and gave His life as a servant in order to transfer and impart His life to those who dare to serve Him.

And because the firstborn Son has plainly and mercifully proved Himself to be the servant of all, are we not constrained with gratitude and compelled by devotion to lift Him up even higher and worship Him all the more fervently as the everlasting Lord, Master and Judge of all!

So there is no doubt: His self-imposed servitude has ended up reflecting as a mirror the greatness of His glory in superb excellence.

And in an ever deepening way, it all redounds to His praise!

THE SPIRIT TO SERVE

One of Jesus' chief concerns was the hope of bringing to birth in His disciples this same kind of *"spirit to serve"* that He possessed.

He knew that carnal pride, greed, jealousy and rivalry among His representatives could render the work of God relatively fruitless, so He went to extreme measures at times to prevent such cancerous attitudes from taking root.

He counted this lesson to be learned so important that in the last few hours of His ministry He even set about the lowly, menial task of washing His disciples' feet.

And when He did, He was careful to remind them - *"I have given you an example, that ye should do as I have done to you."* (John 13:15)

Through this living sermon Jesus was beautifully exemplifying and emphasizing the fact that we should do our utmost never to hostilely criticize, condemn, judge or accuse those who are truly brethren, but rather always be quick to forgive and ready to uphold, strengthen, pray for, and lovingly exhort one another in the name of the Lord. By maintaining attitudes such as these we are, in essence, washing and cleansing one another from the contaminating influence of this world.

Yes, we are called to be our brother's keeper, for we have not inherited the spirit of Cain who shunned this responsibility.

But to be successful in this calling and *title-position* we must cultivate a feeling heart; we must be sensitive in the Spirit, constantly searching out the needs present in the lives of those around us.

In a practical way, we can often *serve* others by performing natural duties in their behalf...always being ready to help, always being available to assist, even in mundane, everyday chores.

(And how often these natural things are overlooked when faithfulness in this area, at times, can be the very key to obtaining greater spiritual responsibilities. For the encountering of such situations is quite often a divinely ordered test of the heart).

We can all *serve* humanity by being channels of love, mercy, faith and all the fruit of the Spirit (the personality of deity) according to the particular necessity.

Furthermore, our reason for striving to develop and manifest this spiritual fruit should be not so much our own enjoyment and benefit, but much more so...the benefit and edification of others.

We serve not only God, but others as well, when we live upright and clean before the Lord, for living an exemplary life is a great service to mankind.

Every day we can serve humanity by prayer, by fasting, or by sharing with any receptive soul we meet the revelation of the Word that God has given us.

We know Jesus came for the purpose of giving away all that He received of the Father...His wisdom, His love, His power, His glory, and His authority.

Now we are called upon to do the same.

• **And it is so true that the more we advance in God, the more we have to give away...and the more we give away, the more we advance in God.**

Spiritual advancement and spiritual generosity are therefore inseparably and reciprocally linked to each other.

It must be mentioned also that sometimes we *serve* by simply curbing our temper, biting our tongue, and holding our peace.

By humbling our flesh this way, we keep the Adam-man under subjection and we emerge in an even greater degree as *servants*...because we are willing to swallow our pride in order to *serve* the good of the whole. This is what God expects of us for - *"the servant of the Lord* must not strive; but be gentle unto all men, apt to teach, patient, in meekness instructing those that oppose themselves." (II Timothy 2:24-25)

• Philippians 2:5 even says - "**Let this mind [this same attitude and purpose] be in you which was also in Christ Jesus.**" (AV, AMP)

In other words, we must also be willing at times to "make ourselves nothing" and "empty ourselves, assuming the condition of a slave". By doing so we "strip ourselves of every advantage" in an earthly sense, but we capture the heart of God, for we go forth to be givers not takers.

And when we strive to multiply our "talents" in the lives of others this way, we find the key to entering "the joy of the Lord"...both now and forevermore! (Matthew 25:14-30)

MAKING THE CHOICE

O, how different this Jesus way is from the normal way of acting and reacting!

The fallen nature that binds us is seething with hostility and longs to strike back.

The flesh part of us feeds on attention and desires the preeminence.

The carnal part of us loves the feeling of independence and self-sufficiency. Often, it even craves the pleasure of exercising authority over others.

• But Jesus said - "it shall not be so among you: but...WHOSOEVER WILL BE CHIEF AMONG YOU, LET HIM BE YOUR SERVANT." (Matthew 20:27)

This challenge sums up one of the high callings of a believer - a mark for which we must constantly reach, in all of our endeavors and in all our human relationships.

We recognize that we have been called into liberty and in a certain sense, therefore, we do not need others now, for we are complete "in Christ".

We have found the true source of fulfillment, therefore we are no longer bound by the need for acceptance.

We need not be bound any longer by the fear of rejection.

Neither should we cringe at the rebuke of the angry, or the mocking refusal of those who do not believe...for Jesus Christ has made us whole.

Our peace no longer hinges on circumstances.

Our joy no longer depends on where we are, or who we are with.

We are not as grossly affected by outward change now for we have inward stability.

If we are right with God, then automatically we are liberated from all this dependency.

We need not lean on the arm of flesh any longer.

If preachers or admired believers around us falter and fail, it should never alter our commitment and stand. We are free!

We belong to Jesus and He belongs to us.We trust in Him alone.

We feel utter security in this blessed divine relationship and we definitely should!

• But still, though we possess this new-found freedom, Paul cautions that we *"use not liberty for an occasion to the flesh, but by love serve one another."* (Galatians 5:13)

To fulfill this Bible command we must lovingly and willfully commit ourselves as bond-slaves to the rest of the body of Christ and to the world.

This is not an imprisoning kind of servitude in which we cower in fear and cringe in sickly submission at the voice of another human being. This is the kind of self-imposed service to others that springs from the heart.

This must no longer be a "have to" but rather a "want to" action on our part, for then love is perfected within us and we become pleasing in God's sight.

• Paul further explained this idea when he said - *"though I be free from all men, yet have I made myself servant unto all, that I might gain the more."* (I Corinthians 9:19)

Paul found his answer to life on the Damascus road and he could have spent the rest of his life rejoicing in his own salvation, developing his own relationship with God and living a life of ease. Instead he chose the route of becoming a bond-servant and a debtor to all men.

He explained what motivated him to make this decision when he said - "the love of Christ constraineth us". (II Corinthians 5:14)

O, how the world would be powerfully affected and the wounds in the body of Christ healed if all of us would just follow this simple rule and lay down our lives for the sake of others.

We are not all called to the five-fold ministry (apostles, prophets, evangelists, pastors and teachers) but we are all called to be *ministers...* **servants of Jesus Christ...**ministering the power of God and the love of God to a lost world spiritually starving for both. (See Ph. 1:1, Jude 1)

• In fact, it is important to note that certain Hebrew and Greek words that are translated into the word *minister* are also, in other places in the Bible, into the word *servant*...for instance, the Hebrew word *sharath* and the Greek word *diakonos* (also translated *deacon*).

So these two words and these two callings are synonymous to a great degree.

We are all called to *serve*; we are all called to *minister*.

And not only to those who love us in return, for Jesus said - "Whosoever shall compel thee to go a mile, go with him twain." (Matthew 5:41)

This refers directly to the customary way that a king's courier, in Jesus'day, would demand help from perfect strangers, but usually no more than a mile's distance.

It speaks to us now of *unlimited service,* going the extra mile to *serve* those who appreciate us, and those who hate us...those who call us friends, and even those who count themselves our enemies.

This is the nobility and the humility of sonship married together in one divine-like attitude.

And this is a reflection of the spirit of Calvary, for Jesus died for the ungodly and the rebellious as well as the righteous.

Yes, we are called to serve even as gracious David who was more than willing to play his harp under the sweet anointing of the Spirit, to compassionately deliver a tormented and demon-oppressed king, even though that same king burned with hate and jealousy toward him at times to the point of murder.

This is a brand of love that only God can give, an agape-love that was fully revealed in the Messiah Himself - a love that He challenges us to possess.

And without a doubt, the generous Saviour has given a generous promise of reward to those who strive to follow His example and be generous with love in this manner.

He said - "he that humbleth himself shall be exalted." (Luke 14:11)

To pursue the love of God and service to others, even to the point of humbling ourselves, is a pattern of life that works - "For God is not unrighteous to forget your work and labour of love, which ye have shewed toward His name, in that ye have *ministered* to the saints, and do *minister*." (Hebrews 6:10)

This attitude definitely worked for our Elder Brother in abundant return for "He humbled Himself, and became obedient unto death, even the death of the cross" (the ultimate service to humanity). But it was certainly not in vain, for the Bible went on to say - "WHEREFORE GOD ALSO HATH HIGHLY EXALTED HIM, AND GIVEN HIM A NAME WHICH IS ABOVE EVERY NAME." (Philippians 2:8-9)

This is one of the mysteries of the kingdom of God...that all dominion, mastery, honor, glory and power will be eternally given to the Son of God though actually He never really sought for it...and in truth it seemed He sought the opposite.

But this is "the Kingdom Law of Giving and Receiving" in operation - and "the Law of Servitude and Mastery" - even in the life of Jesus.

And so shall it be for those who sincerely follow this lowly Nazarene and learn to *serve* as He did..."not with eyeservice, as menpleasers; but as **THE SERVANTS OF CHRIST,** doing the will of God from the heart; with good will doing service, as to the Lord, and not to men." (Ephesians 6:6-7)

With this kind of attitude, by *serving* others, we are in essence *serving* God.

• Jesus even said that inasmuch as we do something kind or beneficial unto one of the least of His brethren, we actually do it unto Him. (Matthew 25:31-46)

So really, if we are to be true *servants*, we should seek out the least - the weak, the unloved, the downtrodden - to *serve* them.

Most people enjoy *serving* the elite and the important, for by doing so they feel that they, to a degree, share in the same elite status and importance. Few make it their goal in life to *minister* to all people, without respect of persons and without self-seeking, ulterior motives. Even fewer make it their passion to administer God's mercy and power to those who are forgotten, despised and cast off in this world.

Yet this is the end of the quest for fulfillment, and though it is hidden from the eyes of many, this is the pulsation of God's heart, the joy of life, and the key to being a true Christian.

No wonder, as He girded Himself with a towel and knelt before His disciples, Jesus said... *"If ye know these things, happy are ye if ye do them."* (John 13:17)

MINISTERING TO GOD

It has been proven quite satisfactorily thus far that we, as disciples, are called to be *servants* to mankind, but there is yet a higher calling of service that needs to be unveiled.

- **As *servants of God* we have received the supreme honor and calling of actually *ministering* to God's need.**

Psalm 2:11 commands first that we - *"Serve the Lord with fear, and rejoice with trembling."*

The psalmist was speaking in this passage of a fear that is somewhat different than our normal definition of the word - it refers to the heart-gripping, reverential awe and deep, trembling respect that we should feel for the holiness, the majesty, and the greatness of our God.

Praise springing forth from such purity of spirit is sure to fill up the heart of the Creator.

Then, Psalm 100 commands that we "make a joyful noise unto the Lord...come before His presence with singing...enter into His gates with thanksgiving, and into His courts with praise"...for by doing these things we *"serve the Lord with gladness."*

What great joy must flood our heavenly Father's inner being, when gladness rises in our spirits toward Him in this way.

This is especially true when we praise Him selflessly without any thought of receiving something in return.

As we joy in the Lord, in a reciprocal way, He will also rejoice over us with joy and joy over us with singing . (Zephaniah 3:17)

And as our joy becomes His joy, His joy becomes ours.

This is the rapture of the relationship and a purpose for which we are ordained...for we have been created for His pleasure. (Revelation 4:11)

SERVANTS TO RIGHTEOUSNESS

When our attitudes are right, we fulfill this purpose of God in a far more perfect and marvellous way...so keeping a right spirit is of the utmost necessity.

- Romans 6:19 declares - "as ye have yielded your members servants to uncleanness and to iniquity unto iniquity: even so now yield your members **SERVANTS TO RIGHTEOUSNESS** unto holiness."

Another translation of the same passage says - "surrender yourselves entirely as slaves of righteousness, for holy purposes." (TEV)

To be enslaved to righteousness this way involves dying more fully to the flesh with its rebellion and self-will, and coming alive more fully to God's slightest desire, so that obedience becomes an unquestioned and immediate response in our relationship with God.

Few ever reach such a place of consecration and spiritual sensitivity, but those who do walk into sweet communion with the Father, for they fill up the calling of a *servant* to the utmost.

• For "being made free from sin, and become **SERVANTS TO GOD**, ye have your fruit unto holiness, and the end everlasting life." (Romans 6:22)

Yet God still asks for more.

• Luke 17:7-10 reveals that if we only do what is demanded of us, we are **unprofitable servants**.

God is searching for those who are willing to do more than just what they consider their absolute duty.

He desires those who will dare to take initiative, in new and innovative ways, constantly searching out fresh means of fulfilling our call to serve the Lord, the body of Christ and the world around us.

As we mature in God and in our calling to serve, our time and our thoughts should be dominated day and night with this burden of the Lord and not with sports, hobbies, pleasurable diversions, or worldly entertainment.

Frivolity, levity and concern over trifling matters of life is foolishness to a true *servant* of God, for the world's trumpet-cry to indulge in these things rings hollow and empty in our ears.

The blood of Jesus has purged our "conscience from dead works to serve the living God" and now we are quite sensitive to what pleases God.

We know that "**No servant can serve two masters:** for either he will hate the one, and love the other; or else he will hold to the one, and despise the other." (Luke 16:13)

We cannot serve God and mammon (earthly riches).

We have a holy charge and a sacred responsibility and we must simply refuse to be distracted by that which is transitory.

We may be blessed materially for a certain purpose in the kingdom, but we refuse to be a servant or a slave to that which is material. We look beyond the natural that passes away into the spiritual that endures forever.

We have only one chief concern and that is serving the pleasure of our Master. Therefore, we must constantly review our attitudes and keep ourselves wholly committed to Him.

THE OLD WILL SYMBOL

• **In the Old Testament, *servants* who were Hebrews were only required to serve for six years. Then, in the seventh year, they were set free, liberally furnished with food, flocks and others goods at the command of God.**

But if by chance that servant truly loved his master, he could make the choice to remain a servant for the rest of his life.

If this was the desire of his heart, the servant's master would carry him to the judges to announce his decision.

After returning to their abode, the servant would then be taken to a door or doorpost in the home where his ear would be placed against the door, or post, and bored through with an aul. (Ex. 21:1-6, Deut.15)

This God-ordained Old Covenant ritual represents an important facet of our New Testament status as *servants of God.*

Surely all of us experience certain times in our walk with God where circumstances pressure us into making a more firm commitment...one way or the other. We may even feel a "loosening of the reins" and sense the Master's voice testing us saying - "Will you go also?"

Challenging situations arise: temptations, oppositions, persecutions, failures or disappointments, and we are forced into making a decision.

We either slacken up or tighten down.

We either draw back or forge ahead.

We either say, "This is too hard of a saying," or we respond to Jesus saying - "Where can we go, for Thou hast the words of eternal life." We either walk out "the door", and flee from the responsibility of being faithful, God-fearing *servants*, crucified with Christ, or because of love we submit all the more by going to "the door", and renewing there, once again, our agreement to *serve* the Master.

Jesus is "the door".

Placing our ears against "the door" to be bored through with an aul represents, in a spiritual sense, the act of utterly resigning ourselves over to His service, His Word, and His will (for the ear is firmly pinned to the door).

It is without question that there are certain times in which we must renew our commitment as *servants of God* this way, and die such a death to self that it lasts a life-time.

The pierced ear also represents inspiration...being able to hear the revelation of both the written and the living Word...and happily, devotedly

226

responding to both.

This is not just a burdensome responsibility.

This is an incomparable, heaven-sent privilege!

Therefore, if we make the right choice, we will present our bodies living sacrifices, holy and acceptable unto God which is our reasonable *service*...that we might hear, know and obey "that good, and acceptable, and perfect, will of God." (Romans 12:1-2)

It is important also to note also that a *door* always symbolizes a new beginning.

This *door* of rededication to service, and reconsecration to the status of a *servant,* will without a doubt open up to God's yielded offspring a new dimension in the anointing.

Therefore, it is clearly not an end; it is always a brand new and exciting start...a blazing sunrise, a cocoon unfolding, a color-filled rainbow, and the bursting of another Spring, a chance for something better.

We must approach every challenge of life and every tribulation with this in remembrance.

We must recognize that every trial is really just another *door* of opportunity challenging us to serve and preparing us ultimately for that grand and glorious day when the *door* will open wider than ever before.

We will then hear those long-sought-after words:

> *"Well done, thou GOOD AND FAITHFUL SERVANT: thou hast been faithful over a few things, I will make thee ruler over many things: enter thou into the joy of thy Lord."*

(Matthew 25:21)

SERVANTS ETERNALLY

In that grand era yet to come our *title-position* as *servants of God* will not pass away; it will rather be established forever. For such a calling is a high honor bestowed eternally on those who truly love God.

How touching it is that Moses was eulogized by Joshua with this very term. He was not called a great statesman, prophet or deliverer of God's people, but simply *"the servant of the Lord"*...for if a man can truly fill this position, he is to be extolled both in heaven and in earth.

We who are blessed will continue in this ordination infinitely - *serving* God's purpose in His kingdom on this earth and then throughout the New Creation to come.

In that glorious age, it seems sure that we will serve God more fully and more effectively than we ever have.

The book of the Revelation (which was given to *servants* - Rev. 1:1) describes this future state so well. At the peak of his vision, John tells us that New Jerusalem will come down from God out of heaven:

"And there shall be no more curse: but the throne of God and of the Lamb shall be in it; and His SERVANTS shall serve Him:

And they shall see His face, and His name shall be in their foreheads.

And there shall be no night there; and they need no candle, neither light of the sun; for the Lord God giveth them light: and they shall reign for ever and ever."

(Revelation 22:3-5)

What an enigma! That *servants* will finally reign as kings!! Yet we know by the Scripture this is the ultimate blessing, the sure reward, and the royal outcome of Christian service. And this is the final destiny of those who call themselves *the servants of Jehovah!*

• It is no wonder that Jesus cautioned His followers to never be slothful in spirit, giving them the following command:

"Let your loins be girded about, and your lights burning;

And ye yourselves like unto men that wait for their lord, when he shall return from the wedding; that when he cometh and knocketh, they may open unto him immediately.

Blessed are those servants, whom the Lord when He cometh shall find watching: verily I say unto you, that He shall gird Himself, and make them to sit down to meat, and will come forth and serve them."

(Luke 12:35-37)

O, praise the name of God! This is the greatest and most beautiful mystery of all...that if we are **FAITHFUL AND WISE SERVANTS** in this life, one day, at the marriage supper of the Lamb, our Saviour will actually *serve* us! (Matthew 24:45)

He will *serve* us with "hidden manna" - revealing in absolute depth the infinite mysteries of God. (Revelation 2:17)

He will *serve* us with "the fruit of the tree of life" - unveiling in us the utter beauty of His flawless perfection and supernal character. (Rev. 2:7)

He will *serve* us with " the water of life" - refreshing our spirits and finally quenching the deep thirst of our hearts to be utterly one with God. (Revelation 21:6)

He will *serve* us and honor us with a new depth of responsibility...for He will make us rulers "over all His goods." (Matthew 24:47)

He will cause us to inherit all that God has, and all that God is!

And, as always, to *serve* His own in such an indescribably abundant and generous measure, will be forevermore the joy and the rejoicing of His heart! (See Isaiah 65:11-16)

Moreover He promised - "when ye see this, your heart shall rejoice, and your bones shall flourish like an herb: and the hand of the Lord shall be known toward **HIS SERVANTS,** and His indignation toward His enemies." (Isaiah 66:14)

O, Hallelujah! We fell compelled to fulfill from the heart Psalm 113:1 - "Praise ye the Lord. Praise, O ye **SERVANTS OF THE LORD**, praise the name of the Lord."

We should never forget or take for granted His intervention in our lives...the great grace, righteousness and peace Jesus has poured forth.

In Isaiah 44:21 the pre-incarnate Christ exhorts - "Remember these, O Jacob and Israel...for thou art **MY SERVANT** : I have formed thee; thou art My servant: O Israel, thou shalt not be forgotten of Me."

•   Having considered this glorious gift, we must be faithful to "utter it even to the end of the earth...The Lord hath redeemed **HIS SERVANT JACOB.**" (Isaiah 48:20)

How very compassionate He was to bring us to that moment of visitation in our lives, when He sternly yet lovingly presented the demand..."CHOOSE YOU THIS DAY WHOM YE WILL **SERVE.**" (Joshua 24:15)

Thank God, we made the right choice! And we have purposed to live in this portion of our "**Promised Land Inheritance**" all the days of our lives. We know He has given us this "land for an heritage...even an heritage unto **ISRAEL HIS SERVANT**: for His mercy endureth forever." (Psalm 136:21-22)

If we spend our lives journeying toward this "mark for the prize of the high calling of God in Christ Jesus" we also can claim three other certainties.

First, God will surely bless our efforts in His behalf - for the Lord "hath pleasure in the prosperity of His **SERVANTS.**" (Psalm 35:27)

Second, no weapon formed against us can prosper...for Isaiah 54:17 declares that "this is the heritage of **THE SERVANTS OF THE LORD.**"

And third, the struggles and the strivings of this life will pass by quickly, like a dream in the night, if our whole motive for service is love.

Genesis 29:20 states that - *"Jacob served seven years for Rachel; and they seemed unto him but a few days, for the love he had to her."*

In like manner...at the end of this long trek from time into eternity, because our hearts have overflowed with sincere and deep love for the Master, we will truly be able to say... *"It seemed but a few days."*

•   In fact, more than likely we will cry - *"O, that our lives had been longer, and our days multiplied in number, that we might have served Jesus all the more."*

VESSELS OF MERCY

VESSELS UNTO HONOUR

VESSELS FOR NOBLE USE

THE MERCIFUL

"What if God, willing to shew His wrath, and to make His power known, endured with much longsuffering the vessels of wrath fitted to destruction:

*And that He might make known the riches of His glory on the **VESSELS OF MERCY**, which He had afore prepared unto glory."*

(Romans 9:22-23)

VESSELS OF MERCY
VESSELS UNTO HONOUR

"What if God, willing to shew His wrath, and to make His power known, endured with much longsuffering the vessels of wrath fitted to destruction:
And that He might make known the riches of His glory on the VESSELS OF MERCY, which He had afore prepared unto glory."

(Romans 9:22-23)

Normally the word **vessel** simply describes a *hollow or concave utensil, such as a bowl, a cup, a dish or a bottle, utilized for holding or containing something.*

But when used in reference to a human being this term means *a person who is filled or infused with some predominate quality of character.*

In Romans 9:23, we see that the offspring of the Most High are called *vessels of mercy.*

It is only right that we claim this *title*, for the magnanimous mercy of the Lord Jesus Christ has lifted us up from the dunghill of sin and exalted us to a position of grand blessedness and inheritance in Christ.

Our lives, our thoughts, our emotions and our very souls have been infused with this beautiful facet of God's personality.

To fully understand what mercy is, though, we must first recognize that there are two slightly different meanings assigned to this one word.

• The first and most used definition of **mercy** is...*compassion or forbearance shown especially to an offender.*

This concept of mercy implies that depth of compassion which produces leniency or restraint in the infliction of punishment, even when justice demands quite the opposite!

This is that mercy which is lofty and beneficent in character...mighty in transforming even the most sin-sick soul.

• The second definition of **mercy** is simply *sympathy expressed!*

The recipient of this kind of mercy is not necessarily some kind of repentant rebel or rogue of society, but rather a person in desperate need and in dire distress.

This kind of mercy first feels, and then extends, pity to those who are in misery. It perfectly relates to the hurt of the hurting, and then does all that it can to alleviate the pain of the pained and assuage the grief of the grief-stricken.

Such is a perfect portrait and a pleasant picture of our God, who is spoken of as being - *"the Father of mercies,* and the God of all comfort;

who comforteth us in all our tribulation, that we may be able to comfort them which are in any trouble..." (II Corinthians 1:3-4)

He extends mercy to us, that we might extend it to others. And miraculously, as we give mercy to those who need it, in return we end up reaping even more than we possessed at the start.

The beatitude promise is sure and steadfast - "Blessed are **THE MERCIFUL: for they shall obtain mercy.**" (Matthew 5:7)

The proverbial pledge is irrevocable - "The **merciful man** doeth good to His own soul." (Proverbs 11:17)

As *vessels of mercy* we are not only called to be recipients of this divine character trait; we are chosen to be His channels...channels of the compassionate tenderness and sympathetic gentleness that can heal any broken life.

JESUS - OUR STANDARD OF MERCY

Jesus showed us how to be *vessels of mercy* when He left His determined footprints in the sands of time and His loving imprint in the aching hearts of those who received His words.

He was the *mercy of God* incarnate in human flesh...the living revelation and the everlasting proof of that side of God's character.

• Hebrews 2:17 declares that - "in all things it behoved Him to be made like unto His brethren, that He might be a *merciful* and faithful High Priest in things pertaining to God."

We can be confident that He understands the weakness and frailty of the human frame. Because "He Himself hath suffered being tempted, He is able to succour them that are tempted." (Hebrews 2:18)

He is just. He is kind.

He judges with righteous judgment, for He always takes everything into consideration.

Ephesians 2:4-5 enhances this truth by saying that "God, who is *rich in mercy,* for His great love wherewith He loved us, even when we were dead in sins, hath quickened us together with Christ."

Notice that the Lord is not spoken of in this passage as being rich in anger or rich in fury. Though rebellion and sin on the part of mankind at times makes this kind of wrathful reaction necessary, still the great wealth of the personality of deity is not measured in these terms.

• One of God's greatest sources of praise is the fact that *"His mercy endureth forever."*

It is somewhat amazing that God's mercy has endured the abuse of an iniquity-laden world for almost six thousand years, yet it is still just as plenteous, just as free, and just as available as ever!

Jeremiah declared, long before the crucifixion of Jesus, that - "it is of the Lord's *mercies* that we are not consumed, because His compassions fail not. They are new every morning." (Lamentations 3:22-23)

If every dawn could bring forth fresh mercy during the ministry-era of this Old Testament prophet who lived under the law of sin and death, then *how much more* is mercy abundantly available now...for the dayspring from on high has visited us "to give light to them who sit in darkness." (Luke 1:79)

He is our perpetual dayspring, bringing forth the dawning of a brand new day every moment that He lives in our hearts.

MERCY AND TRUTH ARE MET TOGETHER

• We know that *truth* became quite powerful when it was fully joined to *mercy* in spiritual wedlock...at the New Covenant, matrimonial altar that we call *Calvary*.

It is common knowledge that in the Old Testament much of the revelation of *truth* only brought judgment and condemnation to the people, for the righteousness demanded by the Law was unattainable. But now -"*mercy* and *truth* are met together; righteousness and peace have kissed each other." (Psalm 85:10)

Initially, this prophecy was beautifully and perfectly fulfilled in Jesus...for when anyone goes to Him they find mercy, truth, righteousness and peace brought together in perfect harmony.

But now this prophecy should also find continuance of fulfillment in us, for *mercy* and *truth* (the Spirit and the Word) came together in a holy, spiritual union in each one of us the very moment that we were born again.

By means of this transformation experience, we became God's hands extended to the world and His heart unveiled.

Now we also are called, as joint-heirs with Christ, to be the living revelation and the everlasting proof of the *merciful* side of God's character and channels of truth in this world.

We are *chosen vessels* as was Paul the apostle. (Acts 9:15)

We are ordained to reveal the name and character of God to the nations. We are also called to - "do justly, and to *love mercy* and to walk humbly" with our God. (Micah 6:8)

If we are seeking to truly shine with Christlike attributes, reflecting the merciful side of God's nature is not an option...it is referred to as one of the weightier matters of the law (Matthew 23:23)...a responsibility, an obligation and an express command. For God has declared more than once - *"I will have mercy and not sacrifice."* (Matthew 9:13)

• Moreover, the Scripture plainly suggests -*"he shall have judgment* *without mercy, that hath shewed no mercy; and **mercy rejoiceth against judgment.*** (James 2:13)

If we refuse to give mercy, we cannot expect to receive it, for Jesus pledged - "with what judgment ye judge, ye shall be judged: and with what measure ye mete, it shall be measured to you again." (Matthew 7:2)

Mature sons of God willingly and rejoicingly exhibit this much needed character trait, for we know that our God "delighteth in mercy."

THE PURPOSE AND LONGING OF GOD

• Unquestionably, the revelation of the character of God is one of the primary reasons for this whole earthly sojourn.

According to our key scripture (Romans 9:22-23) God has allowed the existence of vessels of wrath and *vessels of mercy* in this world...to show His wrath, reveal His power, display His glory, and manifest His mercy!

It never would have been possible for us to experience these extremes of the divine personality in the perfection of the heavenly state.

Experiencing the grace of God, His great compassion and His tender love, will surely seal us, His *vessels of mercy,* into a deeper gratitude, a deeper devotion and a deeper understanding of God than we ever could have received otherwise.

Had there been no strong-armed enemy to defeat then we would have never seen the magnificent display of the divine dominion.

But now we "have seen the end of the Lord; that the Lord is very pitiful, and of *tender mercy.*" (James 5:11)

We have seen that He is mighty to save.

We have seen that His mercy is "great above the heavens." (Ps. 108:4)

We are so blessed and so thankful! But even in our thankfulness we realize that appropriating the benefits of this revelation is our challenge now.

For it is one thing to behold the great beauty and vastness of the ocean. It is something else to actually plunge in with joyous abandon and be immersed in what we see.

THE MERCY SEAT

• The *mercy seat* in the holy of holies was a plate of solid gold (6 1/3 by 2 2/3 feet) that rested on top of the ark of the covenant. The ark itself contained the law on tablets of stone, the book of the law, Aaron's rod that budded, and the golden bowl full of manna.

Two cherubim hovered on either side of the *mercy seat*. Both the cherubim and the mercy seat were made of one piece of beaten gold.

One time a year on the Day of Atonement, the high priest would sprinkle the blood of a bullock on the golden plate to atone for the sins of the nation of Israel. This *mercy seat* was also the place where the Shekinah of God's presence rested and the place from which God communed with Moses and Aaron.

• **This peculiar piece of tabernacle "furniture" represents the angel-thronged throne of grace in heaven from which God presently communes with us.**

At one time God's throne was primarily a judgment seat. But then the sprinkling of the blood of Jesus transformed a throne of judgment into a altar of infinite mercy...something so much higher and more excellent than the law.

• The following point should be reemphasized: that the mercy seat lid was "above" the law...and this is in God's estimation as well as ours.

If this blood-stained mercy seat was removed, observers were dangerously and fatally exposed to the ministration of death found in the ten commandments. Certain presumptous and curious Israelites discovered this to their terror when they thoughtlessly opened the ark without permission from God. (I Samuel 6:19-20)

How significant it is that the same Greek word *hilasterion*, translated *mercy seat* in Hebrews 9:5, is also rendered *propitiation* in Romans 3:25. This passage particularly speaks of being justified through Christ Jesus -

> *"Whom God hath set forth to be a propitiation through faith in His blood, to declare His righteousness for the remission of sins that are past..."*
>
> (Romans 3:25)

The word **propitiate** means *to appease, to placate or to satisfy - specifically to satisfy the demands of justice concerning the sin-debt of the human race.*

How marvellous it is that Jesus accomplished this goal!

"It is finished", He cried on the cross!

Now, for every needy person, the Father has set forth the Son to be a *propitiation*, a mercy seat, a *"place"* where sin can be forgiven and righteousness can be restored.

• Vital to our understanding is the simple fact that the lid of the ark was called a mercy **SEAT**! For this was the only **seat** in the tabernacle area yet no man ever sat on it.

In Hebrews we find the hidden truth explained:

> *"And every priest **standeth** daily ministering...But this man, [Jesus] after He had offered one sacrifice for sins for ever, **sat down** on the right hand of God."*
>
> (Hebrews 10:11-12)

Isaiah foretold such a glorious **finished work** of the Messiah when he prophesied:

> *"And in mercy shall the throne be established: and*
> *He shall SIT UPON IT. "*

(Isaiah 16:5)

Jesus is now in the heavenly holy of holies, in this throne-position of rest, authority and mercy. He has encouraged us to approach this most excellent throne boldly, that we may obtain *"mercy*, and find grace to help in time of need." (Hebrews 4:16)

ESSENTIAL MERCY-TRUTHS

We dare to approach this mercy seat now, in the inner sanctuary of truth, by asking a few very fundamental questions:

How much mercy is actually available to a child of God?
How is it obtained?
And what are the differences and similarities between the grace of God and the mercy of God?

• Psalm 103:17 declares that - *"the mercy of the Lord is from everlasting to everlasting upon them that fear Him. "*

To *fear the Lord* is to deeply respect His utter holiness and His absolute abhorrence of sin, and to act accordingly.

This in itself is praiseworthy.

But in Psalm 86:11, David went one step further when he requested - "O Lord...unite my heart to fear Thy name."

Surely, to fear the name of the Lord is an even deeper measure of reverence, where one counts even the uttering of the name of God a most sacred privilege, an honor definitely not to be taken lightly.

Individuals with this attitude would never dare enter the presence of God without melting their hearts in brokenness...for they have learned to "serve the Lord with fear, and rejoice with trembling". (Psalm 2:11)

Abundant mercy is their inheritance, reaching infinitely into the past, blotting out all their transgression, and infinitely into the future, sealing their heavenly destiny.

Mercy for God-fearing saints is boundless, overspreading their existence, before, during, and after this life, like an endless rainbow bridge of ordination and promise... *"from everlasting to everlasting. "*

Humility attracts this infinite mercy but not humility alone.

• Jude gave an express command to every son of God when he said -

"Keep yourselves in the love of God, *looking for the mercy* of our Lord Jesus Christ, unto eternal life..." (Jude 21)

We often only get what we *look* for.

Therefore, we must dare to *look* for the manifestation of the mercy of God and believe the Lord to abundantly supply this precious commodity from heaven.

How forcible faith is in effecting this end result...faith in the finished work of Calvary and faith in the covenant promises of God's Word.

Faith in the grace of God automatically includes faith for mercy, because mercy is a major ingredient in grace.

God's goodness, God's power, God's compassion, God's abilities and God's mercy are just a few of the many tributaries that all flow together into the great river of everlasting life called *grace*.

We know that *grace* has been defined (letter by letter, *g-r-a-c-e*) as...*God's riches at Christ's expense.*

One of the main spiritual riches made freely available through the terrible expense of Jesus' vicarious sufferings is obviously the great wealth of mercy that is presently pouring out on humanity...healing hearts, changing lives, and miraculously working the impossible.

This is the same "wisdom that is from above...*full of mercy* and good fruits" that has been sent forth into the lives of God's chosen since the fall of Adam. (James 3:17)

MERCY: MANIFESTED AND PROVEN

This mercy has manifested in a multitude of ways.

It was the mercy of God that brought Lot out of Sodom before the heaven-sent holocaust of fire and brimstone fell (Genesis 19:16).

It was the mercy of God that provided a suitable wife for Isaac (Genesis 24:27).

It was the mercy of God that brought Israel out of Egypt's bondage (Exodus 15:13).

It was great mercy that restored David to a righteous standing and followed him, along with goodness, all the days of his life (II Chronicles 1:8, Psalms 23:6, 51:1)

It was mercy that opened Bartimaeus' blind eyes (Mark 10:46-52).

It was mercy that justified the repentant publican (Luke 18:13).

It was mercy that forgave Paul of the deadly sin of blasphemy (I Timothy 1:13).

• **And it was the attitude of mercy in the heart of the good Samaritan that purchased praise from the Master of mercy Himself** (Luke 10:37)

This very parable is a reflection of the character of our blessed

239

Saviour. In a symbolic sense, Jesus is definitely that "good Samaritan" that found us "half-dead on the side of the road" (our bodies were alive, but our souls were dead).

A roving band of merciless thieves from hell had beaten us mentally and emotionally, robbing us spiritually of joy, righteousness, purity, peace, and any hope for victory in this life and the life to come.

But then Jesus came by and "not by works of righteousness which we have done, but according to His *mercy* He saved us", pouring the *oil* and the *wine* into our wounds (the *oil* of His anointing and the *wine* of His love). (Titus 3:5)

He took us to "the inn" (a place of spiritual rest in Christ) and paid our debt in advance.

Knowing these things we are compelled to echo the words of Ethan the Ezrahite - *"I will sing of the mercies of the Lord forever."* (Psalm 89:1)

Surely, as we celebrate His great mercy, we will see the windows of heaven graciously opened all the more!

• Jehoshaphat's singers went out in energetic, activated faith against the armies of Moab, Ammon and Mt. Seir, worshipping Jehovah by singing - *"Praise the Lord; for His mercy endureth forever!"* (II Chronicles 20:21)

God set ambushments against the enemy, and fought the battle for His people. Israel simply collected the spoil and called that battleground **the valley of Berachah** which means *the valley of blessing.*

• Moreover, at the dedication of Solomon's Temple, the musicians and singers lifted their voices, with the instruments of music (the trumpets, psalteries, harps and cymbals) rejoicingly praising the Lord saying - *"His mercy endureth forever."*

The fire of God fell on 120,000 sacrificial sheep laid in heaps around the huge edifice. Then the thick Shekinah glory cloud of God's manifest presence filled the temple...so much so that the priests could not even stand to minister.

As we consider these examples, we come to a final conclusion.

If instead of grumbling and complaining, we will lift our voices daily to sing and declare the *ever-enduring mercy* of the Lord, God will move similarly for us.

He will set angelic ambushments against the hellish forces that constantly pursue us with intent to destroy.

He will fight our battles for us!

He will turn our trials into valleys of blessings!

Our God will consume us with His glorious consuming fire...and send forth the visitation of His Shekinah glory into our lives!

If we will only sing, and shout and celebrate the unchangeable fact that, after all these years, still - *"His mercy endureth forever!"*

GIVING THANKS

In Luke 17:11-19 we read of ten lepers who cried "Jesus, Master, have *mercy* on us."

It is evident that He responded to their plea for they were all miraculously, mercifully cleansed. But only one returned to give thanks.

And as a result, the Bible said that he was made whole.

Apparently, while the others were only cleansed of the dread disease, the thankful one saw the missing fingers and toes, eaten away by leprosy, restored by a creative miracle.

There is a valuable lesson to be learned through this story.

Having been cleansed from the leprous disease of sin and chosen as *vessels of mercy* it is imperative now that we return and give thanks to the God who has so graciously rescued us.

There is quite possibly no better way of doing this than to present Him with a sanctified vessel in which He can comfortably and gloriously dwell, and out of which He can powerfully and gloriously manifest. Most certainly then...not only will we be cleansed from sin; *we will be made whole!*

No wonder Paul said - "I beseech you therefore, brethren, by *the mercies of God,* that ye present your bodies a living sacrifice, holy, acceptable unto God, which is your reasonable service." (Romans 12:1)

We must pursue this measure of consecration as a means of giving thanks *for the mercies of God,* yet at the same time we must realize that successfully and totally consecrating our lives can only be accomplished *by the mercies of God*, as the above scripture states.

In the end, it all redounds to His praise.

For "we have this treasure in *earthen vessels,* that the excellency of the power may be of God, and not of us." (II Corinthians 4:7)

I Thessalonians 4:4-7 exhorts - "That every one of you should know how to possess His *vessel* in sanctification and honour; not in the lust of concupiscence...for God hath not called us unto uncleanness, but unto holiness."

II Timothy 2:20 reveals that - "in a great house there are not only *vessels* of gold and of silver, but also of wood and of earth..some to honour, and some to dishonour."

• Paul went on to say in the next verse, that - "If anyone purifies himself from what is ignoble, then He will be a **vessel for noble use**" - "a **vessel unto honour**, sanctified and meet for the master's use." (RSV, AV)

Toward this target our will should be constantly aimed.

• In Isaiah 52:11 the prophet spurred and prodded the priesthood of Israel saying - "Depart ye, depart ye, go ye out from thence, touch no unclean thing...be ye clean, that bear *the vessels of the Lord*."

If the ministers of the sanctuary under the Old Covenant were commanded to be sanctified and separated just because they bore the silver and gold vessels of the holy place, then *how much more* should we be sanctified and separated, for we have actually become His *holy vessels*.

If we dare to assume this stance...forsaking the world and denying self, then the promise Jesus gave will surely be fulfilled..."If any man serve Me...him will My Father *honour*." (John 12:26)

God will honor us by bringing us into an intimate and effective relationship with Him, having power with God and with men.

God will honor us with spiritual gifts and manifestations of His Spirit.

God will honor us with fruitfulness.

God will honor us with wisdom, understanding and revelation.

God will honor us by honoring our words, even binding and loosing in heaven, what we bind and loose on earth.

All sons and daughters of God are *"vessels of mercy"* and all are potentially and ultimately *"vessels unto honour."*

But during this earthly sojourn, only those who pay the price of discipleship become *the true and manifest vessels of honour, vessels chosen for noble use.*

This, too, is an essentially important part of our "**Promised Land Inheritance**"...something which we must first see, then conquer and defend...with all of our hearts.

Thank God, we know the Captain of the host of the Lord who will subdue our enemy before us.

Therefore we can shout as the Israelites did outside of Jericho's wall, for the Lord has given us the victory...both now and forevermore!!

WE ARE CONFIDENT THAT HE WILL TAKE US ALL THE WAY THROUGH EVERY TREACHEROUS TRIAL AND TRIBULATION UNTIL WE FINALLY ARISE AS **VESSELS OF MERCY** AND **VESSELS UNTO HONOUR**...FOR ALL ETERNITY!

In our heart we hear the echo of a loud Amen...

SO BE IT, SO BE IT...IN JESUS' NAME.